T0269751

GAUTAM ADANI

ADVANCE PRAISE FOR THE BOOK

'Having known Gautam Adani for more than two decades, I have always been fascinated by his untiring perseverance, sharp intellect and relentless energy. Today, Gautam is one of the most admired industrialists and an icon for the new and confident India. It is a story that needs to be told, and, given the capable penmanship of the well-respected R.N. Bhaskar, I can say without hesitation that Gautam's biography will be an inspirational tale for many budding entrepreneurs'—Deepak Parekh, chairman, HDFC Bank

'A few months ago, I said that Adani and TotalEnergies would achieve many great things in the Indian energy market. Here we are! Our agreement is a big step in our alliance and common vision, with respect to the access to low-carbon energy in India'—Patrick Pouyanné, chairman and CEO, TotalEnergies

GAUTAM ADANI

REIMAGINING BUSINESS IN INDIA AND THE WORLD

R.N. BHASKAR

BUSINESS
An imprint of Penguin Random House

PENGUIN BUSINESS

USA | Canada | UK | Ireland | Australia
New Zealand | India | South Africa | China

Penguin Business is part of the Penguin Random House group of companies
whose addresses can be found at global.penguinrandomhouse.com

Published by Penguin Random House India Pvt. Ltd
4th Floor, Capital Tower 1, MG Road,
Gurugram 122 002, Haryana, India

First published in Penguin Business by Penguin Random House India 2022

10 9 8 7 6 5 4 3 2

ISBN 9780670097326

Typeset in Adobe Garamond Pro by MAP Systems, Bengaluru, India
Printed at Thomson Press India Ltd, New Delhi

www.penguin.co.in

Contents

Summary of Charts

1

The Adani Timeline[1]

1962	24 June: Gautambhai born as seventh child to Shantilal Bhudarmal Adani at Ahmedabad, Gujarat, India
1967	June: Young Gautambhai is admitted to Adarsh Vidyalaya, Deesa, Gujarat, India
1972	June: Gets admitted to New High School, Ratanpole, Ahmedabad
1973	August: Goes on a trip organized by his school to Kandla Port, Gujarat, India. This leaves a lasting impression on his mind
1974	June: Secures admission at Sheth C.N. Vidyalaya, Ahmedabad, Gujarat, India
1977	June: Passes SSC and secures admission in coveted science stream in class 11 at C.N. Vidyalaya, Ahmedabad
1978	July: Discontinues studies and leaves for Bombay (Mumbai), India to pursue his dreams to learn and set up a new business

1979	March: Successfully negotiates first deal by selling a small parcel of diamonds at Dhanji Street in Bombay
1982	May: Returns to Ahmedabad and joins Ezy Packaging, a family plastic processing unit, and takes charge of commercial functions (marketing and procurement of raw materials)
1983	21 June: Visits Korea and finalizes his first deal for importing 200 metric tonnes (MT) of polyvinyl chloride (PVC) from Korea on 22 June 1983
1986	1 April: Adani Agency and Adani Associates are formed as partnership companies to deal with export and imports of plastics, metals, pharmaceuticals, etc. 1 May: Marries Pritiben Vora at Orient Club, Ahmedabad, India
1987	7 April: First child, a son, Karan, is born to Gautambhai and Pritiben Adani
1988	1 March: Adani Exports founded as partnership firm
1990	Negotiations with Cargill for salt farms begin
1993	Negotiations with Cargill for salt farm and jetty break down.
1994	1 April: Adani Export Ltd (AEL) gets rated as super star trading house by Government of India 1 November: Adani Exports lists on Bombay Stock Exchange (BSE); initial public offering (IPO) oversubscribed by twenty-five times

	7 November: Second child, a son, Ject, is born to Gautambhai and Pritiben Adani
1998	October: Jetty at Mundra becomes operational December: AEL commences coal trading December: Gautambhai meets Kuok Khoon Hong, chairman of Wilmar International Ltd, Singapore
1999	22 January: Adani–Wilmar is founded
2000	October: Adani–Wilmar—edible oil refinery at Mundra is set up 24 November: 'Fortune' brand of edible oil is launched in India by Adani–Wilmar. Becomes the country's largest selling brand in June 2012 November: Trial runs of Mundra to Adipur railway line commence (as a Public Private Participation [PPP] project) for connecting the port to the Indian Railways network; first of its kind in the country
2006	April: Mundra special economic zone (SEZ) and Mundra Port merge to form MPSEZL Coal mining operations start in Indonesia
2007	27 November: MPSEZL listed on BSE and National Stock Exchange of India (NSE). IPO oversubscribed by 116 times; Gautam Adani is listed among top richest 10 Indians by Forbes. The honour continues (June 2012)
2009	20 August: Adani Power gets listed on BSE and NSE. IPO oversubscribed by 21 times in a depressed market 1 October: Adani Power's first unit of 330 megawatts (MW) thermal power at Mundra becomes operational

	GAIMS at Bhuj inaugurated
2010	15 April: AEL rights issue US$0.30 billion 29 July: AEL's qualified institutional payment (QIP) of US$0.80 billion is floated 3 August: AEL acquires Linc Energy coal mines in Australia 17 August: AEL acquires two capsized ships (*M.V. Rahi* and *M.V. Vanshi*) 1 September: MPSEZL becomes a subsidiary of AEL 22 December: Adani Power Ltd (APL) commissions the country's first energy-efficient, supercritical technology-based thermal power generation unit of 660 MW 23 December: MPSEZL commissions the world's largest coal import terminal at Mundra Commencement of Udaan project
2011	Senior citizen health card is introduced
2012	Acquired Abbot Point Port in Australia and Carmichael coal mine in Queensland Commissioned India's first-ever private-sector high-voltage direct current (HVDC) transmission line Adani Vidya Mandir school at Bhadreshwar inaugurated 12 March: Entire 4620 MW of power generation comes on stream at Mundra 18 May: APL commissions country's first energy-efficient 1000-km-long HVDC power transmission line in private sector. 24 June: Gautam Adani turns fifty, decides to celebrate by instituting the following:

	50 scholarships of Rs 1 lakh per annum till completion of the course /maximum 4 years (B Tech/MBA as applicable) each to students from Gujarat securing admission to IIT/NIT/IIM (25 for IIT/15 for NIT/10 for IIM with no income restriction) 5 scholarships of Rs 1 lakh per annum maximum of 5 years or till completion of bachelor's degree (B Tech./B Pharm. /MBBS/BDS/5-year LLB/BAMS/CA/others) each to students securing ranks in Adani Vidya Mandir (4 from HSC science stream and 1 from HSC commerce/arts stream) 31 December: AEL commissions a 40 MW solar power plant at Bita, Gujarat
2013	Mundra Port becomes No. 1 private port in India Adani Vidya Mandir football academy is inaugurated at Sarguja Mangroves plantation undertaken System of rice intensification (SRI) technique is introduced to Tiroda farmers
2014	Adani Power becomes the largest private thermal power generator with 9280 MW Adani Ports acquires Dhamra Port from Tata and L&T
	Automotive Skill Development Council (ASDC) is inaugurated at Mundra Adani Vidyalaya at Kawai starts
2015	Completed the demerger of Adani Ports and Special Economic Zone Ltd (APSEZ), APL and Adani Transmission Ltd (ATL) from Adani Enterprises Ltd

	Adani Realty teams up with the US's Brahma Management to build a 150-acre township in Gurgaon
2016	Commissions one of the largest solar power plants in the world with a capacity of 648 MW at Kamuthi, Tamil Nadu Adani ventures into defence, partners with Elbit systems for unmanned area vehicles ATL completes acquisition of GMR Energy's transmission assets Foundation spreads its footprint at Vizhinjam, Udupi and Godda Udaan project expanded to Hazira, Kawai, Dhamra and Tiroda
2017	Starts manufacturing solar photovoltaic (PV) panels Adani Ports forms a joint venture with France's CMA CGM to operate container terminal at Mundra Port Relief work in Banaskantha and Ockhi Swachagrah is expanded to 18 states ASDC is inaugurated in Sarguja Adani Ahmedabad Marathon begins, an initiative for the Indian soldiers
2018	Demerger of Adani Green Energy and Adani Gas from Adani Enterprises Fortune emerges as largest fast-moving consumer good (FMCG) brand for food in India Takes over R-Infra's Mumbai electricity distribution, Adani Electricity is launched Adani Gas becomes largest city gas distribution player

	Adani Enterprises acquires Alpha Design Adani Logistics Ltd. and NYK Auto Logistics (India) Private Ltd announce formation Announces formation of rail logistics joint venture APSEZ completes acquisition of Kattupalli Port—southern India's new EXIM gateway from L&T Gyanodyay programme begins in Godda Partners with Kalinga Institute of Social Science (KISS) residential school in Odisha Relief work in Kerala Spreads footprint in Kattupalli
2019	Emerges as No. 2 IRM player in the world Adani Group moves into global headquarters in Shantigram Ventures into sports, wins the inaugural boxing league Adani Power completes acquisition of GMR Chhattisgarh Energy Ltd Adani becomes first Indian port operator to record 200 million metric tonnes (MMT) cargo movement Korba West Power Co. Ltd of 600 MW is acquired by Adani Power Adani Transmission completes acquisition of Bikaner-Khetri transmission project. Adani Transmission completes acquisition of 100 per cent stake of KEC International Ltd in KEC Bikaner Sikar Transmission asset at Rajasthan APSEZ completes acquisition of Krishnapatnam Port

2020	Adani Gas become 50:50 venture, joins with TOTAL Energies to create India's premier integrated gas utility Wins the mandate to operate 6 airports, starts operations at Ahmedabad, Lucknow and Trivandrum Adani Green Energy wins the contract for the largest solar project in the world, leapfrogs towards goal of 25 gigawatts (GW)
2021	12 April: Flipkart enters into strategic partnership with Adani Group to strengthen logistics and data centre capabilities 19 May: Adani Green Energy to acquire SB Energy's 5 GW India renewable power portfolio 13 July: Adani Airport Holdings Ltd (AAHL) takes management control of Mumbai International Airport from the GVK Group 23 July: ATI is first in India to issue sustainability bonds 16 August: Adani Group to acquire MBCPNL portfolio from Sadbhav Infrastructure at an enterprise value of Rs 1680 crore 22 September: APSEZ fully unlocks India's eastern hinterland with Rs 6200 crore acquisition of Gangavaram Port 29 October: Adani Group to invest in Cleartrip, deepens strategic partnership with Flipkart 20 December: Adani Enterprises bags India's largest expressway project 24 December: Adani Green Energy to acquire SB Energy's 5 GW India renewable power portfolio

2021- 22	EdgeConneX and Adani Group form 50:50, ventures into creating data centre Converts Adani Vidya Mandir school in Ahmedabad into covid care facility Adani takes over Chhatrapati Sivaji Maharaj International airport from GMR Adani Group's *Sportsline*-backed player Ravi Kumar Dahiya wins silver medal at the Tokyo Olympics 2020
2022	21 February: Adani Group announces memorandum of understanding (MoU) with Ballard for hydrogen fuel cells in India 22 March: Adani Ports' cargo volumes accelerate to 300 million metric tonnes 8 April: International Holding Company to invest US$2 billion in Adani Group's green portfolio 22 April: APSEZ acquires Ocean Sparkle 15 May: Adani to acquire Holcim's Stake in Ambuja Cements and ACC Ltd 23 May: Gautam Adani is listed among *TIME* magazine's 100 influential list 26 May: Adani Defence Systems and Technologies signs a deal with General Aeronautics for its military drone and artificial intelligence and machine learning (AI/ML) capabilities and provide end-to-end solutions for the domestic agricultural sector 28 May: Adani Green switches on India's first hybrid power plant

2022-23	The Adani–POSCO steel unit agreement signed
	Adani Group pledges to produce green hydrogen
	APSEZ and Indian Oil Corporation (IOC) to build on relationship at Mundra Port
	Adani Green raises US$288 million for construction facility; increases the construction revolver pool to US$1.64 billion
	Adani Ports cargo volumes accelerate to 300 MMT
	Adani Power, IHI and Kowa collaborate for environmentally sustainable power generation
	Adani Total Gas Ltd (ATGL) forays into electric mobility infrastructure sector
	Adani Group accelerates enterprise-wide digital transformation strategy with Google Cloud
	International Holding Company (IHC) to invest US$2 billion in Adani Group's green portfolio
	April 2022: Gautambhai addresses 2022 Bengal Global Business Summit promising to invest Rs 10,000 crore and create 25,000 jobs
	Adani acquires India's largest marine services company, Ocean Sparkle
	Adani–Wilmar buys Kohinoor brand (rice) to strengthen its leadership in the rice and food business
	Adani Enterprises announces that IHC, Abu Dhabi will invest Rs 7700 crore (US$1 billion) through preferential allotment route
	Adani Enterprises achieves financial closure for Navi Mumbai Airport for Rs 12,770 crore

Mumbai International Airport raises US$750 million from Apollo Enterprises Ltd

April 2022: Adani Enterprises Ltd forms Advance Media Group (AMG) Media Networks, an arm it said would be in the business of 'publishing, advertising, broadcasting, distribution of content over different types of media networks'

April 2022: Adani University is accorded private university status by Gujarat Legislative Assembly. Joins the company of Elon Musk, Jeff Bezos, and others—the newest $100 billion man

May 2022: Adani Portfolio Companies complete Rs 15,400 crore primary equity transaction with IHC[2]

Gautambhai addresses the audience at Davos, outlining his plans for sustainability and the world's unwillingness to understand the problems confronting developing nations

June 2022: Gautambhai acquires Essar's Mahan-Sipat transmission project[3]

On Gautam Adani's sixtieth birthday, the Adani family commits Rs 60,000 crore to charity. Donation to be utilized in healthcare, education and skill development

June 2022: The Adani Group gets into copper production, achieves financial closure of Kutch Copper Limited project, and raises entire debt of Rs 6071 crore. Aims to accelerate refined copper production for India's transition to renewable energy[4]

July 2022: The group announces its foray into the telecom space, but in a limited way. It participates in the 5G spectrum auction to provide private network solutions along with enhanced cyber security in airport, ports and logistics, power generation, transmission, distribution and various manufacturing operations. The group also announces plans of developing its own digital platform encompassing super apps, edge data centres and industry command and control centres, will need ultra high-quality data streaming capabilities through a high frequency and low latency 5G network across all their businesses

The Adani Group and Gadot win the tender to privatize Israel's Haifa Port. A consortium comprising India's APSEZ and Israel's Gadot Group has secured the rights to buy 100 per cent shares of Haifa Port Company Ltd with a concession period up to 2054

Adani Group enters the sectors of higher education and medical education

April 2022: ATGL, India's leading city gas distribution company, announces its operational and financial performance for the first quarter ending on 30 June 2022[5]

August 2022: ATGL announces that it has over 6 lakh piped natural gas (PNG) consumers, 349 compressed natural gas (CNG) stations and has increased revenue from operations by 113 per cent to Rs 1110 crore

	The group starts making PVC through coal The group signs a deal with the Odisha state government to invest Rs 57,575 crore for setting up two projects—Integrated Alumina Refinery and a 30 million tonnes per annum (MTPA) iron ore (value addition) project. Exposure to and involvement in defence-related projects increases. The group gets into maintenance, repair and overhaul (MRO) operations as well
	The list will keep expanding . . .

2

Gautam Adani: The Man
Who Changed India

The roots of this book lie in two events.

The first event took place, quite by accident, in 2007. I was then working as a consulting editor with LOG.IN—the Indian branch of a German publishing group called DVV Media.[6] The Indian publication closed shop in 2009. But in 2007 it was quite active and vibrant, and one of the assignments I chose to pick was a trip to Mundra, a small place in Gujarat where someone called Gautam Adani was building India's first all-weather, deep-water port (privately held port, because almost all other ports were government-owned). I managed to dig up a few connections who could help me locate the place and show me around.

The visit remains unforgettable to this day. I was given access to the entire management team. Shortly thereafter, on 2 November 2007, Mundra Port and Special Economic Zone Limited (MPSEZL) filed its prospectus with the Securities and Exchange Board of India (SEBI) for raising money from the investing public.[7] I was lucky because I got a preview of the group's plans even before the company went public. And I was given an overview that few journalists had ever been given before. That privilege is what I continue to enjoy even today.

A clarification is required here: MPSEZL was not the first company in the group to go public. Adani Exports Ltd had gone public on 1 November 1994. But it was still a trader's company, involved essentially in exports and imports. The inputs Gautambhai[8] got from this business were incredible, as we shall see later in the book. He began getting a flavour of what was involved in going public. By the time MPSEZL was ready, the homework was a lot better.

But the early signs of strategy were already visible. The first unique way in which Gautambhai differs from other industrialists also began to be perceived.

What makes Gautambhai different

Gautambhai does not like raising money from the investing public before the enterprise begins making profits. This is quite unlike many other industrialists in India who first raise funds from the public, and then begin setting up the venture and even obtaining the required clearances. This was to become the hallmark of Gautambhai's ventures. It is a trait that has made him immensely endearing to the investing public. More on this too a bit later.

I subsequently wrote a cover story article for LOG.IN titled 'The Man who could change India'.[9] When I look back, I realize how prescient the title was. Gautambhai truly has changed India.

My first meeting with Gautambhai was extremely pleasant. It is still fresh in my memory. He was affable (and continues to be so). He did not, and does not, speak much, except when required. One reason is that he continues to be very self-conscious about his English (my own Gujarati, the language he was most comfortable with, is extremely limited). Another reason is his reluctance to speak; he would rather focus on listening. And he is incredibly good at maintaining relationships.

The second major factor that influenced this book was an earlier book on Gautam Adani which the family commissioned me to bring out.

2.2

Gautambhai releases his biography in June 2013

from L to R – Gautambhai and his wife Pritiben; with brother Vinod Adani; with author. The title of the book is Gautam Adani: Game Changer.

The Game Changer

While writing the previous book, *Gautam Adani: Game Changer* I got access to various members of the Adani family and the professionals who were in charge of various businesses; and I got a peek into the processes involved in picking up a business opportunity, and more importantly, the factors that made Gautam Adani grow from a diamond and plastics trader into one of the most formidable industrialists in India.[10] That in turn gave me an insight into the man and the company, and in this book I have used several quotes from the meetings and notes I exchanged with them at that time.

As I studied Gautambhai closely, five factors stand out which make him different from many other industrialists in India, and possibly the world.

2.3
The book brought out on his fiftieth birthday

The first, which has been stated above, is his unwillingness to raise funds from an investing public till a business has begun generating money. Undoubtedly, such an approach does allow him to get higher valuations at the time of raising funds through the issuing of shares. But, more importantly, Gautambhai is known to follow a policy of not forcing risks on others. When a business deal goes wrong, he will try and help the person/client with other opportunities which will help them tide over the losses they have made in the past. This, in turn, has nurtured a sense of loyalty towards Gautambhai in a way that many other industrialists have not been able to command or nurture.

The second is his ability to build and maintain relationships. He does not like going back on any deal that he has entered into. Nor does he try to buy out or squeeze out his partners. His motto is simple. He would like to keep his partners with him all through the journey. If some partner wants to leave, he will try and dissuade them. But if they still insist on leaving, Gautambhai will not stop them. When a deal does not work out the way it was expected to, Gautambhai usually sits down with the partner and arrives at a resolution—either the business grows to the levels which are acceptable to Gautambhai, or it is shut down. The two partners invariably part ways amicably.

There are hardly any non-compete agreements that he has asked his partners to enter, as far as my exposure to various business heads goes. He succeeds in maintaining relationships even if common sense might demand a re-evaluation of relationships. Take for instance the Adani–Wilmar venture story (more on this later). It is a 50:50 venture, where Wilmar and Adani hold equal stakes. Not once—since it was set up in January 1999—has Gautambhai entertained any desire to make his stake go up and make Wilmar the junior partner. He believes that businesses grow when competence marries enterprise. And if the other party combines competence with enterprise and enters into a relationship with the Adani Group, a 50:50 relationship is the most desirable. Currently, Adani–Wilmar is one of the top five players in the FMCG sector in India. It is the largest seller of edible oil. And yet the relationship survives,[11] and is thriving. And as the following pages will show, the 50:50 formula has been the hallmark of many other relationships as well.

Maintaining relationships extends even beyond family and his corporate group. His relationships with political and social leaders, across all types of party lines, have made him acceptable to every government. He has concluded projects under the Congress government, the Bhartiya Janta Party government, the National Democratic Alliance, the left parties in Kerala and even the mercurial Mamata Banerjee of the Trinamool Congress in West Bengal.

West Bengal has become extremely important for Gautam Adani because he has emerged as the highest bidder for West Bengal's Tajpur deep-sea port.[12] And he has bid for other ports as well. In a much-publicized speech in that state, Gautambhai promised to invest Rs 10,000 crore in West Bengal and create 25,000 jobs.[13]

Maintaining relationships plays a major role in his recently announced project in partnership with South Korea's POSCO (formerly known as Pohang Steel Company Ltd).[14] The entire corporate structure for the steel production deal has not been announced. However, South Korea as a country has been close to Gautambhai. He began his move into big-time trading in plastics in June 1983 with a South Korean company. His journey into wealth began with this connection, though there were several other contributors as well. POSCO has been involved with the Adani Group in building the 200-kilometre-long railway line in Australia as well.[15] More about the steel plant a bit later.

The third factor which differentiates Gautambhai from many other Indian industrialists is that he does not block the chances for anyone to grow or compete with him. Unlike some other Indian industrialists who like to block the growth of competitors, Adani likes to push himself harder to grow faster than those who want to compete with him. Sometimes, this ability to push himself makes him take risks that many would call foolhardy. But like most shrewd traders-turned-entrepreneurs, he knows how to hedge his risks and how to take steps to mitigate any resultant losses. This is what happened when he persuaded the government to create a rail link policy for ports, which would allow ports to build their own railway lines to connect to the national railway network. Obviously, he wanted this for the Mundra Port, but he did not get exclusive benefits. It was a policy change for the country. More on this too a bit later.

2.4								
Port incomes for the Adani Group								
							figures in crore rupees	
Particulars	Cargo		Revenue		EBITDA[#]		Free Cash Flow	
	FY22	FY21	FY22	FY21	FY22	FY21	FY22	FY21
APSEZ*	282	247	15,934	12,550	9,811	8,063	5,261	5,800
GPL	30		1,206		796		1,293	
Total	312	247	17,140	12,550	10,607	8,063	6554	5800

Notes : GPL- Gangavaram Ports; *APSEZ financials don't include Gangavaram Port numbers; # EBITDA excludes forex mark-to-market loss/gain. EBITDA of FY21 excludes one-time donation of Rs 80 crore, EBITDA of FY22 excludes one-time expenses of Rs 60 crore related to acquisition of SRCPL.
Source: Adani press release of 24 May 2022

The fourth factor is that he is of the firm belief that when a corporate group's interests are closely aligned with national interests, growth can be assured. Of course, other management inputs also matter, especially project implementation capability, finance and strategic vision.[16] But aligning with a country's interests is crucial. This started with coal, ports, agriculture and logistics, and now with defence as well. There are times when ports, defence and national strategies get blended to give this group unusual advantages and heft.

The last and the fifth factor, he respects fair play. In some cases, where he wanted to buy out a shareholder, he paid him more than what the market price was. This is what happened when Gautambhai had to request the state government of Gujarat to give up its stake in the Mundra Port. As A.D. Desai, IAS (Retd), formerly vice chairman (VC) and chief executive officer (CEO), GMB; formerly secretary ports, Government of Gujarat, explains,

'At a time when Gujarat was marked by minor state ports (Kandla was under the central government), Mr Adani marketed to the state government the vision of how more ports would catalyse the state's economy. At a time when the government began to agree that what he was saying was right, he succeeded in getting the state of Gujarat to become a minority stakeholder in the Mundra port. When the government wanted to allot the port to the highest bidder, he was able to demonstrate his credentials which included a captive jetty and road. The result is that Gujarat's port capacity has increased from 24 million MT in 1996 to 280 million MT in 2012 [the latest figures are given in chart 2.4]. However, what I like best about this big achiever is that he is polite and down to earth. Most large industrialists would send their senior executives to visit bureaucrats; Mr Adani would always come in person.'

The Mundra Port deal was exceptional in two ways. First, it was possibly the only deal where he had to buy a shareholder out. And second, this was a rare deal that was won without an open tendering process. The group's defence deals would also fall into this category, because it is not possible to finalize defence deals based on tendering. The Mundra Port project was soon to become the lynchpin for all his group's activities.

Looking back twenty years, it is now possible to realize why the Adani–POSCO deal could be another watershed moment for the group. With this project, Gautambhai has got into the core of infrastructure building. He has got into steel-making. Going by the group's track record, and an insight into the way the group thinks, this project could be a big exporter of steel in addition to supplying the metal for local consumption. And this project could propel Gautambhai's plans of becoming India's largest player in green energy. If all goes well, he could become the world's largest player in the green segment.

On 13 January 2022, the Adani Group signed an MoU for comprehensive cooperation for making high-grade steel, and for introducing carbon reduction technologies in India.[17] POSCO had a nightmarish experience in India while setting up a steel plant in Odisha.[18] After several years of trying to set up a steel manufacturing facility there, it gave up all attempts. POSCO's other venture in Maharashtra continues to function well.[19] But it is landlocked and hence limited in size and capabilities.

Even though the Maharashtra unit was set up in June 2014, its production still remains small—at 1.8 million tonnes of cold rolled steel a year. Moreover, it is landlocked, and the best synergies for steel units get unleashed when they are near the coast, thus, allowing for easier import of raw material and easier export of finished goods. Location matters in making steel units extremely competitive and efficient. Moreover, the Maharashtra plant faces occasional disruptions in production.[20] POSCO was looking for a better location and one where labour problems too would not be disruptive.

That is where Mundra makes immense sense. It has an all-weather, deep-sea port, a management team that has excellent links with South Korea, big plans for setting up manufacturing facilities in the abundant land it has in the SEZ next to the port, and most importantly, a partner who could help it secure all the clearances that it might require from time to time. The state of Gujarat, and more specifically the Adani Group's plants, have an excellent labour record.

All these factors played a part when the MoU between the Adani Group and POSCO was signed. They agreed to explore business cooperation opportunities, including the establishment of a green, environment-friendly integrated steel mill at Mundra, Gujarat, as well as other businesses. The investment is estimated to be up to US$ 5 billion.

2.5

The Adani-POSCO steel project should help both, even India

Pix: Press release from the Adani Group and POSCO media teams

The investments could grow for the simple reason that the group wants to be in the sector where it could be the largest or the second largest in the country. In March 2022, the Jindal Group (JSPL) announced its plans[21] for setting up the largest single-location steel plant in Odisha. The High-Level Clearance Authority of Odisha, headed by Chief Minister Naveen Patnaik, approved JSPL's proposal to expand the capacity of its steel plant to 25.2 million TPA (tonnes per annum) at Angul by 2030. This would be the world's largest and greenest single-location steel plant, thus pitching Odisha's USP (unique selling point) on the global steel map. JSPL's investment in Odisha is slated to grow to Rs 1,25,000 crore from Rs 45,000 crore at present. That would be almost ten times the outlay announced by the Adani–POSCO venture. We can expect the Adani–POSCO venture to be scaled up significantly. Also expect the Australian connection that Adani enjoys to play a crucial part in bringing the best ore to this plant by sea, more efficiently than if it had been mined in Odisha. The steel industry is likely to witness a turbulence seldom expected before in India.

Moreover, POSCO is already setting up the world's largest facilities for hydrogen production in Saudi Arabia.[22] But that was before the Adani–POSCO deal was signed. It is now quite possible that India's hydrogen production capabilities will exceed those of Saudi Arabia.

The steel production centre becomes even more important because this one project alone will take away the harshest of criticisms levelled against the Adani and Ambani groups.[23] Economist Arvind Subramanian called their growth 'stigmatised capital'. He said that both had benefitted from government favours, protection and clearances. He also said that unlike the *chaebols*, neither group was known for its focus on exports that made South Korea the powerhouse it has become.

It's true that most of the Adani projects are not export-oriented. But they aid exports. Ports enable more efficient exports and imports. Without ports, India would face an export bottleneck. Moreover, even though all earnings by ports are in foreign exchange, especially from foreign ships docking there, their expenses too are in foreign exchange, leaving the net figure very small if not negative.

Cementing another business

Another recent acquisition—the Holcim-ACC-Ambuja cement plants in India[24]—could find huge synergies with Adani's steel plants, power plants, and even at Kutch and Saurashtra (where the group's operations are the largest). Kutch has abundant limestone, a key raw material for making cement. Adani has the largest solar plants in that region that will give him cheap clean power to make cement, which is energy intensive.

The steel plant will produce clinker and slag which can be used for cement production. The thermal power plants (both Adani's and Tata's) in the region produce unbelievable amounts of ash, which can be blended with cement. And the combination of iron and steel as well as cement makes him the most formidable player in the infrastructure segment. It is possible that Adani will not be content with remaining the second-largest cement producer, and soon become the largest instead.

Gautambhai did think of going into cement production in the 2000s but gave up that idea because the capacities would have been small. He refuses to get into any business where he cannot be one of the leading companies in India.

The ports will be used for shipping the cement through the coastal route around India, and even for exports.

Adani–Wilmar does export some of its produce, as does Adani Agri Fresh in very limited quantities (more on this too later). But big-time exports will come through this steel project

Otherwise, most Adani Group projects are in the service industry sector. Power is a service offered to people. So is gas distribution. Ditto with ports, airports and railways. The steel and cement projects promise to be different. So do those relating to agriculture (more on this later). There are other similar projects in the pipeline.

With the Adani–POSCO project, the group actually becomes a big exporter and reduces import of steel into the country. Moreover, the new defence projects being set up in the country by Adani and other industrialists will increasingly require more special steel. It is possible that India and the Adani defence projects will seek to export military hardware and services as well.

2.6	
Adani's railway network	
Railway line	Km length
Mundra	74
Dhamra	69
Krishnapatnam Rail Co	113
Kutch Rail	301
BDRCL	63
Total	620

Note : Does not include the group's overseas rail network, especially the one in Australia which accounts for 200 km. Moreover, according to a 24 May 2022 press release, APSEZ acquired 70 km of Sarguja Rail from another Adani Group.

Source: APSEZ presentation of March 2021; https://www.adaniports.com/-/media/Project/Ports/Investor/Investor Downloads/Investors-Presentation/APSEZ---SRCPL-Presentation_Final.pdf

This steel project actually unleashes all the visions and plans that Mundra had spoken of in 2007. Gautam Adani has finally begun bringing industries into his SEZ to make them coast-based industries. This is what Nitin Gadkari spoke of when he was union minister of ports and shipping (among other portfolios).[25] While other coastal economic zones (CEZ) have remained on the drawing board, the Adani–POSCO project (and some other projects like cement) is likely to release energies unheard of in India.

Rail connectivity and synergies

The proposed railway network will have easy access to the port, a captive airport (for now), power plant (for both energy and electrolysis to produce good water to cool the steel and power station boilers), thermal electricity, solar farms, and lots of land for stocking raw materials as well as finished products. It will

further the group's dream of transitioning into green power—
solar and green hydrogen being the key drivers in addition
to gas. That is why the MoU talks about renewable energy,
green hydrogen, and logistics in response to carbon reduction
requirements. It mentions how both parties are examining
various options to cooperate and leverage the technical,
financial, and operational strengths of each company. It may be
mentioned here, that POSCO already has a key role with the
Adani Group in Australia. It is helping the group to build the
200-km railway line connecting the mine to the existing railway
line which reaches the port at Abbot Point in that country.

As Choi Jeong-woo, the CEO of POSCO explains, 'POSCO
and Adani are able to come to great synergy in the steel and
environment-friendly business with POSCO's state-of-the-
art technology in steel making and Adani's expertise in energy
and infrastructure. I hope this cooperation will be a good and
sustainable business cooperation model between India and South
Korea.'[26]

This project also highlights the way Gautambhai identifies
potential partners, and then goes all out to woo them, comfort
them and make them business partners as well.

This does not mean that there are no disputes.

There have been differences of opinion which have sometimes
resulted in court cases. The first terminal of MPSEZL was
developed by P&O which then got taken over by Dubai Port
Works (DPW). It wanted to be involved in developing other
terminals at the port as well. But Gautam Adani had other plans.
He used his own group's management skills and native genius to
develop these terminals. DPW continues to remain the operator
of the first terminal. But all other terminals at MPSEZL and other
ports have the Adani Group itself as principal developer, owner
and operator (more on this later). Nonetheless, the relationship
survives. DPW is today a partner as well as a competitor. But
Adani has outgrown the earlier relationship. Such instances are

rare. With Gautambhai, the norm is that partners and the Adani Group must grow together.

One way of minimizing disputes, say admiring group insiders, is the marvellous knack Gautambhai has developed of not letting a good man's mistakes unsettle him or his mood. He prefers to overlook a mistake when it had been done in good faith, and not out of incompetence, negligence or greed. His colleagues still talk of how a coffee trader employed with him ran up losses of a few crore rupees. Aghast at the outcome of his trades, the man approached Gautambhai with his offer to resign. Gautambhai is said to have replied with a twinkle in his eye, 'You have learnt your lessons at my cost; do you think I can afford to let you go?'

That ability allows many of the wrinkles to be ironed out, forging stronger relationships and even undying loyalties.

Where government can help

Like many industrialists, Adani too has sought favours from the government. For instance, he wanted the government to grant him permission for connecting his Mundra Port with the railway network of the Government of India. The closest railway junction was Adipur. So, Gautambhai lobbied for a port-railway-network connectivity policy which the government granted in November 2020.

'Gautambhai acquired 17,000 acres to complete 64 kilometres of rail link,' says Dr Malay Mahadevia, director, Adani Ports and Special Economic Zone Ltd, and a key member of the Adani management team. 'When the last part of the rail project became difficult, he assumed direct control. This one-of-its-kind project would have normally taken four to five years elsewhere; it was completed by him in one-and-a-half years. The result was the creation of the first private railway line in India which led to the enunciation of a national PPP policy on port linkages.'

But that concession from the government was not exclusive to the Adani Group. It is for the entire port industry. Today, that single policy has made the entire ports sector for the entire country extremely vibrant. With hindsight, it is now obvious that this policy has helped the Adani Group with its other ports as well. At the time of getting this policy introduced in the country, Gautambhai had no idea that he would be developing so many ports. Today, port connectivity alone accounts for 620 kilometres of railway lines in India[27] (more on this later).

In the final analysis, Gautam Adani has changed India. And in the following chapters, I will attempt to explain the factors that helped propel Gautambhai to where he is today.

Restructuring group management

2.7			
Key management personnel in the Adani Group			
Family		**Non-family**	
Gautam Adani	Chairman	Angshu Mallick	CEO, Adani–Wilmar
Priti Adani	Wife	Anil Sardana	MD and CEO, Adani Transmission; MD, Adani Thermal
Rajesh Adani	Brother	Ashish Rajvanshi	President and Head, Chairman's office
Pranav Adani	Vinod Adani's son	Gaurav Gupta	CEO, Adani Capital
Karan Adani	Gautam Adani's son, CEO, Adani Ports and SEZ Ltd, President Group Finance	Jayant Parimal	Advisor to Chairman
Jeet Adani	Gautam Adani's son, Vice President Group Finance	Jeykumar Janakraj	CEO, Adani Global, Singapore & Adani Connex
Sagar Adani	Rajesh Adani's son; Executive Director, AGEL	Jugeshinder (Robie) Singh	Group CFO
Pranav Vora	Pritiben's brother, CEO Shipping	Lucas Dow	CEO and Country Head, Adani Australia
Samir Vora	Executive Director, Adani Australia	Malay Mahadevia	Director, APSEZ and CEO, AAHL
Notes : The brothers of the Adani family are not mentioned as key management players —Vasant, Vinod, Mahasukh and Vasant—have opted to stay away from the group and tend to their respective businesses. Vinodbhai is actively involved in almost every overseas financial negotiation.		Sudipta Bhattacharya	CEO, Adani Group, North America and CTO, Adani Group
		Suresh Manglani	CEO, Adani Gas
		Vikram Tandon	Group Chief Human Resources Officer
		Vinay Prakash	Director, Adani Enterprises and CEO, Natural Resources
		Vneet S Jaain	MD Adani Green Energy
Source : *Names have been gleaned from https://www.adani.com/About-us*			

A massive restructuring of the group is under way. With tremendous growth come restraints on management time. Hence meetings with key managers are not as easily fixed as before. Fortunately, material collected over the past seventeen years has been of immense value. Plus, discussions with merchant banks, former employees, investors and people still close to the Adani Group have helped me fill in the gaps.

And I wanted this book to be out close to his sixtieth birthday (in June 2022). I am also aware that with a growth rate as stupendous as the one notched up by the Adani Group (see chart no.10.5), more opportunities will emerge, and new companies may get born. Maybe a revised edition will be required within a few years. But what has been achieved till now is spellbinding.

At the core of Gautambhai's empire is the mix of professionals and family members (who too boast of excellent qualifications), most of them having studied overseas and are extremely competent at their jobs. Without such a mix, it is doubtful if Gautambhai could have created such a large empire.

Coupled with this is a decision to stick to a terrain that he understands well. He prefers being in Gujarat, and in Ahmedabad to be more specific. While many industrialists opt to move to a metropolis like Mumbai, Delhi, Bengaluru or Chennai once they become large and pan-India, Gautambhai has preferred to stay in his native state capital instead. This has meant that he had to travel to Mumbai occasionally to meet bankers and merchant bankers. But as he began growing, all of them have opted to make a beeline to his corporate headquarters at Adani-Shantigram—even though it is 12 km away from the city airport, which itself is some distance away from the main city.

But Shantigram has allowed Gautambhai to expand his corporate office in a way that he is comfortable with—all key offices of the group are within the same complex. There are very few distractions of going out for lunch to the city's fancy restaurants (you will notice similarities between the largest corporate groups worldwide and the Adani approach). Shantigram boasts of its own hotels (also used as guest houses for important visitors). The air is better, and key officers stay within the Shantigram complex.

Three factors influencing structures

Three factors have contributed to the group's structure.

The first would be the DNA and culture factors.[28] That is a key contributor to the sharpening of what many call intuition. It is interesting to note that way back in 2008, this is what Gautambhai himself had to say, 'The corporate credo of Adani Group is based on a piece of advice that even I do not know where it came from. "When everything gets really complicated and you feel overwhelmed, trust your intuition." There are times when we find that we are caught in a maze … Our strategy is three-pronged. First is survival, for which I often trust my intuition… [the second kicks in when] After getting out of this, we study why it happened and how we can avoid such a contingency or adversity when it does occur again. Third, we think out of the box for ideas that take us forward.'[29]

The trading instinct and the urge to clinch bigger deals, with the keen sense of going in for risk mitigation when required, is the second factor.

Luck is a third factor. In many ways Gautambhai is destiny's child. He has escaped accidents, major trading crises and even terrorist attacks.

For instance, in January 1998, much before he became a big industrialist, Gautambhai and Shantilal Patel, an associate, were kidnapped. Adani and Shantilal Patel were abducted at gunpoint after they left Karnavati Club in a car and headed for Mohammadpura Road in Ahmedabad. A scooter reportedly forced the car to stop, and then a group of men came in a van and abducted both men. They were taken to an unknown place in a car before being released, the police chargesheet said.[30]

But an Ahmedabad court in end November 2018, nearly twenty years after the alleged incident, acquitted two main accused—Fazl-ur-Rehman alias Fazlu and Bhogilal Darji alias Mama. Kunal N. Shah, the lawyer of the two accused, said that Additional District Judge D.P. Patel acquitted his clients as the victims refused to press charges.

One reason for not pressing charges could be that a large ransom was paid, estimated at $1.5 million. People close to the family confirm this, but refuse to confirm the ransom amount. In any case, Gautambhai has also gone public with the fact that he was indeed kidnapped.[31]

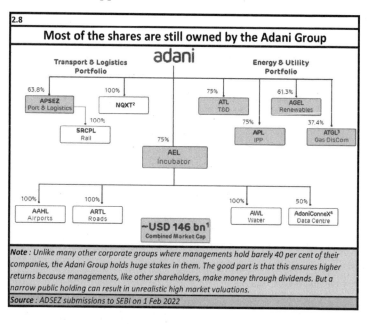

2.8

Most of the shares are still owned by the Adani Group

Note : Unlike many other corporate groups where managements hold barely 40 per cent of their companies, the Adani Group holds huge stakes in them. The good part is that this ensures higher returns because managements, like other shareholders, make money through dividends. But a narrow public holding can result in unrealistic high market valuations.

Source : ADSEZ submissions to SEBI on 1 Feb 2022

On another occasion, on 26 November 2008, he was having dinner at Mumbai's iconic Taj Hotel when it was attacked by terrorists. It was the deadliest terrorist attack that Mumbai had witnessed. Adani hid in the basement as terrorists killed over 160 people inside. He was able to escape safely when commandos took control of the situation and engaged with the terrorists.

Eventually, all three—he, his colleague Sandeep Mehta and the Dubai Port CEO Mohammed Sharaf—escaped (the story is that the DPW CEO was still trying to persuade Gautambhai for giving his company a bigger say in the Mundra Port. But there is no confirmation for this narrative). In any case, people can hear what Gautambhai himself has to say about his miraculous escape.[32]

The hotel staff helped the guests, including Gautambhai, to move to the basement. A couple of hours later when it became too suffocating in the basement, they were then moved to the Taj chamber hall on an upper floor.[33]

Among the top ten richest people

Take all the achievements listed above, and you then begin to understand how this man has grown to become the richest person in Asia,[34] and among the top ten richest in the world. There was no family wealth involved. Vision, grit and luck together cemented more and more deals.

Another interesting aspect about the Adani Group is that the management continues to hold substantial stakes in all the companies (see chart 2.8). Unlike many Indian managements, who transfer much of the company ownership to shareholders, the Adani Group prefers owning significant stakes in all companies in the group. The group has also not been involved in collusive mergers and demergers aimed at benefitting the management over shareholders. Similarly, there has been no attempt to delist companies when they have become profitable as some entrepreneurs are known to have done. In doing this, he is closer to the likes of Azim Premji—who continues to hold substantial stakes in Wipro—than many other contemporaries.

This lends confidence to investors, bankers and potential partners, as they know that the management's own profits will come from future dividends. A substantial holding also enables a management to maintain a long-term vision for the company, rather than looking to maximize returns every quarter. Such a structure can also reduce the public float and help manage very high valuations.

Memorable traits

Talk to his friends, and even employees, and you will learn that Gautambhai has some unusual traits.

Harinarayan, secretary to Gautambhai, recalls, 'He is always in a rush to complete the jobs on his plate.' But that is because he 'manages several meetings a day, responds to about 150 phone calls and about 150-200 emails. The bottom-line is "Be quick!" The result is that if I receive a fax, it must be scanned and uploaded to his iPad within 60 seconds (wherever he is in the world), anyone asking for an appointment must specify the precise number of minutes required (when those minutes are consumed, Gautambhai's body language will change); if a visitor has a meeting with him at the office, I am expected to track the visitor across Ahmedabad and ensure that he/she reaches five minutes ahead of schedule; when he is traveling, my job is to send him a comprehensive email every 30 minutes on the name, time, purpose and contact numbers of those who called in his absence—so that he can respond within five minutes, whether he is in Melbourne or Mundra.

'Despite setting a relentless pace for himself and colleagues, Gautambhai makes himself accessible to everyone—even peons. They just have to come and place the request with me, I will communicate to him, and he will somehow squeeze time in during the day. To this extent, he likes to be interrupted, so that he can respond to micro-meetings in a jiffy and then return to what he is doing.

'What amazes me is that for a man who lives every minute and is known to take large risks across a number of businesses, I have never seen him use an expletive; he addresses colleagues as *bhai* even if they are a day older.'

Another trait was his ability to get into mischief. His relatives called him *toofani* (loosely translated as a typhoon-like turbulence). Girish Desai, a cousin, says, 'If there is one word to describe him when he was young, it would be "toofaani". So much so that my father would quietly indicate to his mother, who was my father's sister, that she should never make the mistake of sending Gautam to our house alone during the holidays.

'On one occasion we were playing around a building that was under construction. We had gone up the stairs to the second floor; when it was time to come down, we took the usual route. Gautam walked to the edge and jumped into a *ret no dhaglo* (mound of construction sand). His antics were such a source of concern that the family approached a *jyotishi* (astrologer) for advice. The jyotishi studied the charts for some time and told our much-relieved family that this boy *"Kyaan thi kyaa aagar nikalshey* (loosely, will go places)." Despite his *dhamaal-masti*, (noisy mischief) if there was someone he feared, it was my father, his maternal uncle. On one occasion when the family iron (we called it 'press') did not operate for some reason, he absconded for fear that he would be apprehended, walked to the nearest bus depot in Palanpur and took a bus 45 kms to his residence in Deesa without telling anyone. He was just ten years old.'

Desai pauses and adds, 'Later, we [Prakash, Gautam, and I] worked together in diamond trading. And this was what we did: we bought diamonds standing on Dhanji Street, we showed diamonds standing on Dhanji Street and we sold diamonds standing on Dhanji Street. Gautam had an appetite for large trades. On the occasions when he bought a larger quantity than our prudent inventory norms warranted, his single reassuring line to the partners was *"Vechaasey!* (I will conclude the deal!)" Thereafter, he scouted for low-cost diamonds, blended them with the high-priced inventory, reduced the overall holding cost and fished around for an exporter to sell the entire blend to for a profit. This is the way diamonds are traded, because different traders need a variety of assortments. Much of the profit comes by blending the right mix of gemstones that the potential buyer might like.

'Those were interesting days; he would sleep on the train from Vile Parle to Charni Road and on a number of occasions would wake up only when the train had overshot his destination and reached Churchgate. He was an unusual diamond trader; we would read *Stardust* from cover to cover whereas he would also subscribe to *Scope*, a science magazine.

'This idyllic life came to an end nearly two years later, when Mahasukhbhai called one day to tell [brother] Gautam that he had bought a packaging factory and needed family hands to run it. The result was that we had to pay Gautam around Rs 2 lakh as his share of the profits that had been invested in our business and he returned to Ahmedabad.'

Risk mitigation, intuition and delegation

However, no matter how audacious the deal, Gautambhai always believed in de-risking any transaction. As Kaushal Kabra, general manager (Chairman's Office Adani Group), recalls during an interview, 'I was a member of the Adani treasury department.

'I made some trade investments in blue-chip equity shares which suffered extensive losses during the 2008 slowdown. The company was compelled to take a sizable loss on its books. I owned up my responsibility and submitted my resignation. This letter reached Gautambhai who called me for a meeting. He said, "The organisation takes the responsibility for the loss. If we had the right systems in place, we would have cut our losses early enough." The result of this surprising turn of conversation was that the quantum of trade investments has declined at the Adani Group and systems have been created to address contingencies. Besides, the company allocated me to a role where my capabilities are utilized better, and I now work with a fire in my belly to recoup the loss incurred by the company. The company transformed me into a resource once again.'

And underlying all this is Gautambhai's intuition that was mentioned earlier. As Utkarsh Shah, a friend, says, 'Some of the most successful people normally challenge themselves intellectually all the time. Let me give an instance. I solve a Sudoku puzzle in about 12 minutes. Gautam cracks the same game in about 4 minutes. So, one day I asked him, "How is this possible?" He said, "I usually begin in the conventional way like everyone else, but once I am a minute or two into the puzzle, I let my intuition take over. I say, 'If there is a 7 here then there must be a 3 here.' After some time, there is no logic to it, but it works perfectly."'

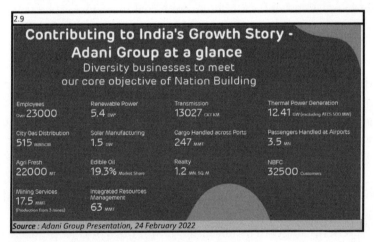

A niece of Gautambhai, Darshini Patel, also points to his inclination for completing the jobs on hand, 'Not many people know that Gautam kaka (uncle) starts his day with a large sheet of paper on which are scribbled hundreds of tasks lined up for the day. As he completes each, he folds that part of the paper and moves on. The smaller the sheet gets, the bigger seems to be his sense of achievement.'

When one looks back on the journey of just three decades, one realizes how far the group has come (see chart 2.9). Its core focus remains nation-building, even as the group grows into businesses that it had not envisaged earlier. It employs 23,000 people (before the cement and other mergers) and touches over 3 million lives. And, if there is one word to describe the group it is 'awesome'.

But most of all, Gautambhai is remembered for his enormous flexibility in decision-making and the willingness to delegate, as well as his unassuming nature.

On the first of these qualities, one of the best instances is provided by Harsh Mishra, former group president (international business), Adani Group: 'As president of corporate planning, I was given the freedom to negotiate mining assets in Australia. When I finally rang him with a proposal—we pay up to $500 million and a $2 a tonne royalty-based arrangement for twenty years in exchange for about 7.8 billion tonne coal mine in Australia—he was on holiday in the UK. I told him that this was probably the largest coal tenement in the world and about three times our budget. I told him that on the other hand, this would represent the group as game changer. He heard everything . . . and ended one of the most critical "meetings" in the history of the group in just 5 minutes with a "Go ahead!" Any other person in his place would have flown out to the mines immediately. In fact, he never visited the mine or met the seller for two months, delaying this [visit] to just a couple of days before the deal, which I signed on his behalf.' The deal was brilliant. The owners actually wanted $1.5 billion upfront. More details can be found in Chapter 8.

On his ability to handle crises, Jayesh Buch, former president, corporate affairs at Adani Group, says, 'I have noticed how most truly successful people are essentially grounded.

'During the setting up of the Gujarat Adani Port, the company defaulted technically on a loan repayment, so Mr Adani could not take his salary for the month. I asked, "*Ghar kevi reetey chaaley?* (How does one manage one's household?)" He said that he would give his wife Rs 10,000 every month to manage the household expenses, that when he travelled, he usually stayed at the company's guest house, and he bought a new coat and shoes once in six months, twenty-five tailored shirts once a year and stayed with that and no more.

'This attention to micro-detail extended to his time management. When we needed to travel from Ahmedabad to Mundra, most people would leave Ahmedabad at 8 a.m. and reach the port by early afternoon; but Mr Adani would leave at 4 a.m. so that he could be at the site office at 11 a.m. to catch up on the day's business.'

3

The March of the DNA

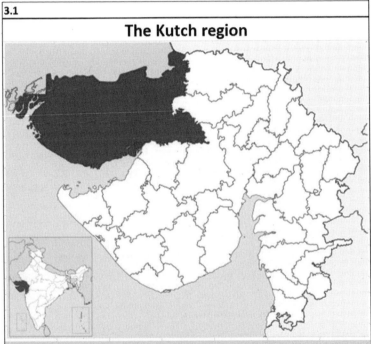

3.1

The Kutch region

Notes: The area is dry and was once almost inhospitable. But these lands bred a tenacious people, among whom are some of the country's finest etrepreneurs.
Source: Wikipedia; https://en.wikipedia.org/wiki/Kutch_district

Why being a Kutchi matters

'Where does one draw the line between tradition and the individual talent?' That was a question T.S. Eliot asked,[35] and several others before and after him. There are countless theories.

But most people agree that both play a part. And there are times when the DNA of a community gives the marching orders. Yet, there are times when the individual may choose to ignore them, even muffle them, for better or worse.

It was possibly the very DNA—of the community in which he was born—that allowed Gautambhai to dare to dream big and become bigger. The Jews call this chutzpah (pronounced kuds-pah).

Many studies, worldwide, have shown that the most successful entrepreneurs come from communities with very strong family and social connections. It is this collective-community-knowledge that creates the petri dish in which ideas for entrepreneurship germinate easily. And since the family and community become the safety net when things go wrong, the ability for chutzpah, to dare to do something bigger and better, even unconventional, manifests itself that much more easily.

Land and sea trade

Gautambhai was born to a family that hailed from the Kutch region in Gujarat. This is an arid region where little grows by way of crops. Its people used to rear goats and sheep in the past, and many migrated to other regions to become farmers. Many other became traders. Some traders remained on land. Some took to the seas and rivers. It is interesting to note that Gujarat has as many ports as the rest of India put together.

This was a territory of traders, even seafaring traders—almost akin to the trading territories of South India.

Yet, funnily enough, religious practices did not allow the largest community of Hindus to excel in trading across the shores of India. This was something non-Hindus would engage in. For

the Hindus, the sea was forbidden territory, even inauspicious.[36]
If a Hindu crossed the oceans, he had to go through a purification
ceremony (*shuddhikaran*) on his return. One can dive into the
history of the country to see that. Except for a solitary incident
of a Chola king sending across a ship full of armed soldiers, the
territory called India did not have a navy.

It may be recalled that even Lord Rama, when trying to
locate Sita, was faced with the same dilemma. When he reached
Kanyakumari, an ocean separated him from Sri Lanka. The Lord
invoked the sea god, who advised him not to use boats, but to
build a bridge instead. Boats were common in those days, if one
recalls the story of the Kevat. But those were on rivers, not oceans.
Hence sea trading was avoidable for most Hindus.

But when it came to land-based trading, few could match
the Gujaratis, especially Kutchis. The sparseness of the terrain
made them hardy, observant, thrifty and extremely careful in
financial dealings. Not surprisingly, many Kutchis became traders
and shopkeepers. Many intrepid and innovative ones grew from
trading to entrepreneurship to becoming business magnates.

Kutch is part of Gujarat which has spawned some of
the biggest industrialists in India. But it has its own unique
characteristics. A Kutchi, typically, considers education to
be less important than starting one's own business. That is
why you will find many Kutchis going into trade—hardware,
pharmaceuticals and chemicals are among the top favourites.
Many Kutchis opt for working as accounting consultants to
medium-sized and small businessmen. Some go into trading
in diamonds and plastics. Most Kutchis would shun being
employees, though. This has been changing, but it is common
to find extremely well-educated Kutchis opting to start their
own small businesses, rather than join the top echelons of a
corporate house. Unless they are from the same family, and
work together to grow the business.

Gujarat, on the other hand, values education even over starting one's own business. Consider Azim Premji for instance. He was born into a Gujarati family, and his father, Muhammed Hashim Premji, incorporated Western Indian Vegetable Products Ltd, based at Amalner, a small town in the Jalgaon district of Maharashtra. The family produced cooking oil under the Sunflower Vanaspati brand, and a laundry soap called 787, a by-product of oil manufacture.

Azim studied at Stanford, and would possibly have continued his studies there, if not for the sudden demise of his father. What Azim did, after taking over the company, was amazing. He professionalized oil trading and made it grow. He soon diversified into bakery fats, ethnic, ingredient-based toiletries, hair care soaps, baby toiletries, lighting products and hydraulic cylinders.

Later, as computers began making their appearance in India—and also because of a huge vacuum created by the exit of IBM from India[37]—the company's name was changed to Wipro and Azim diversified into computers and Information Technology (IT).

Today, he straddles both the IT and consumer goods sectors. He is a legend, primarily for his success in the IT sector. But he is equally successful in a variety of consumer brand products in India and overseas. He is one of India's most illustrious industrialists also because he has grown without seeking favours from the government. He has also emerged as one of the biggest philanthropists in India,[38] largely focused on school education through his Azim Premji Foundation.[39]

Ambani and Adani

Another Gujarati who shot into prominence during the 1980s was Dhirubhai Ambani, founder of Reliance Industries. He too began his career as a trader—of plastics and yarns—till he got an industrial licence from the government for producing synthetic yarns in India. India was under the Licence Raj then, and Dhirubhai succeeded in obtaining one government licence after another for enhancing his production capacities and then for producing the raw materials that went into the making of yarn. He even tried to go into retailing synthetic fabrics under the Vimal brand, but that business has not taken off as yet—it is not one of the top five textile brands in India even today.

He then became the petrochemicals giant in India. In the late 1990s he managed to get the government to transfer the right of some lucrative oil fields that the public-sector Oil and Natural Gas Corporation (ONGC) owned and moved into oil exploration, production and refining, setting up one of the largest refineries in the world. After Dhirubhai's demise, his two sons fought over succession rights. A patch-up followed, but the younger son lost out on many fronts. The elder son—under the Reliance Industries umbrella (RIL)—decided to expand the power generation, green energy and mobile telephony businesses for the group. Till such a time that RIL did not get into power generation and green energy, it was not competing with the Adani Group. But once it entered these sectors, both groups have been keenly competing.

However, as the figures show (see charts 10.5, 10.6 and 10.7) Adani has registered a blistering pace of growth, which could see him maintain his current lead over the Ambani group in the coming years. Gautambhai likes to play down such comparisons and said, 'I don't compare myself with others. I just do my best.'

Today, Mukesh Ambani of RIL and Gautambhai are neck-to-neck in terms of being the richest industrialists in India.[40] At the time of writing this book (May 2022) Gautam Adani ranked at 7 and Mukesh Ambani was 10. It must be mentioned here that these rankings change constantly, and Bloomberg updates the numbers daily.

Early years

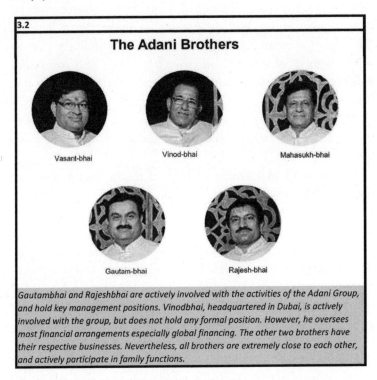

The Adani Brothers

Vasant-bhai

Vinod-bhai

Mahasukh-bhai

Gautam-bhai

Rajesh-bhai

Gautambhai and Rajeshbhai are actively involved with the activities of the Adani Group, and hold key management positions. Vinodbhai, headquartered in Dubai, is actively involved with the group, but does not hold any formal position. However, he oversees most financial arrangements especially global financing. The other two brothers have their respective businesses. Nevertheless, all brothers are extremely close to each other, and actively participate in family functions.

Gautam Adani was born into a Jain family—a community that has excelled in producing some of the finest professionals, industrialists and entrepreneurs engaged in gems and jewellery among others. In fact, almost the entire diamond cutting, polishing and export-import businesses related to diamonds is controlled by a section of the community known as the Palanpuri Jains.[41]

For this community, trade takes place usually by word of mouth. A spoken contract is as sacred as a written one. And while written contracts may be disputed in the corporate world, a spoken contract within this community is seldom broken. If a man defaults, it is customary for other relatives of the family to pool in their resources to redeem the family name. To help the family achieve this, the community itself offers the unfortunate relatives some opportunities and suggestions to make the redemption possible. If a member reneges on a deal, it is unlikely that any other member of this very enterprising, closely knit community will ever do business with him again, except with the most iron-clad guarantees.

Gautambhai was born, at Ahmedabad, in 1962. He was the youngest in the family—the fifth child born to Shantilal and Shantaben Adani.

Being born in a family of limited means meant that there was no great wealth to start a major enterprise. In many ways, Gautambhai seldom forgets his roots—that he is part of the Tharad Jain community.

The community itself originated from Banaskantha, an arid part of Gujarat where harsh conditions have helped forge, over the centuries, people who have learnt how to innovate and prudently manage scarce resources. This has made them entrepreneurial even under the most intimidating conditions. Most members of this community are self-employed entrepreneurs; seldom does a member of this community seek employment.

As mentioned earlier, the Adani family was into commodity trading. It used to enter future contracts for castor seed, and it graduated to textile trading by the late 1960s. Those were the days, when the best of traders had something to do with textiles—either in the cotton trade, fabrics, processing or even trading in garments. It was the backbone of Indian industry, and this is where most enterprise found expression. It is a pity that the government let this industry slip into near irrelevance.[42] Now, however, there are signs of this sector picking up, though import tariffs are structured in such a way that they favour producers of synthetic yarn or man-made fibres.

Gautambhai began his schooling in the small town of Deesa where the family ran a commodity trading business. He completed his primary education in this very town and was acknowledged to be good at studies.

Once, during the summer vacations, in 1978, he was mulling over what the next step should be, when his maternal uncle gently prodded him to think out of the box.

His uncle pointed out how Gautam's elder brothers had gone through university education, but finally landed in family business. Would it, therefore, not be more prudent that Gautam too tried his hand at some business or the other to find his own calling?

Adolescence to adulthood

As the boy moved from childhood to adolescence, the first signs of a sharp intellect and the urge to be ahead of others became evident. Whether it was walking on the parapet of his maternal uncle's two-storey house in the village or challenging his peers to solve *ukhana*, verbal puzzles in Gujarati, each situation provided one more opportunity to test the frontiers of what could be dared, and achieved. 'Impossible is a word that does not exist in Gautambhai's dictionary,' says Jay Shah, a long-time friend. The childhood games and pranks were probably the breeding ground for such a disposition.

Gautambhai has always believed in daring to do the unconventional. And what many thought as being brash was his way of testing his own mettle to see how far opportunities could be tapped.

For Gautambhai, life is all about transformation. First, he transforms himself, and then he expects this from others as well. And while he is great at delegation, he expects every member of his team to report to him directly on the progress of the work he has been assigned. He lends a hand, if the job has hit an unexpected obstacle and helps to decide quickly on the go/no-go options. Even today, he works for nearly eleven to twelve hours a day at his office.

In earlier years too, nobody ever thought of him as a contented child, or at peace with the world. For him, life offered, at each stage, one more opportunity to push forward, one more chance to dream the impossible dream. As the previous chapter stated, the favourite word to describe him was toofani. Gautambhai moved to Ahmedabad with his parents in the early 1970s, and his academic competence won him an admission at Sheth C.N. Vidyalaya, in 1974, a highly reputed school in Ahmedabad. He appeared for his secondary school exams (SSC) in 1977; his performance won him admission in the coveted science stream in Standard XI at the school.

After heeding his uncle's advice, the teenager decided to move to Bombay (now Mumbai) to pursue his dreams. He stayed with his elder brother Vinodbhai, a wholesaler of cut-piece fabrics for Bipin Mills and Rajesh Mills, and decided to try his hand at trading in diamonds.

Gautambhai would have preferred to embrace the earn-and-you-learn model for growth and development. But the fates had other plans for him.

Diamonds beckon

Gautam studied for a couple of months at a South Mumbai college. The diamond trading office was very close to the college. He went to the diamond markets in the morning, learned diamond sorting and assessment at Mahendra Brothers and then went to college. But in his attempt to excel at business, he found it difficult to mark attendance at college. Realizing that he could not meet attendance norms as well as do business the way he wanted to, he decided, within six months of life as a college student, to become a full-time diamond trader in Dhanji Street.

Devendra R. Amin, who has now retired from the Adani Group, and who was senior VP, corporate communications, says, 'Gautambhai is not constrained by a "formal" education. Formal education teaches you what has been done and how it has been done in the past in a variety of disciplines ranging from science to business. Gautambhai was lucky that he did not go through such an education, which normally produces consultants and not entrepreneurs, or say, "worker bees" and not the "queen bee". What is needed for growth and progress is the queen bee. A lack of formal education allows him to think out of the box and make swift decisions.'

Vinod Adani recalls how within a month of joining college, Gautambhai had begun to feel burdened by the pressures of attending college and coping with the demands of the diamond trade. He would be so tired that he would often go to sleep in the suburban train, overshooting the station he was supposed to get off at. Everything conspired to the eventual decision to give up studying. He began to solely focus on diamond trading instead.

He entered into a partnership with his maternal cousins, Girish and Prakash, to trade in diamonds. In many ways, diamond trading honed Gautam's instincts in finance.

Diamonds, being very precious stones, are traded on wafer-thin margins—just a few basis points. Just to give an idea on how the diamond trading works: trades must be concluded quickly, because diamonds are purchased in one country and in one currency, sorted and traded in another country, then (usually) cut and processed in India. The process pipeline is usually three to six months. They are then sold to a fourth country. The longer the time, the greater are the exchange risk variables, and the interest burden on the inventory. One has, therefore, to meet other diamond traders in quick succession, show them samples of the stones you have, make a quote, and quickly strike a deal. Most commitments are oral in nature, and trades are settled in cash within a couple of days at best. Deals, at the smallest broker's level, were worth a few thousand rupees in those days (in today's values the trades would be upwards of Rs 1 lakh),[43] or a few tens of thousands at most.

Even in those days, Girish talks about Gautambhai's overarching desire to strike big deals. He recalls how one day, Gautambhai had gone out with some diamonds, had sold them to a trader without informing his office, and then left for a couple of days' holiday. When Girish returned to his office, he found the inventory short by diamonds worth Rs 1.5 lakh,[44] a princely sum in those days. But there was nothing to show that a corresponding amount of money had been deposited in the bank. He waited for Gautambhai's return.

A few days later, Gautambhai returned to Mumbai and breezily informed his cousins that he had struck a deal with another trader for this huge amount and had happily gone back home to his native place, confident that a spoken deal was enough to ensure that he would get his money back.

Unfortunately, the trader could not pay back in time, and failed to turn up at the diamond market. Nor would he take telephone calls. Promptly, Gautam and Girish worked out a plan. They decided to go to the trader's house at 6 a.m. when the milk delivery boy rang the doorbell. The wife was surprised to see two young boys there.

They then explained their purpose, and finally met the trader. The trader said that he had fallen on bad days and, after a bit of negotiation, finally settled his part of the trade with an offer of another set of precious stones. There wasn't much profit that Gautam and Girish made in this transaction, but the deal got squared off. That was perhaps Gautam's first brush with the unexpected factors in trading. He also realized that even though the spoken word matters, steps should always be taken to ensure that risk should be mitigated within a given time frame.

The three cousins continued to trade in diamonds and even made a tidy sum.

The decision to give up his studies did not come easily to this bright student. His relatives recall how he had a raging fever for the few days before this decision was to be made. Another school friend, Mahendra Vora, who currently runs very successful businesses in Ohio, USA, remembers how he exhorted Gautambhai not to make this foolish mistake, and how Gautambhai calmly told him that while Mahendra should continue his studies, he himself had a lot to do and that studies could not help him in pursuing his plans.

Gautambhai was resolute. Business first. Studies could come in later.

In a way, Gautam had seen what had happened to his two elder brothers Mahasukh, who did his master's in polymer engineering from the US, and Vinod, who is an engineer. Both had ended up as traders. If trade was the goal, how much could studies help him grow? He was constantly reminded of his maternal uncle's advice. Clearly, the odds favoured giving up studies. But it wasn't easy.

After all, Gautambhai's quest for knowledge was almost insatiable. For instance, both Girish and Prakash were aware of how Gautam's thirst for knowledge far excelled their own. 'When all of us, as college boys, were enamoured by glamour and girls, and used to go through cine magazines avidly, Gautam would only go through "Scope" a science publication, that he would devour cover to cover. His eagerness to understand how technology works and how the world deals with situations, was "unquenchable",' recalls Girish. That thirst remains undiminished even today.

The family calls him

But what finally tilted the scales against diamond trading in Mumbai was brother Mahasukh's decision to get into plastic processing. Mahasukh had decided to diversify away from textiles and had acquired a small plastic processing unit, as polymers and polymer processing were sunrise sectors of the Indian economy in the early 1980s. The plastic processing unit was purchased from another entrepreneur, a member of the Tharad Jain community and a family friend, Sevantilal Vora. Gautambhai did not know at that time that Sevantilal would play an extremely important part in his life soon.

Sevantilal had a master's degree in mechanical engineering from the US and had worked with General Electric for a few years. However, the entrepreneurial instincts prompted him to return to India, and he started manufacturing PVC-suction hosepipes for agriculture. 'I had worked in glass factories earlier, and the principles of extrusion and injection moulding were common to both plastics and glass. So, I set up my own unit, got raw material from Shriram Chemicals, Chemplast, DCW and NOCIL,' explains Sevantilal.

He soon set up couple of additional processing units and moved to both making and trading in PVC film, a premium packaging material in those days. Demand was robust, as textile goods were being wrapped in PVC film. That was when two of the four partners who had started the PVC processing units with Sevantilal opted out. Sevantilal began looking for some competent individual to whom he could hive off one of his PVC processing units.

As luck would have it, Mahasukh, Gautambhai's elder brother, was already trading in PVC film and was a trained polymer engineer from the US. Sevantilal sold his factory (Ezy Packaging) to Mahasukh with all assets, which included a car. (In those days it was difficult to get a car, as the availability was highly restricted on account of a licence regime. Ownership of the car became an added attraction. Gautambhai, however, preferred to move around on his scooter, as he visited one potential customer after another.)

Sevantilal gracefully agreed to continue as mentor to the Adani brothers and help them develop their newly acquired polymer business. Mahasukh requested his brother, Vasant, who was in Bombay, to come down to Ahmedabad and help manage the new acquisition. They, in turn, after some time, requested Gautam to join them in the business as they were unable to cope with the complexities of business. Mahasukh himself was over-burdened, as he was responsible for managing the family's textile trading business as well at Ahmedabad.

That call clinched the issue. Gautambhai gave up diamond trading in Bombay and opted for the family's new venture—processing of plastics and trading in it. He felt that the challenge was bigger than trading in diamonds, as it involved multiple dimensions, raw material procurement (supply chain management), hiring, training and retaining skilled manpower, managing technology, marketing, production planning, finance and cash flow management, compliance with industrial, labour, commercial laws and so on. Young Gautam, who had a penchant for taking up challenges and successfully combating them, found this to be a godsent opportunity.

Discovering core values

As Gautambhai got into the nitty-gritties of business, he began to understand and respect some core values that had come down through generations. Mahasukh Adani, his brother, recalls how the 'two operative words of Gautam's personality are *neeti* (loosely translated as behaviour, way of doing business) and *dharma* (value system). These are derived from the underlying culture of our family. During the early days we lived in a modest locality where our family was better off than most neighbours. So, on one occasion, when my father bought my mother some jewellery he did so with a condition: she would never wear these so that *padosiyo ne dukh na thaay* (the neighbours would not feel unhappy or pained) as they would not have been able to afford it. As a result, much of the jewellery that my mother got was only meant to be kept in the box. There were other family manifestations of this modesty: Gautam still wears a watch he bought years ago, and in earlier days Karan would travel from Ahmedabad to Mundra by train even though he could have taken the corporate jet.'

The other value system that Gautam inherited was trust-worthiness. Mahasukh adds, 'In the early days when he traded large quantities of plastic raw material, a number of buyers would inevitably come to my father to request him that Gautam honour his delivery commitments when prices jumped. Father would assure them that if Gautam had made a commitment, it would be honoured, no matter what. He would tell them, "*Chinta na*

kartaa, Gautam maal aapshe (Don't worry. Gautam will deliver)."
The buyers would go back assured. And that is how it always was—
without any documentation or written contracts as transaction
proof, *"zabaan ni keemat* (The value of the spoken word)" became
our family recall.

'My father took this sense of fairness and trust one step
further. When some traders were caught on the wrong foot and
would have lost money, sums would be advanced to help them
tide over. Besides, it was usual for someone to come and tell father
that they were owed such and such money following such and
such transaction by a member of the family; the money would
promptly be paid without even cross-checking. That is how we
operated. Gautambhai also nurtures these values. If a trader loses
on a trade he is involved with, he will help him out, so that the
obligations can be squared off over some time.

'This is not to say that our business survived on generosity.
Father was engaged in active castor speculation. He had some
ground rules: prices could go up and he would keep positions
open, but the moment prices began to decline more than his risk
appetite dictated, the position would be immediately squared. The
result was that even though we lived on everyday fluctuations, we
never went bankrupt.'

This is the culture that Gautambhai injected into his business
model. It could be as large as he wanted, but it would be extensively
de-risked; it could be as profitable as he desired but it would never
lose the human touch.

Such sentiments find an echo in what Laxmi Prasad
Chaudhary, a director with the Adani Group, has to say, 'Vision
and trust. These are what good businessmen are made of.

'When Gautambhai imported plastic raw material in small
vessels through some of the smaller ports like Okha, Porbandar
and Mundra in the Eighties, he began to see how port inefficiency
was eating into his competitiveness. A 5000 DWT vessel would
unload only 500 MT a day; such a vessel would take nearly 10

days to unload; for every day that the ship spent at the port, he would have to pay demurrage. That is when he began to think: if we graduated from trading, which is an unpredictable business anyway, to the creation of an efficient port, we would help importers and exports reduce their costs and in turn create a profitable property. We tried to dissuade him. We said, "Gautambhai, *yeh sab apna kaam nahi hai*! (this is not our work!)" But his philosophy was "*Suno sab ki, karo man ki* (Listen to everyone, but do what your mind tells you)." During our trading days, Gautambhai made **trust** the foundation of his business. Since he had looked after so many traders during volatile markets by delivering material to them even after prices had risen, that, in turn, made traders take care to pay him on time. So, while other traders suffered defaults and delays, Gautam could sleep with the thought that all his outstanding would come. We traded Rs 700 crore with a Bangalore trader across some years and because our dealings were so clean, I never had an occasion to ever meet him. Today, this is unthinkable.'

Opportunities and responsibilities

As Gautambhai's trade dealings increased, so did his ability to articulate the values he believed in. Mahendra Vora, his childhood friend, recalls, 'On one occasion I asked Gautam about how he could continue to focus on a new opportunity even while the existing business was yet to stabilize. I remember his words, "Business is like a body with a straight line running from the top to bottom. On the right side are the problems of the day that I need to address. On the left are all the opportunities of the world. Both sides are mutually exclusive. So even as the business may be passing through one of its biggest challenges, that will not stop me from prospecting some of the biggest emerging opportunities. Both are not connected."'

Another family friend, business associate and well-wisher, Chintan Parikh, who is also chairman of the Ashima Group says,

'Gautam Adani went into business when things were license-based; he succeeded at a time when success was vision-based.

'In the private port sector in India, this was the right approach at the right time. There were no existing national benchmarks. So even though his industry experience was largely limited to understanding the nuances of trading, freight, and shipping, he was willing to be led by common sense on the one hand and the experience of colleagues on the other. It was a green mind more than a greenfield project.

'And there was one thing that he knew well: whatever the government did, he could do better. For instance, he could see that the port cranes could be used for longer than they currently were; he was aware that jetties constructed by the government over four years could be built in six months; he could sense that ports needed to be linked to consumption centres through rail or road. He had not done his ROIs for these activities, but these ideas represented small gut feelings that aggregated into a larger gut feel, on the basis of which he entered the business of port creation and management.

'The same gut feel was evident when he proposed to bid for the ultra-mega power plants. If he succeeded in the bid, he would bring the coal into the country (which he was doing anyway in his capacity as the country's largest coal importer) and generate the power. If he did not succeed in the bid, he would create his own UMPP (ultra-mega power plant)—faster and larger—and here again, he would import his own coal and manage the logistics. And if he did neither of the two, he would still continue to bring in the coal as a trader and manage the logistics for the other power plants that needed these resources. So, while most people questioned his logic of assuming large risks, the reality was that the Adani business model was extensively de-risked.

'Then there was the big question of delegating the project commissioning to an EPC contractor. His argument was that given the size of his projects, no EPC contractor would be able to manage his risk better than himself. Since he intended to commission nearly 20,000 MW over the decade, he felt that it also made sense for him to build the first plant himself, create a knowledge repository and leverage the knowledge to commission successive plants with speed and economy.

'The result is that in commissioning his power plants faster than any other company in India—and possibly the world—he has raised the bar for EPC contractors everywhere.'

Vasant adds, 'We believe that a man is holistically successful if he has addressed the needs of society, community and family. Gautam has lived that philosophy. He observed our father's deep ethical sense from close quarters. Our father would often say, *"Gareeb ni haayi koi deevasey bhool-chuk thi pan leta nahin* (Don't ever take anything from a poor man, even by mistake)." That became our family value system. Besides, our father was the kind of man who when he was out on *ughraani* (collections), would inevitably end up giving money to someone with a hard-up story enroute (after some time, the partners politely relieved father of this responsibility). There was this occasion when someone who owed the family business a significant amount brought his wife's jewellery to liquidate the debt, our father refused to accept and told him *"Jyaarey rupiya aave tyaare aapjo!* (when you get the money, give it to us then)."'

To grow a business, even after observing and promoting such values, calls for immense integrity and commitment. That is what young Gautambhai had begun to show.

4

The Quest Begins

In retrospect, it was the foray into plastics that brought out the businessman in Gautambhai. It brought in global connections. It made him think in terms of volumes, not just value, per transaction. And it taught him how to look at imports and exports. That in turn taught him to study ports, which in turn helped him become a five-star export house.

Diamonds taught him the need for quick trade. It taught him how to calculate money, interest, time and foreign exchange. Plastics taught him the basics of import-export, and the need to think in terms of huge volumes.

Had he not got into the plastics business, he would at best have graduated from being a diamond trader into a diamond exporter and importer. Plastics got him to think in terms of large corporate structures and actual expansion. It taught him a lot about global competitiveness.

Several other factors helped him along the way too. His ability to probe deeper, tenacity, determination to pursue larger volumes, willingness to go a step further, ability to become friends with the people who could show him a way out and—most importantly—his ability to spot an opportunity that many others might have just missed as being 'not my cup of tea'. These were the qualities that would come into play. Gautambhai became sharper, more discerning and more daring with each passing year. Together, they marked the metamorphosis of the boy and the emergence of the man.

And unknown to him at that time, Sevantilal was to play an even more significant role in his life. He was to become the person—both by observing and guiding each move of Gautambhai—who would then decide that this boy could become the best matrimonial match for his daughter, Priti. But that was to come a few years later.

The grooming begins

Gautambhai assumed the role of a marketing person under Sevantilal's watchful eye. Vasant managed the factory, while Gautambhai looked after marketing and procurement of raw materials. His friends recall how Gautambhai would ride his scooter across the city, almost tirelessly, looking for a trade opportunity and then reporting back the day's exploits to his brother and Sevantilal. Mahasukh overlooked the business and also continued the family's textile trading in Ahmedabad with Vinod continuing his textile trading in Mumbai.

The plastics processing business was booming, which prompted Vasant and Gautambhai to start two more processing units—thus looking over three units in total: Ezy, Eco and Elite. The first unit, Ezy, was built on a land which was taken on lease. The other two were on lands that they purchased from the government. The process of asset formation had already begun. Business was booming and there was always a shortage of skilled technical manpower and raw material.

Rajeshbhai, his brother, recalls, 'Even when our packaging unit had an annual turnover of only Rs 2,00,000, Gautambhai was always scouting for the next opportunity. For someone as restless as he was—and still is—it was not a surprise that his interests outgrew our small packaging unit. In this business, we would buy raw material, process it, and sell it. He recognized that the margins lay upstream with the traders, so he thought of new ways and means of buying the raw materials more efficiently.

'When this route had been exhausted, he decided he would import without a bank facility, even though we had no more than Rs 5 lakh in cash at that time. Our family was upset, *"Gaando thayi gayo chhey?* (Have you gone mad?)"* Within the first year, he made more money from trading in raw material than manufacturing PVC film. He was only twenty-one. Within three years, he had moved from buying 20 tonnes of raw material to importing complete shiploads of around 70,000 tonnes. Within three years, we had also moved from buying one raw material to importing a basket of polymers across different grades with a good idea of which customer needed what quantity of which material at what time and of which quality/grade.

'When our customers suffered losses during volatile markets and considered the idea of exiting the business altogether, Gautambhai would tell them, "I will bear 50 per cent of your loss and over the next few transactions will help recover your loss for you. Don't lose heart." The result was that after some time, buyers paid a "commitment premium"—which was unthinkable in commodity markets because they knew we would never renege on our commitment and would also bail them out if they went bankrupt. The other traders who reneged often would come and complain, *"Tamey amaari market bagaado chho!* (You are spoiling the market for us)."

'Gautambhai would normally sell 60 per cent of the polymers he imported as soon as he bought them. The rest he traded on the markets. On the one occasion this strategy backfired was after the historic July 1991 Budget, when custom duties crashed while we were sitting on an inventory of 5000 tonnes. This meant that material which had been imported against a high customs duty would now have to be liquidated at lower prices. Overnight, we had lost Rs 25-30 crore. Most traders liquidated their inventory at a loss. Gautambhai said, "Let us not lose our cool. The polymer markets are tight and even though customs duties will stay down, I expect prices to firm up." Within ten days, Saddam Hussein had invaded Kuwait and polymer prices peaked. We exited with a nominal Rs 5 crore loss.

'The amazing thing is that when faced with probably the biggest loss of his life (until then) following the 1991 Budget, he was busy reading the newspapers the following morning. "It is important to see what opportunities we might be missing," he said.'

Rajeshbhai also recalls how he insisted on changing the way traders treated vendors. The trigger was his waiting in their Delhi office for some executives to arrive for a meeting. That is 'when he saw number of company's vendors protesting to the receptionist about how they were being treated—being made to wait for hours, spoken to badly and often sent back without their payment. Gautambhai returned and immediately called a meeting of our 25 purchase officers. He laid down a standard operating procedure related to vendor treatment: all vendor accounts would be automatically credited by the eighth morning; no vendor who came to the office would be kept waiting; in the event of an unavoidable delay the purchase officer would apologise to the vendor in person; and the vendor would be treated with the respect due to a partner during the meeting.'

Intuitively, Gautambhai had discovered that businesses are built and grown when foot soldiers are cared for.

Preparing for Korea

By 1982, the sourcing of plastics became a bit more difficult, compelling the Adani family to look for other suppliers in the open market. Dhirubhai Ambani had also begun making his foray into the world of plastics, yarn and all the raw material that went into making them. Obviously, this was an area where both were occasionally competing for the same customers.

That is where Gautambhai did something none of them had bothered to do till then. He watched how the supplier of the raw material was careful enough to remove all tell-tale marks of the source from where it had originated. But there was something he had overlooked—a trademark on each sack. Gautambhai asked Sevantilal and Vasant to begin looking for the party who owned the trademark. Everyone scoffed at his idea. 'We are plastic processors. Our job is to process and mark up on the price at which we get the raw material. Why should we take the additional trouble?' they asked.

The quest to identify the source brought him to two traders in Mumbai—Jay Shah and Jatin Kotecha—both wholesale dealers in plastics and plastic additives. They dealt in consignments of 2000 tonnes or more. But Gautambhai managed to persuade them to sell him smaller quantities—starting with 20 tonnes and then going up to a few hundred. Gautambhai's persuasive charm and his energy brought him closer to Jay and Jatin, and gradually even these friends began to realize that Gautambhai was a person who dreamt bigger than anyone else they knew. It was a relationship which was proving to be beneficial to all three.

In fact, they chuckle when they recall young Gautambhai always trying to spend more time with them. To do this, he even travelled with them on night train from Mumbai to Ahmedabad every weekend. Gautambhai had a second-class ticket, while Jay and Jatin travelled first class. Still, unwilling to lose the opportunity of being with them, he would boldly travel first class, sleep on the floor at night, but spend as much time with both of them as was possible.

Through them, he learnt a lot about the way business was done and the basic rules of export and import of large quantities. But more importantly, Gautambhai would keenly observe their mannerisms, their way of dressing, the way they used the knife and fork—each of these would be cultivated by him as he climbed the social ladder.

As Rajesh Mandapwala, then director general manager, corporate affairs, Adani Group, explains, 'I joined the Adani Group when it was just a packaging unit in 1982. My employer (Gautambhai) was just twenty. It appeared (to me at least) that the future lay in building a bigger packaging unit. I felt that with our raw material which could be bought from anywhere; what the world would need was more and better packaging material.

'Gautambhai felt exactly the opposite. He had quickly recognised that the packaging unit was at best a steady business where the realization of the end product would be largely fixed and the cost of raw materials variable, sometimes dangerously so. If we had to make a bigger profit, it would have to come from identifying a stable source of lower cost raw material; but since vendors were largely the same, this too was a problem.'

Gautambhai never gave up. He kept scouting for material, whether it was from NOCIL, Chemplast, DCW, Shriram or through imports. This quest provided him an information lead, which tells us exactly how his mind can link two unconnected realities for sizable gain.

Rajesh Mandapwala says, 'Somebody must have told Gautambhai around the mid-1980s that while the Gujarat State Export Corporation (GSEC) would export handicrafts and earn credits against which it could import anything duty-free, it was not doing so. The result was that GSEC had built up a large "bank" of unused credits. So, on the one hand, a trader like Gautambhai was always seeking ways and means of importing at lower costs and here was GSEC, which could import at zero tariff, but was constrained from doing so because plastics trading was not their business.'

Mandapwala continues, 'Gautambhai connected these two realities. He gave GSEC a deal it couldn't refuse. He would buy GSEC's unused import credits, he would give them a fee for every rupee's imports, and he would insulate them from any business risk. The bureaucrats at GSEC sat up; this twenty-three-year-old was giving them an attractive income for their inventory of unused import entitlements.'

At some point they asked Gautambhai how much he intended to import. The annual figure that both parties eventually settled for was Rs 2 crore. The imports began; Gautambhai's duty-free imports provided him with a large pool of plastic raw material to trade at a handsome profit. The proceeds were immediately redeployed in ordering the next consignment. When the numbers were added at the end of the first year, GSEC was most surprised that this youngster had exceeded his target by 500 per cent. Gautambhai had imported Rs 10 crore worth of plastic raw material in the first year!

Vasantbhai remembers how, 'Gautam first visited South Korea when our packaging factory's raw material appetite was only 20 MT per production cycle. While he was there, he ordered 200 MT in one go and then sent us a message to immediately open an LC (letter of credit) for that quantity. The bank officer rejected our application by saying, "What will you do with such a sizable quantity?" When Gautam came down, he personally went to see this officer. I don't know what charm Gautam used but within 10 minutes, the LC was cleared.'

Gautambhai's persuasive skills were now being noticed and admired.

The key to Gautambhai's success in those days—and even today—was his capacity to be unfazed by fleeting adversity. On one occasion, the vessel in which he had imported a 5000-tonnes consignment of polymer capsized, resulting in a sizeable immediate loss (recouped through insurance). Gautambhai responded by opening an LC for an even bigger import consignment!

In the first quarter of 1983, Gautam got the details of the biggest supplier of plastics and plastic additives in Korea.

On 21 June, in the same year, he visited South Korea (it was his maiden trip overseas), and the story is that he kissed the ground when he reached the country. He knew that this was the place from where his fortunes could be made. He clinched his first deal for importing 200 tonnes of PVC from Korea the very next day.

Jatin explains with a smile and a shake of his head, 'We took him with us—it was his first trip overseas—and he was so delighted to learn about how other countries worked that he insisted on opening his account with a token import of 200 tonnes, even though the price was not the lowest at that point of time.'

'He just wanted to leave the first stamp of his trade in Korea,' adds Jay with a chuckle.

Studying Exim

By this time, Gautambhai had begun to study and learn the entire process involved in the import of raw material. He began reading up on ships, ports and delivery schedules. It also got him close to the South Korean suppliers who were introduced to him by Jay and Jatin.

He had begun to realize that if he had to get the raw material at competitive prices, he had to import larger quantities. So, he decided to use half the material to meet his factory's raw material requirements, while the rest could be sold to other processors. His bankers, who also realized how his business with them was growing rapidly, helped him understand the rules. It was this type of working knowledge that enabled him to discern which port in India was best suited for what type of material. This taught him the rules governing all export and import, which in turn helped him navigate the rocks when getting into the import-export business as an export house which was to be set up in March 1988 as a partnership firm.

Soon he began to think in terms of shiploads of 5000 tonnes or more. To be able to do this, he had to sell off these large volumes quickly in the market. That is why he first began going to large importers like Prince, Finolex and Supreme and found out what their requirements would be. He was confident that his price would be the most competitive because of both his sourcing and the volumes. Just the knowledge of their requirements would suffice. Competitive pricing would clinch the deal.

Armed with the knowledge of volumes, he then began working on shipment schedules, so that the goods arrived just when these large users would require them. 'Gautam began looking at the CIF (cost, insurance and freight) value of consignments in terms of all the three,' explains Jay Shah.

'In terms of cost—could he negotiate with the principal suppliers directly? In terms of insurance—could he talk to the insurance companies and reduce the insurance premium payable? And in terms of freight—which ship would give him the most competitive rates?' Jay adds.

'We tried to tell him that this was not our business—that we could still make money if we just played the margin game, and leave the rest to others,' adds Jatin with a laugh. 'But Gautam would not listen.' He wanted to get to the source, and shave off every layer of the price. Soon Gautam was collecting import licences from bigger players—the Lalbhais, Metro Cycles and Finolex. He even tied up with Gujarat Export Corporation of the Government of Gujarat and got their consent to use the import licence to further enhance volumes imported and further lower purchase costs.

Wedding bells

Meanwhile, back in Ahmedabad, Sevantilal continued observing intently the zest of this young boy and suggested to his daughter, Priti, that Gautam could be a good match for her. She wasn't sure because Gautambhai had not finished his graduation, while she herself was pursuing dentistry. But Sevantilal let the idea germinate in his daughter's mind.

He kept hinting to her that the best man was one who had the intelligence to discover more than one way to stand on his feet, and to make others grow with him. Gently, he persuaded both Gautambhai and Pritiben to meet and to converse with each other. Gradually the doubts melted away, and they got married on 1 May 1986.

Those days were tough on the marriage. Gautambhai's ambitions took him away from home for several days. His work hours became more intense. Yet, as his wife Pritiben recalls, Gautam had the ability to switch off work once he came home, so that he could have quality time with his family and friends. He continued to do so even after his first child, Karan was born in April 1987.

Another quality that Gautambhai exhibited in great abundance was the ability to forget a bad transaction. 'It is done, and over,' he would tell his colleagues in Gujarati. 'Let's proceed to the next item.'

A quality that won him his employees' respect was to overlook a mistake when it had been done in good faith, and not out of incompetence. Gautam knew that if a trader cannot take losses, he will never be able to grow. The man who made a big mistake and had offered to resign (mentioned earlier in this book) continues to be an important part of Gautam's operations even today.

Linked to this trait is yet another aspect, which has been talked of earlier in this book. Gautambhai is uncomfortable whenever any party who has done business with him runs into losses on account of some transaction. If the loss related to a transaction with Gautam, and if it were on account of market conditions, Gautambhai would do whatever was possible to give him a better deal next time, so that the earlier losses could be squared off. That, more than any other thing, has allowed him to build a loyal circle of associates around him, who stand by him through thick and thin.

4.1

The old and the new Adani headquaters

The old office was at Navrangpura in Ahmedabad; the new office is in Sadani-Shantigram, 12 km from Ahmedabad airport.

In fact, in order to minimize losses even in trading, Gautam began professionalizing the business with more and more systems put in place. How much of an exposure should a trader be allowed? What are the margins within which he could play independently, beyond which a ratification might be needed? There were many such queries. Thus, while many other export trading houses of those times faded into oblivion, Adani Exports thrived. Part of their success was on account of trading skills, but it was also on account of professionalism that allowed him to scale up and expand the breadth and depth of his operations.

This was to work its way further into systems and processes that Gautam continues to introduce for the entire group even today. 'His passion for systems is understandable,' says Devang Desai, former CFO and executive director, Adani Enterprises. 'If you have to grow big, you need systems in place. What goes to Gautam's credit is that he has retained the spirit of entrepreneurship, in spite of bringing in systems.'

Ten years ago, Gautambhai worked out of his Ahmedabad office and people could walk into the office with relative ease—though the chairman's office which was on another floor was kept out of bounds for most people. Today, there is a huge security screening before anyone gets inside Adani Towers at Shantigram, 12 km from Ahmedabad airport. The distance from the city airport, and the security screening for accessing the Adani corporate headquarters have filtered out the needless visit by people to the hub of the Adani empire.

His unquenchable desire to grow is confirmed by some of the most astute merchant bankers like Vallabh Bhanshali of Enam Securities. He says, 'Gautam has a quiet intensity to grow. He decides where he should be, and then tries to find out the process that will take him there. Another trait is his ability to think big. A quality that defines him is that he is also a family man. He makes time for his family.'

Nimesh Kampani of JM Financial adds one more quality to the list—simplicity. 'It is his unassuming nature, and his willingness to help others in difficulty, and his commitment to social relationships, that have endeared Gautam to others,' says Nimesh.

A great deal of credit also goes to the way Pritiben has coped with the situation. She focused solely on bringing up their children. Karan is now thirty-six, with a major in economics from Purdue, USA and is the CEO of APSEZ. Jeet, the younger son, now twenty-nine years old, is VP, group finance for the entire group. He joined the group in 2019, after attending the School of Engineering and Applied Sciences, University of Pennsylvania.

And, as Vinodbhai's wife Ranjanben puts it, 'Pritiben strengthened the bonds with the other members of our family. Today, the Adani family is united in everything it does. Our family is often cited as an example by our entire community, as a model one should emulate.'

Social bonding creates a resource pool, that in turn ensures that the path to further growth becomes less formidable.

5

From Imports to Exports

By 1992, economic reforms were ushered in, and import duties slashed. Plastics came under the Open General Export Licence (OGEL). Margins between international and domestic prices narrowed. Import alone was less attractive than import backed by export.

For the innovative mind, when one door closes, another opening is discovered. Not surprisingly, Gautambhai decided to get into exports too, because that is what the country needed. Once again, almost intuitively, he realized that when corporate and business interests are aligned with the interests of the nation, growth can be faster and more assured.

India faced a huge foreign exchange crisis and had to even pawn its gold reserves in January 1991 to meet its import needs. India desperately wanted to build its forex reserves. 'What Gautam did is that he integrated all the processes he had learnt before. He joined the dots and began doing bigger business than even the earlier years,' recalls Sevantilal. By 1995, the three plastics units were closed.

So, what did Adani Exports send out of the country? Almost anything that had a market. 'We sold toothpaste, shoe-polish, seafood, cosmetics and lots of other commodities,' says Vinod. 'What mattered was that export of the item from India was not banned, and that there was a market which could give us a good profit margin.' These exports found their way to the

US, Europe and the Middle East among other places. While Gautambhai was busy in commercial innovations, back-office work and day-to-day affairs of the trading were managed by his younger brother Rajesh, who joined him after graduation in the late 1980s.

Today, Rajesh is president and head of the chairman's office. He has been developing business relationships and assisting his brother. He works closely with his brother and manages the regular affairs of all Adani businesses.[45]

Becoming nationally relevant

Once again, Gautambhai began to see the advantage of dovetailing his business interests to national needs. There was a business opportunity, and there was a national need. When both get aligned, the tide itself upholds the swimmer. 'We must align ourselves to national priorities,' is a remark he often makes. With a focus on the port, coal and power generation lines of business, the remark carries more weight and wisdom now, than it did before. He is getting into defence and data management. Both have tremendous synergies with the government, and the need to work closely with government will become that much more crucial.

But the emergence of this vision found its first expression in 1992. The trader was beginning to recognize the tremendous benefits of being nationally relevant.

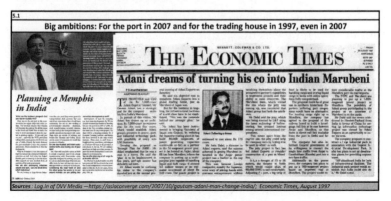

5.1

Big ambitions: For the port in 2007 and for the trading house in 1997, even in 2007

Sources: Log.In of OVV Media —https://asiaconverge.com/2007/10/gautam-adani-man-change-india/; Economic Times, August 1997

And that is also when he began thinking of becoming much bigger. P.S. Anantharaman, a journalist who interviewed him in the late 1990s, recalls that Gautambhai always dreamt big. He wanted to become the Marubeni Corporation (Marubeni of Japan is one of the world's largest trading conglomerates) of India. At other times, he visualized making Mundra the Memphis of India, a vision that was articulated by one of his key lieutenants—Capt. Sandeep Mehta.[46]

In a way, this is precisely what Nimesh Kampani, one of the most astute investment bankers in India, means when he says, 'Gautam Adani is an ideal example of an empire builder who did not owe his growth to any of the new-age technologies. Instead, he chose to be part of the development scene of the country and achieve success through the contributions he could make to society.'

The social connect works in several ways. National interests work at the macrolevel. But there is a micro-connect as well. People talk about how he has taken care of some of his loyal workers when they have faced stressful conditions.

Others point to over 200 dwellings he built in Ahmedabad for the economically challenged members of his community. Still others point to the manner in which he organized one of the biggest pilgrimages (1100 people) to Samet Shikharji in West Bengal for all his associates and relatives, just because it was a lifelong desire of his mother. Many employees recall how he has personally attended wedding ceremonies of his most junior staff if he was in the city at that point of time. That was at the microlevel.

But much of the gratitude, loyalty and relevance will eventually come from the work the Adani Foundation[47] has been doing—to shape livelihoods for common folk by empowering the children of schools with quality education and even vocational skills. More on this in the chapter 'The Taste of Goodness'.[48]

Thinking big

Gautambhai had begun to master the art of flitting with great ease between the macro perspective and the micro demands of relationships. The first excited him, and the second created a fabric of supporters on whom he could depend on when he needed to. Was this deliberate? Was this a calculated strategy? Or was it the natural outcome of a person who is intuitively endowed with qualities that a leader ought to have? It could be all of them.

But gradually, such actions and responses are being streamlined, so that they can be replicated, again and again. So that there is predictability. And more importantly, if something has to be scaled up, it must first be standardized and then properly defined for replicability.

By the 1990s, the country's foreign exchange position became precarious. To shore up its forex reserves, it had begun giving incentives to exporters in the form of Replenishment Export Permits (REPs) which would entitle the exporter to import freely those goods that were on the country's negative list. This was the type of permit that diamond traders often used to import diamonds. Thus, any exporter had several benefits. If he managed his sourcing and his procurement prices well, he could make decent profits on the goods he sold. He could then take the REPs and sell them at a premium in the markets or import other items and sell them at a profit in India. Gautam did both and, in no time, he became one of the few Star Export Houses in the country. He became one of the key players in the REP market. He was active in the rupee-rouble trade too—which too yielded very high returns.

By 1993, the first annual report of Adani Exports was out, and it recorded merchant exports of Rs 18.88 crore and a profit after tax of Rs 78 lakh. Working capital was sorely needed, and that is when Gautam toyed with the idea of raising funds from the public. By April 1994, Adani Export got rated as a super star trading house by the Government of India, and by November 1994, Adani Exports got listed on the BSE after being over subscribed twenty-five times. It made an IPO of 12,50,000 shares and raised Rs 18.75 crore. The issue was oversubscribed and the shares were listed on 1 November 1994. This company was later to get rechristened, appropriately, as Adani Enterprises.

And as Dame Fortune looked on benevolently, Gautambhai and Pritiben had their second son in November the same year.

The trader had transformed into an exporter. The latter brought with it connotations of respectability and also national relevance. The difference was only in terms of perception of the marketplace. In reality, the trading instincts remained the same. The purchase-selling and hedging qualities remained the same. What had changed was the way the world had begun to perceive him. He was being metamorphosed into an industrialist. This would be the man who would dovetail his strategies with national priorities and move in tune with national needs.

But export-import can be treacherous as well. It is one activity where what one perceives as a genuine opportunity can easily be reinterpreted by someone else as a sharp trade practice. Eventually such disputes land up in court.[49] India has an unfortunate history of cases being filed against industrialists, by social activists and by vested interests. The slow pace of Indian courts makes adjudication in such cases extremely complex and long-drawn-out.[50] Hence the number of cases against such parties or individuals can be very large. But most of such cases are either thrown out or dismissed by Indian courts eventually. They can be irritants, taking away productive management time. To be successful in India, entrepreneurs must have the ability to withstand and triumph over such irritants. More on this later, especially in Chapter 10.

Gautambhai's brothers normally looked after court cases and oversaw the work that lawyers were expected to carry out.[51] More on the vexatious nature of litigation is discussed in the Chapter 10 too.

Lately, however, Mahasukh and Vasant have opted out of day-to-day involvement in the Adani Group activities and have preferred to nurture their respective businesses instead. Vinod remains actively involved with the group, especially when negotiating international finance and connections. But he does not hold any formal position with the group.

Articulate

Notwithstanding allegations and charges, Gautambhai's actions have invariably stood vindicated. Perceptions play their part and the loser invariably is one who cannot express his point of view articulately enough. Gautambhai was both savvy and articulate, and he was clear about what he was doing. Not surprisingly, his business kept growing by leaps and bounds.

Exports, thus, brought in the first opportunity to effect a transformation once again—Gautambhai was soon to metamorphose from being an exporter to becoming an industrialist. Adani–Wilmar and Mundra Port completely transformed the vision of the group, and its growth strategies. Both were accidental and had key connections with traders. Mundra owes its origins to the trading group Cargill, while Adani–Wilmar to the trading group Wilmar, set up by Kuok.

They were opportunities that just appeared unexpectedly. And as the old saying goes, 'Fortune favours the prepared mind.'[52] It was so with Louis Pasteur, who just observed and discovered pasteurization. It was thus with Isaac Newton who began asking questions about why the apple fell on his head. All of a sudden, the commonplace becomes a special quest. It becomes a mind-blowing opportunity.

6

Mundra: A Gateway to the World

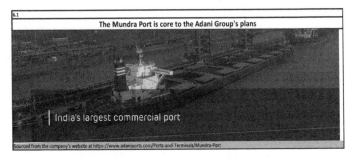

6.1
The Mundra Port is core to the Adani Group's plans

India's largest commercial port

Sourced from the company's website at https://www.adaniports.com/Ports-and-Terminals/Mundra-Port

In retrospect, the biggest deal that Gautambhai could have made in his career was the one involving the Mundra Port.

6.2					
How efficient is Mundra					
Top 5 ports and more					
The CPPI 2021: Global ranking of container ports, from 370 ports surveyed					
ADMINISTRATIVE APPROACH			**STATISTICAL APPROACH**		
Port Name	Rank	Total Points	Port Name	Rank	Index Value
King Abdullah Port	1	217.914	King Abdullah Port	1	93.387
Salalah	2	197.675	Salalah	2	87.372
Hamad Port	3	194.823	Yangshan	3	83.522
Yangshan	4	183.455	Hamad Port	4	82.146
Khalifa Port	5	182.649	Khalifa Port	5	81.052
Ningbo	7	170.696	Ningbo	7	76.077
Jeddah	8	161.493	Jeddah	8	73.527
Colombo	24	117.493	Djibouti	24	52.476
Pipavav	26	109.823	Tianjin	26	51.441
Halifax	46	91.744	Mundra	46	35.568
Mundra	48	86.563	Laem Chabang	48	34.706
HongKong	50	83.775	JNPT	50	33.142
JNPT	54	79.672	Bremerhaven	54	29.896
Notes : This is a ranking of container ports alone. It does not refer to dry bulk, liquid or gas. Pipavav ranks #34 on the statistical approach. But the Adani ports perform better than any of the 'major' government owned ports.					
Source : World Bank Group and S&P's The Container Port Performance Index 2021 — https://cdn.ihsmarkit.com/www/pdf/0522/Container-Port-Performance-Index-					

It does not involve the biggest investment. Nor can it be called the most glamourous. But when you consider the unfolding of the Adani strategy, Mundra Port had a lot to do with it. Gautambhai forayed into many businesses—edible oil (Adani–Wilmar), power plant at Mundra, coal operations, foray into food and agriculture, railway plans, Maruti Suzuki's export hub at Mundra, defence, steel and many more. All of them can find their roots in or connections with the Mundra Port.

It is this port that gave him the confidence of building port terminals on his own and then developing other ports. Today, he has become one of the most formidable port developers in the world and rubs shoulders with the likes of DPW and PSA (the Singapore port developer). It is among the most efficient ports in India, outranking all the government-owned ports when it comes to container management. But it must climb the rankings a bit more when it comes to other global ports.[53]

It is possible that very few of the Adani businesses would have emerged without Mundra Port. This is also true of the strategic oil reserves at Mundra which are connected by a pipeline to the Bhatinda refinery. Mundra Port was crucial to many of these ventures.

6.3
Kandla and Mundra—not far apart

Note : Kandla and Mundra are just 134 km apart by road. The sea route would be shorter.
Source : Google maps

In fact, the Food Corporation of India's (FCI) grain operations at Mundra led it to sign a deal with the Australian Wheat Board (AWB) to build the first few prototype grain storage silos for the government. These were the latest in storage technology. They allowed the first in grain to be the first out through a top-loading facility. They also allowed for adequate airing and even fumigation if required. These could become the prototypes for all grain storage in India in the next few decades. But more on this later.[54]

Similarly, Adani's foray into power generation—first at Mundra, then elsewhere—made him think of transitioning into green energy—first into solar power, and now into green hydrogen as well. That in turn made him realize the synergies that lie with the Korean POSCO which has an MoU with the Adani Group. Steel production involves the use of and even the generation of hydrogen. Incidentally, POSCO is already helping Saudi Arabia set up one of the largest hydrogen production facilities in the world[55] in collaboration with POSCO Steel of South Korea. The Korean connection (initially in plastics) is revisited, but with a bigger vision, a bigger plan.

Enter Cargill

Actually, the decision to get into ports was purely accidental. But as Louis Pasteur had once remarked, 'Chance favours the prepared mind.'[56] Gautambhai had already acquired, by the time the Mundra opportunity emerged, the requisite understanding of what this meant. Once it came, he pursued it with a focus and frenzy seldom observed in India.

By 1990, Gautam was already reckoned as one of the savviest businessmen in Gujarat. His ability to move things in and out of India, as a trader, was by now indisputable. His ability to get the government to listen to him for obtaining requisite clearances for introducing innovative ways of doing business, which would also be in the interest of the state and the country (foreign exchange earnings was one such justification), brought him close to people who wanted to get things done.

6.4
Land acquired by MPSEZL
The multi-product SEZ covering the Mundra Port and its surrounding areas covering an area of 2406.8 hectares (approximately 5947 acres) in relation to which we have received a notification from the Government of India dated 23 June 2006 and on 3 July 2007, we received a subsequent notification with respect to an additional 251.4 hectares of land, resulting in a total of 2658.2 hectares (approximately 6568 acres).
We have been granted the right to use and develop 3404 acres of land around Mundra Port for thirty years under the Concession Agreement, and pursuant to the merger with Adani Port Limited in 2003 and Mundra SEZ and ACL in 2006, we now have approximately 15,665 acres of land available to us.
. . .while approximately 16,688 acres of additional land are at various stages of being transferred to us. We plan to utilise the approximately 4000 metres of undeveloped waterfront land in growing our port operations.
Following the mergers of ACL and MSEZ into our company, we now have approximately 15,665 acres of land available to us while approximately 16,688 acres of additional land are at various stages of being transferred to us.
On 23 June 2006, we received notification from the Government of India with respect to land covering Mundra Port and the surrounding areas of 2406.8 hectares (approximately 5947 acres) and on 3 July 2007, we received a subsequent notification with respect to an additional 251.4 hectares of land, resulting in a total of 2658.2 hectares (approximately 6568 acres).
Note : This is in addition to land acquired for the oil farm, the railway line connecting Mundra to Adipur and other such facilities
Source : DRHP for the company filed in 2007 -- https://www.sebi.gov.in/filings/public-issues/nov-2007/mundra-port-and-special-economic-zone-limited_9514.html

One such opportunity was brought to Gautam by the global commodities trader, Cargill.[57] In 1990-91, Cargill approached Gautam to source several million tonnes of salt from India. (This was a commodity that is available in abundance in the Kutch-Saurashtra region, which is also why soda ash companies like Tata Chemicals set up their facilities here.) Negotiations began, and a back-of-the-envelope costing was done. The price at which the salt could be made available was arrived at and communicated to Cargill. The next question was whether it could be evacuated from a port or jetty close by. The first thought was the Kandla Port. But then, Cargill, with its access to some NASA maps and advice from some people familiar with water depth and currents, came up with Mundra as the best possible location.

There were several reasons why Cargill liked this location.

It had a good draught (draft or draught of a ship's hull is the vertical distance between the water line and the bottom of the hull or keel). The greater the draught, the easier would it be for bigger ships to get docked at the jetty or port.

It was not far from the biggest free trade zones (FTZ) in the Middle East.

And it was a location where vessels could come in and get docked throughout the year. The Kandla Port is a bit inside the waterway.

Mundra had always been a small port—even today dhows from different parts of the world come to the old Mundra jetty. The location appealed to Gautambhai as well, as he was familiar with this area. It was like reviving history, making it relevant to modern wealth generators. Both Cargill and Gautam began working on their respective plans and agreed to set up a 50:50 joint venture to build the jetty and establish salt farms. This could involve investments of around Rs 100 crore.

Gautambhai was, at that time, focused only on the jetty and the salt trade. Little did he realize how this would metamorphose in the coming years into something extremely big. It would catapult him into becoming one of the biggest infrastructure players in the country. This jetty was to transform the very landscape of the country. But all this was to unfold over the next decade.

Land acquisition

Intuitively, he immediately realized that a good jetty—like a good port—would require lots of land. Moreover, like most Indian businessmen, he was also aware that there was little downside to land acquisition. Like most investors, he knew that any piece of forlorn land becomes valuable when connected to a port, airport, road or railway line. It is an age-old business practice worldwide—not just in India.

Much of the land was marshy land, under brackish water, and some of it was used as salt pans. Nobody wanted these lands, and hence they weren't worth much. Yet, Gujarat's bureaucrats sat tight over the papers which would allow transfer of these land to Gautambhai. Finally, according to some versions, Gautambhai actually hired a plane, took the bureaucrat to show him the lands that he wanted to purchase. 'But these are marshes' is what the bureaucrat is believed to have said. 'Exactly,' explained Gautambhai. 'Nobody wants these lands. I want to fill up these marshes and create jobs.' The bureaucrat finally gave his consent to the transfer.

The government made money on this land, and so did the owners/salt workers. Everyone was glad to get a price for them. Hence, today, when critics unfairly accuse Gautambhai of purchasing land at a throwaway price, they forget that this was precisely what it was worth at that time. The land acquisition spree would gain momentum as the concept of the jetty metamorphosed into that of a port.

Gautambhai had learnt—through all his dealings as an exporter and importer—that almost every port makes profits from its lands and not from port operations. The port operations are essential, and, yes, they help recover costs. The real profits come from renting out storage space for the consignments, either before they are put on boats, or afterwards. Known as demurrage in the industry, this is what makes a port profitable. So, the greater the land area available to the port, the more profitable it could become.

In fact, even India's government-owned port has shown, for several decades, that it is more profitable being a landlord rather than being a port operator. Jawaharlal Nehru Port Trust (JNPT) has leased out its terminals to other players and takes a revenue share (of around 30 per cent) of the business they do. Today, JNPT makes more money from being a landowner and renting out assets, than from the single terminal it operates by itself.

This realization also had an unexpected effect. Aware of the way demurrage works, Gautambhai was hypersensitive to paying demurrage costs anywhere. Saurin Shah, president, Adani Group, says, 'While we were into trading and shipping, Gautambhai would keep tab of a single number—demurrage. It told him more about his business than any other number—how efficient his staff was and how driven his team was. He would happily take a Rs 5 crore loss on a trade—which he said provided invaluable learning opportunities—but would bring the house down if even Rs 500 had been paid as demurrage.'

It helped him hone efficiencies even further.

Moreover, Gautambhai had other plans. He wanted to be a port operator as well. Gradually, this too would change, and he would don the role of a developer. But that happened a bit later.

Work on the jetty

Going along with Cargill's discovery, a jetty was set up under Adani Exports (later to be known as Adani Enterprises) for moving salt. By then the unexpected event took place.

By 1992, the Government of India, desperate for foreign exchange inflows, decided to allow foreign investors to own 100 per cent equity in state-owned ports and jetties. Till now all the key ports—twelve of them, also referred to as major ports—were owned by the Central Government.

Suddenly, this announcement changed Cargill's perspective. Predictably, they now wanted to own a higher stake in the Mundra jetty.[58] Cargill suggested that Gautambhai be content with a lower stake (some people suggest that the figure was as low as 11 per cent) while the rest could be taken up by this commodity giant. Gautam refused to consider such a proposal. He believed that a deal was a deal and it could not be broken.

Cargill pleaded with the Gujarat chief minister (CM). But the CM refused to intercede. He said that since this was a business arrangement, it should best be settled between the two parties. The state government would not intervene in this matter. Not satisfied, Cargill decided to approach the union ministry instead. The minister for ports was the mercurial George Fernandes (now deceased) and he wrote to the Gujarat CM to consider Cargill's request.

The CM is believed to have told the union minister that Mundra was a state port, and that this was a state government's jurisdiction. Furious at being rebuffed, Fernandes suggested he would sweeten the deal for Cargill by offering it a full terminal instead at the government-owned Kandla Port nearby. Kandla is just 134 km away from Mundra by road. Though, by water, the distance is considerably shorter. Mundra has an advantage of being close to the mouth of the gulf.

But Kandla is close to the hinterland. It was also a fully developed port and had ships docking there almost every day. Getting a terminal there would significantly enhance the profit potential for Cargill. The alternative proposal was agreeable, and Cargill washed its hands off the Mundra jetty.

But those plans went awry. The plans to take over the terminal proved abortive, partly because of a port strike which lasted for long.[59,60]

Mundra Port is born

In the meantime, work at the Mundra jetty continued at a frenetic pace. Gautambhai made a presentation to the Gujarat government that he be allowed to convert the jetty into a full-blown port, with the state government holding 26 per cent of the equity share capital.

The state government's port policy was ready by 1995, which was aimed at promoting the development of ports in Gujarat. MPSEZL began operating its port under concessions and licences granted by the relevant government agencies.

On 17 February 2001, the Gujarat maritime board (GMB), an organisation of the Government of Gujarat, entered into a concession agreement with MPSEZL granting it the right to develop, operate and maintain a port at Mundra for thirty years.[61]

MPSEZL also entered into a separate lease and possession agreement with the GMB whereby it was granted the right to use approximately 3404 acres of land as its port and the right to use the foreshore land and waterfront. That deal was crucial because it gave Gautambhai access to more land. Gradually, the contours of an SEZ began emerging.

MPSEZL has also a sub-concession agreement between Mundra international Container Terminal or MICT (formerly Adani Container Terminal Ltd) and the GMB dated 7 January 2003 and amended on 17 April 2003. Through this agreement MICT has the right to operate and maintain the container terminal-I and the container freight station and collect charges from users for providing container handling services at the container terminal- I and the container freight station.

On 15 May 2003, MICT was acquired by P&O Ports (Peninsular & Oriental Steam Navigation Company), which was subsequently acquired by Dubai Ports World (DPW in February 2006, causing the management and ownership control of MICT transferred to DPW or Dubai Ports Authority).

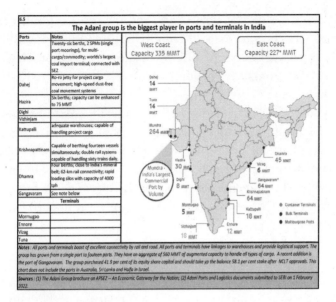

6.5			
The Adani group is the biggest player in ports and terminals in India			
Ports	**Notes**		
Mundra	Twenty-six berths, 2 SPMs (single port moorings), for multi-cargo/commodity; world's largest coal import terminal; connected with SEZ		
Dahej	Ro-ro jetty for project cargo movement; high-speed dust-free coal movement systems		
Hazira	Six berths; capacity can be enhanced to 75 MMT		
Dighi			
Vizhinjam			
Kattupalli	adequate warehouses; capable of handling project cargo		
Krishnapattinam	Capable of berthing fourteen vessels simultaneously; double rail systems capable of handling sixty trains daily.		
Dhamra	Four berths; close to India's mineral belt; 62-km rail connectivity; rapid loading silos with capacity of 4000 tph		
Gangavaram	See note below		
Terminals			
Mormugao			
Ennore			
Vizag			
Tuna			

Notes : All ports and terminals boast of excellent connectivity by rail and road. All ports and terminals have linkages to warehouses and provide logistical support. The group has grown from a single port to fourteen ports. They have an aggregate of 560 MMT of augmented capacity to handle all types of cargo. A recent addition is the port of Gangavaram. The group purchased 41.9 per cent of its equity share capital and should take up the balance 58.1 per cent stake after NCLT approvals. This chart does not include the ports in Australia, Sri Lanka and Haifa in Israel.

Sources : (1) The Adani Group brochure on APSEZ – An Economic Gateway for the Nation; (2) Adani Ports and Logistics documents submitted to SEBI on 1 February 2022.

When Gautam Adani, to diversify his risk, wanted terminal-II to be developed by another party, DPW objected citing its ROFR (right of first refusal).

Gautam Adani, in 2007, stated, 'We had a private jetty, and we decided to build it further as a joint venture with the state government which wanted to hold 26 per cent while we held 74 per cent. In 2006, the state government divested its holding at a price of Rs 120 (US$2.95) a share compared to its original investment at Rs 10 (US$0.25) a share.'[62]

Instead of getting into a prolonged dispute, Gautambhai brilliantly took up the development and management of the subsequent terminals at Mundra Port himself. He and his people had studied the ways in which ports were built and operated. They had the confidence of now being the developers and managers of their own destiny.

Mundra was profitable from day one. MPSEZL's monthly terminal royalty from MICT (10 per cent of the gross revenue received) generated Rs 52.9 crore as income from container cargo, including royalties for fiscal 2006, and the income from related marine services, was Rs 5.29 crore (US$13.23 million in 2007), or 13.8 per cent of MPSEZL's income from operations, and for fiscal 2007, container income was Rs 7.2 crore (US$17.88m) (12.3 per cent).[63]

Today, the Adani Group operates several ports and terminals in India, in addition to a major one in Australia, and a strategically important one in Sri Lanka. It wanted to build one in Sittwe (Myanmar) and Chittagong (Bangladesh) as well. The Sittwe Port had to be abandoned because of lenders objecting to funding a military state.[64] The first salvo had already been fired by Nordic fund KLP.[65]

Discussions about Chittagong are still under way.

This is also true of West Bengal, where Adani hopes to build at least one if not more ports. The group is already the highest bidder for the Tajpur deep-sea port in that state.[66] He hopes to get more ports in West Bengal which would open up trade across the Bay of Bengal right up to all the North-eastern states. That is why, the speech he gave in West Bengal in April 2022 is crucially important. He promised the government that he would invest Rs 10,000 crore in that state and create 25,000 jobs.[67]

Meanwhile, in July 2022, the Adani Group signed an MoU with the Israeli Innovation Centre which in turn helped in acquire a significant stake in Israel's Haifa Port. As Dror Bin, CEO, Israel Innovation Authority said, 'The Israel Innovation Authority is pleased to partner with the Adani Group in cementing Adani's and India's strategic collaboration with Israel, following the group's historic acquisition of Haifa Port.'[68]

This port is extremely interesting because of several reasons. First, it gives the Adani Group a foothold in the Middle East and even Europe given Israel's linkages with the countries there. Second, it further strengthens the bond between Adani and Israel, which is already a partner with this group for its defence projects and its Innovation Centre.

Strategic Sri Lanka

One of the ports that the Adani Group is building, in Sri Lanka, could have immense implications both for global maritime movement as well as geopolitics.[69] In September 2021, the Sri Lankan government allowed the Adani Group to build, own and operate a port near Colombo.

According to media reports, the Adani Group will join with John Keells Holdings, a local Sri Lanka conglomerate, becoming the largest foreign investor in Sri Lanka's ports. In a letter to the Colombo Stock Exchange, John Keells said that a Build, Own, Transfer Agreement was executed on 30 September. The partnership will build and operate the terminal for thirty-five years before it transfers it to the Sri Lanka Ports Authority(SLPA).[70]

APSEZ will own a controlling 51 per cent of the new company, with John Keells Holdings (JKH) holding 34 per cent, and the remainder held by the SLPA. The total cost of the project will be approximately $650 million topping the estimated $500 million invested by China in building its facilities in Port of Colombo. Sri Lanka issued an official letter of intent in March 2021 for development of the new West Container Terminal-1.

It will be a deepwater terminal with approximately 1.4 km of quay length and will have an annual handling capacity of 3.2 million TEUs (20-foot equivalent units, a measurement used to denote the size of containers). Construction is due to begin in 2022 with the first phase opening in about twenty-four months and expected to complete the total development within forty-eight months.

This port has several implications. First, because it is part of the Colombo port—which is quite an efficient port[71]—shipping traffic already moves into this area. So, no change of shipping routes will be required. At best, the ships only dock at another terminal, preferably one which has the best charges and the greatest efficiencies. Both are areas where the Adani Group has proved its mettle.

Second, it could be the best transhipment port India and the Adani Group could have asked for, especially for ships that move from Africa to Australia or Japan or other eastern countries.

This effectively means that the traffic that the China-owned Hambantota Port expected to dock at its newly built port may not be easily forthcoming. It could be Advantage Adani. All ships headed to Australia, Japan and South Korea may opt to dock at the Adani port instead.

6.6

Sittwe would have benefitted all three

Adani, India and Myanmar

Notes: *The Sittwe Port would have benefitted Myanmar, the Adani Group and even the Government of India. Myanmar grows agricultural produce, which India needs frequently. India can export its engineering goods to Myanmar. But most important is that Myanmar touches several North-eastern states —Mizoram, Tripura, Manipur, Nagaland and Arunachal Pradesh. That could mean tremendous benefits for the defence forces of India, and for trade with the North-east.*

Source: Google Maps

However, it is unlikely that Gautambhai would seek to antagonize the Chinese. He is a businessman and knows that having good relations with China will be important. Firstly, both India and China represent the largest consumer markets in the world. These countries are where the growth opportunities lie. Secondly, China will need to acquire coal and iron ore in addition to other minerals. They could re-emerge as a customer for Adani's coal mines, if he can bring about a settlement between Australia and China. Thirdly, there is no denying that China is already the largest trade partner for India. Effectively, Adani will soon slip into the realm of geopolitics as well.[72]

Yet, there is no denying that, once again, group interests and national interests have converged brilliantly in the Sri Lankan port. The new West Container Terminal will compete with the Colombo International Container Terminal and the southern port of Hambantota, both of which are operated by China Merchants Port Holdings.

The new West Container Terminal-1 will be a deep-water terminal with approximately 4500 feet of dock at a depth of 65 feet. The terminal will have an annual capacity of 3.2 million TEUs. Construction is due to begin in 2022 with the first section opening within twenty-four months and completion within forty-eight months.

At the same time, the group is also on the lookout for ports that it could acquire in the US and in Europe.[73] At the rate at which the group has been growing, it won't be long before it acquires ports in those regions as well.

Sittwe is desirable

Another port that Gautambhai almost developed and operated was the Sittwe Port in Myanmar.

In 2015, everything seemed to be going smoothly for Gautambhai. Myanmar was willing to let the Adani Group develop and operate the Sittwe Port. That would have made the group much more active in and around the Bay of Bengal. Moreover, much of India's pulses, whenever there is a shortage, come from Myanmar. That country also needs India's engineering goods. And it wanted to balance its dependence on China with Indian investments (China already operates a port in Myanmar). Moreover, Myanmar touches more North-eastern states in India than any other country. Hence it could easily become a route for galvanizing trade with the North-east regions as well.

In fact, funding was being tied up beautifully. The Gulf-based GFH Financial group came forward with money.[74] By 2019, the Government of India also agreed to bring in money.[75]

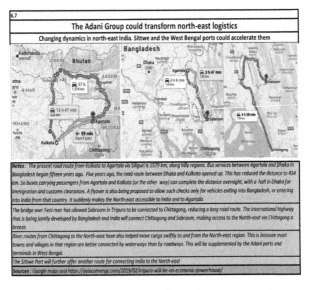

But global lobbyists, opposed to the Adani Group, forced major global financiers to stop funding the Sittwe Port.[76] They also wanted to escalate the war to cover all international projects of the group, including the big one in Australia (see the chapter on Australia). The argument put forth was that such investments would make the military rule in Myanmar even stronger. Worried about the domino effect this could have on the group's investments elsewhere, the Adani Group stopped all work on the Sittwe Port.[77]

But by now the governments of India and Myanmar were determined to have this port, recognizing the strategic significance of the Adani Group operating the Sittwe Port and the immense benefits it would bring to both countries. So, in July 2021, another Indian venture, Bharat Freight group stepped into the crease and decided to set up this port.[78]

The move was welcomed by multilateral agencies.[79] And India's interests have been protected. But had the Sittwe Port been developed by the Adani Group, the synergies would have been mind-boggling.

6.8

The Mundra Port oil tank farm

The Mundra Port boasts of one of the largest oil storage terminals in India, connected by a pipeline to the Bhatinda refinery
Photograph sourced from the Adani group

In any case, both India and the Adani Group have been looking at the north-east (NE) states to help them in their economic development. The Adani Group is said to be looking at the opportunity to develop the overhead connectivity between Kolkata and Agartala.[80] It is similarly into negotiations with the West Bengal government to take up the development of its ports and use them both for international cargo movement as well as connecting the port to the rivers that intersect and connect most villages in the NE region. In the region, river transport is more popular and widespread than road transport.

Sittwe would have fitted in with such plans giving the group immense access in developing the NE region.

All the same, expect more action by the Adani Group in the east and the NE. It has already announced development of rooftop solar in the north eastern region,[81] and it will not surprise many, if the Adani Group actually manages to acquire the Sittwe Port sometime in the future.

Strategies for profitability

Meanwhile, in order to make Mundra Port even more vibrant, Gautambhai did two things:

- He created new lines of business, for which, when required, he entered into strategic partnerships.
- He got into building new terminals with an amazing strategy which saved costs, and enhanced income streams.

The group entered into strategic long-term contractual arrangements with Indian Railways relating to the railway links and cargo services to and from Mundra Port (more on this a bit later).

The group has entered into a long-term relationship with IOC for the handling of crude oil cargo. To ensure that this business kept rolling in, the group persuaded both IOC and industrialist L.N. Mittal to build a large oil tank farm and also an oil pipeline connecting Mundra with Bhatinda Refineries. That in turn made Mundra the preferred port for import because the logistics and costs were taken care of. Today, this IOC association has expanded into gas distribution.[82]

In 2007–08 itself, MPSEZL began getting substantial income from some very large customers (which included group companies like Adani Enterprises Ltd and Adani–Wilmar).

In fiscal 2006, each of four customers—Adani Enterprise, Indian Oil, Indian Railways and Indian Farmers Fertiliser

Cooperative (IFFCO)—contributed to over 5 per cent of MPSEZL's income from operations. Together, these four customers and MICT accounted for 39.7 per cent of MPSEZL's income from operations in fiscal 2006 (Adani Enterprises contributed 10.9 per cent).[83] During fiscal 2007 too, each of four customers, including FCI, Indian Oil, Indian Railways and Adani Enterprises along with MICT contributed to over 5 per cent of MPSEZL's income from operations. Together, these four customers and MICT accounted for 50.9 per cent income (FCI's contribution was the largest—18.8 per cent).

Likewise, MPSEZL has entered into transactions with other Adani Group companies, such as Adani Enterprises and Adani–Wilmar. Both Adani Enterprises and Adani–Wilmar are significant customers of MPSEZL's bulk cargo and related marine services, and together the two companies accounted for Rs 527.5 million and Rs 466.2 million (US$13.19 million and 11.66 million), or 13.7 per cent and 8 per cent, as income from operations for fiscal 2006 and fiscal 2007, respectively.[84]

MPSEZL received an approval from the Government of India permitting it to establish a multi-product special export zone (SEZ) in an area measuring 2658.2 hectares covering Mundra Port and the surrounding areas, resulting in several fiscal incentives and other benefits for SEZ developers and their customers, including exemptions from income tax and duties. More land meant more opportunities.

As Gautambhai said around that time, 'Although we did not understand anything about building ports ten years ago, we think we have one of the finest teams in this business today. So, when Dahej which has an LNG import facility wanted to get into solid cargo, it approached us and we took up a 50 per cent equity stake in this business. The same was with Dholera.'[85]

One port followed another, making the Adani Group the biggest port developer and manager in the country. And there were some unique strategies that he adopted, first in Mundra and then for every other port that he managed to get.

But crucial to the building of a port was the manner in which each part of the port was made to generate revenues, even while another section of the port was being built. This is where Gautambhai redefined the phases of port building. Devang Desai says, 'While we were working on the master plan of the Mundra port, the creek and basin phasing needed to be done. The consultant presented us with a comprehensive diagram of coastlines and jetties after spending months on it. Each one of us saw the big vision of how the place would be transformed.

'But Gautambhai saw the diagram like a sequential transaction: what would come up first and where, how it would be linked to the second part and how all this would stack up in terms of financial viability. This meant that the man, who knew much less about port design than the consultants, was making the most significant contribution to the deeper understanding of how the port would work. The result was that the port design had to be altered.' It was an unusual type of lateral thinking making money even while spending it.

Such efficiencies were applied in other areas as well. Vinay Prakash, COO, Adani Natural Resources (including coal), explains how Gautambhai 'had studied other ports; he felt 10 rakes per day were possible. Since we were not precise as to how we could get there, he spoke to a few hands-on people at the port (not necessarily senior). Within hours he had realized that the port needed specific investments that would debottleneck capacities. Today, we manage 10 rakes per day, which we know is an Indian record based on our presence across 16 Indian ports. The lesson this taught us is that it is not necessary to work on a minimum cost basis all the time; it is important to increase selective investments that can increase volumes (and hence reduce costs per unit).

'The man can see farther than most. Until some years ago, we were importing coal through Supramax vessels (50,000

DWT, geared). Gautambhai asked, "Why are we not using more Panamaxes (75,000 DWT, gearless)?" I told him that there was not much of a costing differential; anyway, we were better off than most as we were doing a 20-80 Panamax-Supramax split whereas others were working with a 0-100 split.

'He said that he would not go into operational issues, but advised us to seek an advantage, however small, grow it and move towards a 50-50 split as "it will help you". That is all he said. So, we began to look into this possibility; in those days, there was a large market for Supramaxes, low share for Panamaxes and no market for Capesized (1,50,000 DWT) vessels. Thereafter, we progressively evolved our vessels mix: today, only 15 per cent of our exposure is with Supramaxes, 45 per cent with Panamaxes and 40 per cent with Capesized vessels.

'What is more important is that we account for 95 per cent of all Capesized vessels and 90 per cent of all Panamaxes coming into India. We are able to move as much coal in a month that most players can move in a year. Because of the frequency of our import, we are able to provide coal every few days to customers, which help them to nurse a lower inventory and consume less working capital. Today, the prudent selection of vessel sizes is strengthening the competitiveness of our customers.'

Wilmar arrives

Even while he built the ports, he kept adding lines of business for the ports as well.

He first started importing coal, grain and oil for the Government of India. He saw a huge opportunity in coal trading—something which he began from December 1998. It also led him to acquire coal mines—first in Indonesia and then in India and Australia.[86]

The same month he met a Malaysian businessman (of Chinese descent) in Singapore. His name was Kuok Khoon Hong, chairman of Wilmar International Ltd. This was a Singapore-based edible oil trading company, belonging to a group which also owns the Shangri-la Hotel chain, and accounts for a market capitalization of some $30 billion. Kuok agreed to look at Mundra. On his first visit to Mundra, the tremendous zest and long-term vision that Gautambhai showed resulted in a deal being signed in January 1999, leading to the formation of Adani–Wilmar—a 50:50 joint venture to import and refine edible oil at Mundra.

Atul Chaturvedi, director, Adani–Wilmar, and earlier CEO at Adani Agro Business in 2013, explains, 'When Kuok Khoon Hong came to Mundra, I had to take charge of showing him around, and Gautambhai asked me to take care of all formalities. He trusted me with all negotiations and cleared the final proposal when it was made to him.' Chaturvedi adds, 'Kuok had understood India better than most of us. He had seen the manner in which China's markets had exploded and was sure that this would happen in India as well.'

Kuok was a trader by instinct, and so was Gautambhai. Both understood each other almost immediately, and there has been no looking back since then. What started as a 600 tonnes per day (tpd) plant is now processing 3400 tpd of edible oil (cumulatively, taking all seven plants all over the country), it has a refining capacity of 10,000 tpd, majority of it is sold under the 'Fortune' brand, which has become the largest brand among edible oils in India.[87]

The edible oil refinery was set up at Mundra. Unrefined edible oil imports were channelled through the port, making both the edible oil plant and the port develop synergies and thus benefitting each other.

This was possibly the second time that Gautam showed his ability to select the right people to negotiate a deal, and then delegate the responsibility to the chosen managers to arrive at a recommendation. Earlier, this ability to delegate and empower was in evidence when the P&O deal was concluded. This time it was the Wilmar deal.

By October 2000, the edible oil refinery of Adani–Wilmar was set up at Mundra.[88]

Then as city gas distribution (CGD) licences began being given out, Gautambhai bid for as many as he could and became the largest owner of CGD opportunities. While this was going on, he realized that CGD would require LNG terminals with regassification facilities. He has thus become a formidable player in the LNG terminals space at his ports.[89] From 1998 to 2005 Gautambhai combined his trading skills and project implementation capabilities in ways that few could imagine. In retrospect, it became evident that Gautam's quest for efficiency and effectiveness was primarily responsible for transforming Mundra into the vibrant port it is today.

Transforming Mundra

6.9		
Upcoming LNG terminals		
		figures in MMTPA
Location	**Company**	**Capacity**
Already commisioned		
Mundra	GSPC Adani	5
Ennore	Indian Oil TIDCO	5
Under construction		
Dahej (expansion)*	Petronet LNG	5
Kakinada	APGDL	2.5
Dhamra	Adani	5
Jafrabad (FSRU)	Swan Energy	5
Jaigarh	H-Energy	2.5
Planned		
Gangavaram	Petronet LNG	5
Kolkata Port	H-Energy	2.5
Chhara	HPCL & Shapoorji Palloni	5
Krishnapatnam	LNG Bharat	2.5

Notes : (*) post the ramp up, the Dahej capacity will be 20 MMTPA; While the Adani group may not own many LNG terminals, its Dahej capacity is huge. It is also the biggest coastal shipping player. Moreover, it is bidding for ports in West Bengal. That could make the group's gas plans formidable.

Sources : CARE Ratings (now CARE Edge) report of May 14, 2019 titled Natural gas FY19 review; Company filings, PPTs; Petronet LNG

Mundra was a barren piece of land, marshy in many places, but with a coastline which dipped sharply giving the location a remarkable edge that suited a port. But managing a port was not easy. Gautam had absolutely no idea about how to construct ports and manage the same. He started from scratch, thought out of the box, hired the best contractors for construction and created infrastructure for what could be called a modern port. Yet, over the years, he had learnt that a port succeeded only if it had three major prerequisites.

As mentioned earlier, the first is water depth, which is actually a gift from the gods. The alternative would be to blast and dredge the rock bottom and create depth. The initial costs are prohibitive, and the recurring costs involved in constant dredging can haemorrhage a port financially.

The second—as described above—is land. Ports require huge amounts of land to store goods either for putting them on to ships, or for storing goods that have been evacuated from ships or to process them in an industrial unit to add value. Gautambhai had already begun acquiring land, first for the salt pans, and then for the port. By 2006, the Adani Group had acquired almost 15,665 acres of land. But as chart 6.4 shows, the figure could be upwards of 30,000 acres.

Gautambhai wanted land for yet another reason. He knew that the best exporting countries had industries located near ports. He wanted the land on which he could resettle industries next to the port. That has already happened with Maruti Suzuki's automobile export hub. It will happen with Adani–POSCO. It has already happened with power and edible oil as well. Expect more units to come up on this land—benefitting both from the SEZ status and proximity to the oceans.

The third was connectivity to the hinterland from where goods would come, and to the destinations where they had to be sent. First came the road connectivity—linking Mundra to the national highways. But much of cargo arrives through rail (rail transport is also cheaper than road), so a rail linkage was crucial. Mundra was 64 km away from the nearest rail junction.

Rail linkage

Gautambhai promptly began building a 64-km railway line with the consent of the government. By November 2000, trial runs between Mundra and Adipur began, and with this Gautam was soon to become one of the key influencers in changing national policy when the Central government announced that all port linkage rail connections could now be built on a public-private partnership (PPP) basis. The Mundra railway line terminates at Adipur junction from where goods can be sent to any part of India. Simultaneously, Gautam began impressing on the state government of the urgent need to develop road connectivity to all ports, and thus to the Mundra Port as well.

Today, all of the Adani Group ports have some of the best linkages, especially by road and rail. Please refer to chart 2.6 for details on rail linkages.

Today, the Mundra Port has become the virtual gateway of the country for many of the goods India requires. The port has become so central to Gautam's corporate empire, and means so much to him, that it has become the prized jewel in the group. It is not surprising to see dignitaries—both from politics and industry, in addition to media representatives—flocking to the port to see the marvel that has come up in India.

There is an emotional side to such visits as well. Gautam recalls how, when he was a child, he had been taken to see the port of Kandla, and how impressed he had been then. Today, he wants other children to have the same benefit as well.

He now gets his group to arrange for school buses to ferry children to Mundra every day. These buses travel—under escort, from Ahmedabad to Mundra and back to Ahmedabad, every day. The children stay overnight at the port, visit the Adani–Wilmar plant, see the power generation facilities, and return to home base. At least 30,000 students have benefitted from such trips during less than a year, and the numbers continue to swell. It is Gautam's way of telling children how to think big, and how a barren piece of land can become central to a nation's pride and economic growth.

Airport—Civil and defence

In Mundra, he even built a 2.2-km runway—good enough for the largest aircraft. While no plans have been announced for this 'airport' as yet, expect it to play a big role. Adani has already bagged licences for airport management. It is only a matter of time, the Mundra airport—currently used for captive purposes, and for bringing key visitors to Mundra—will be operationalized either as a cargo airport, or even as a full-fledged commercial airport. Alternatively, it could be used as major support for his defence and MRO[90] related projects.

Adani's foray into defence business will make both the airport and the port become extremely profitable and nationally relevant. For instance, the group is looking at the MRO business which involves maintenance and repair of aircraft. This is one of the most lucrative businesses in the world.[91] The Adani runway will come in extremely useful because the MRO business requires access to an airstrip and technology partners. So do the production of missiles, drones and other items which involve avionics. Access to a runway can be a huge advantage, even a prerequisite.

Then the group has already signed major deals with aircraft producers for defence purposes. These include a $20 billion deal with SAAB of Sweden.[92] Then there is Israel's Elbit,[93] Airbus,[94] the Italian Snam,[95] Hindustan Shipyard for a Rs 45,000 crore submarine project[96] among others.

In the coming decade, it will not be surprising if these begin to generate more money—and national relevance—than all the projects put together.

Shrinking timelines

Gautambhai's experiences as trader and importer came in handy at this point of time. He realized that speedy turnaround time of vessels was essential for the success of his port, as ships are hired on time charter basis. He opted for the highest possible level of mechanization at the port for the entire range of operations, right from loading/unloading to storage and packaging.

The entire back-end work including traffic management and product movement was fully computerized from day one. All these led to high level of efficiency and in turn rapid growth in business as anchoring at Mundra became the most cost-effective option for imports as well as exports. Gautambhai also knew that the other essential part of port operations was to ensure and maintain quality of the product handled, this was achieved by opting for highest level of housekeeping and adopting best practices.[97]

The result is that Mundra is today probably the only port which has a floating pontoon for loading/unloading of automobiles in ships. This ensures round-the-clock and speedy loading, making Mundra the preferred destination for automobile export. The country's largest automobile exporter is Maruti Suzuki, and its entire automobile exports are through Mundra.[98]

Dredger ownership

At the same time, he decided that, unlike other Indian ports, he would own the dredgers, instead of just hiring them. It was a toss-up between time and cost. Since dredgers were not easily available, their timely procurement was uncertain, and the costs were extremely high. Owning dredgers would prove to be cost-effective for a port that had to grow very rapidly. Today, Adani has sixteen dredgers—each costing between Rs 50–250 crore.

But there was a need to get someone to manage one of the jetties which was to be converted into a container terminal at the port. Gautam had little knowledge of how to manage a container terminal.

He ordered a search worldwide for potential partners. There was a bigger problem as well. The port had taken up a lot of money, and Gautam was terribly short of funds. For the first time, the group's finance managers were getting worried at the rapid depletion of funds, wondering if there would be enough money left at the end of each month to pay salaries to the employees of the group.

Dr Malay Mahadevia, director, Adani Ports and Special Economic Zone Ltd, adds, 'While we were building the Mundra port, it was a given that we would appoint contractors to do the dredging for us, as is done at every port in the world. Gautambhai resolved to buy every single of his dredgers and become his own contractor. Two things happened as a result: he created a commercial global market for dredgers for the first time in the world and created a jetty service in just 10 months against a 24-month standard.'

Mahadevia, a childhood friend, has other anecdotes to share. He says, 'Whenever you want Gautambhai to achieve the impossible, all you need to do is to tell him that *yeh nahi hoga* (loosely translated, it means, this is not possible). When one of his friends told him that "setting up a port *apna kaam nahi hai* (this is not our job), we are traders... *bus khatam!* (that clinched the situation)." Gautam responded, "*Woh bola kyun?!* (Why did you say that?)." He says, chucklingly, that if his friends want Gautambhai to do something, they should make it appear impossible. Gautambhai then rises to the bait, quite often.'

Another anecdote he mentions is the way Gautambhai does not like protocols and pomp. 'Once when he reached Mundra by jet, there were four cars, security, and a reception team at the airport. They were scolded, "Don't you have any work for the day? Why are you not at your desks?" Thereafter, nobody ever went to receive him.'

The Maruti Suzuki opportunity

But the plans he had for Maruti Suzuki were a bit different. Had they worked out, almost all the cars produced by Maruti would have gone to all coastal regions using ro-ro ships.

Gautambhai's team made presentations to the automobile manufacturer. They pointed out that even though the company was the largest producer of automobiles, almost 40 per cent of the market had been grabbed by the likes of Ford and Hyundai. Both had their plants in south India, near Ennore Port. They pointed out to Maruti Suzuki's bosses that one reason why these south-based automobile producers had succeeded in India was because their logistics costs were lower.

Intrigued, the Maruti Suzuki bosses asked for elaboration. The Adani team pointed out that in order to cater to the south Indian market, Maruti Suzuki had to send vehicles by road. But since there was no cargo to be picked up from south India, trucks could be had at a discount. Thus, the two south-based automobile producers had a lower cost advantage—thanks to trucks which had brought in Maruti Suzuki vehicles begging for return cargo.

What they suggested was that Maruti Suzuki should transport cars by rail to Mundra, load them on a ro-ro boat and then reach the southern market. The logistics costs would be lower (rail costs are lower than road costs, and shipping costs even lower than rail costs).[99] Maruti Suzuki liked the idea because rail transport would have cut short time and cost. Moreover, the accidents and damage road transport cost the company could be reduced. Trials were initiated. A ro-ro ship was pressed into operation, and everything seemed to go well. It could have actually hit Ford and Hyundai very hard.

Then there was trouble. There were few ro-ro ships available, and the operator increased his fares. It was no longer viable. Second, there were too few ports under Adani control then in the southern and eastern region. And ro-ro ships need specially trained drivers to put cars on to ships and then drive them off to the destination port. But Maruti Suzuki was so impressed with Mundra that it built its export hub there. Drivers are specially trained to take vehicles up the gangway on to the boats, and to tether them properly. That in turn has helped the automobile giant boost its export business enormously.

It will not be surprising if within a few years, all automobile players will begin adopting the coastal route because the Adani Group has more ports all around (see chart 6.5). Moreover, with the emphasis on linkages and training that the group has insisted on at all its ports, the only gap is the ro-ro vessels. Expect the Adani Group to enter this line of business as well. After all, as Paresh Pujara, former chief information officer, Adani Group, explained almost a decade ago, 'The annual import of nearly 40 million tonnes of coal into India has resulted in 400 Adani ships being out at sea at any given time and 1,00,000 tonnes being discharged at pan-Indian ports every day. Gautambhai has been acquiring or chartering ships all the time.' At the right time, he will either give orders for building the required ro-ro ships, or will take them on a long-term charter. This possibility cannot be ruled out.

Gautambhai's strategies were not lost on other entrepreneurs across the country, who also began to work on ways to connect their respective private ports to the hinterland. They also began to work on acquiring large parcels of land. However, even today, no other port has the land bank that Mundra Port enjoys which, in turn, has benefitted the port in two ways.

First, it helped Gautam store goods, and even build container freight stations, for customers. It allowed him to build excellent cargo evacuation systems—whether it was for containers, or bulk grain, or oil, or automobiles, or even coal. Second, it permitted Gautam to even develop some of the land as SEZs.

Had this land not been available, it is unlikely he could have persuaded a variety of units to locate their manufacturing facilities at Mundra.

7

King Coal

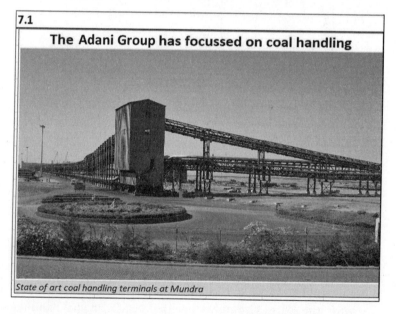

The Adani Group has focussed on coal handling

State of art coal handling terminals at Mundra

No activity of the Adani Group has been as controversial (or profitable and economically relevant) as his dealings in coal—whether through trading, shipping or mining.

But coal remains crucial to the group's plans and there are several reasons for this.

First, after PVC, the item that he has traded in most has been coal. This was even before the Mundra Port was built.

7.2

New coal-fired power capacity by country (MW)

Global Coal Plant Tracker, January 2022 in MW capacity—top 10 given

Country	2000	2005	2010	2015	2020	2021	Total 2000-2021
China	17,530	46,966	64,172	65,787	41,386	25,237	1,002,935
India	1,705	3,325	12,276	20,750	2,000	6,445	186,767
Indonesia	1,720	0	630	2,291	3,376	2,790	33,472
South Korea	1,000	500	250	0	0	3,098	28,268
United States	101	434	5,879	50	0	0	25,714
Japan	4,204	276	1,010	74	1,957	1,830	25,637
Vietnam	0	0	300	4,475	1,288	2,400	22,172
Germany	1,980	0	85	3,382	1,100	0	13,775
Turkey	317	495	1,390	1,140	55	145	13,259
Malaysia	1,000	0	0	1,000	0	0	12,580
Total of top 10	29,557	51,996	85,992	98,949	51,162	41,945	1,364,579
World	34,640	53,877	89,489	107,013	56,772	44,975	1,455,120
India and China	19,235	50,291	76,448	86,537	43,386	31,682	1,189,702

Note: Anyone who believes that coal is dead has not looked at these numbers closely enough. Except for 2020 and 2021, both COVID-19 years, demand has kept on growing as have supply sources. Expect this trend to resume.

Source: Global Energy Monitor – https://globalenergymonitor.org/

Second, as soon as the port got built, and coal imports were likely to be more predictable (and profitable), Gautambhai purchased a coal mine in Indonesia.[100]

Third, Adani continues to be the largest importer of coal in India, for the county—much of it from his coal mines in Indonesia and Australia.

Fourth, demand for coal continues to be strong, and is likely to remain so for at least the next decade. New sources of energy have yet to replace coal for most countries because of the lack of reliable storage devices. Hydrogen may work, but it is more difficult and hazardous to handle.

Fifth, the Adani Group has invested heavily in coal handling terminals in many of its ports in India and overseas.

And, lastly, it must be stated that the Adani Group has not been involved in any of the coal scams that have rocked the Indian parliament, time and again and have made media headlines. The group has imported coal, or traded in it, or has acquired coal mines through a process of tendering. The controversies surrounding coal mining activities are actually a result of other factors, as has been explained later in this chapter.

7.3			
Production of Raw Coal			
2020-21 figures in million tonnes			
			million tonnes
Sector	Coking	Non-Coking	Total Coal
Public	38.9	647.0	686.0
Private	5.9	24.3	30.1
All India	**44.8**	**671.3**	**716.1**

Source : Ministry of Coal – Provisional Coal Statistics 2020-21; https://coal.gov.in/sites/default/files/2021-06/Provisional-Coal-Statistics-2020-21.pdf

Gautambhai's very first terminal in Mundra began setting up coal handling systems so that it could be evacuated at high speeds from vessels, put on a conveyor belt and then deposited in areas where coal dust would not create problems. Today, sophisticated coal handling facilities can be found at Adani ports and terminals in Mundra, Dahej, Mormugao, Tuna and Vizag.

In the initial years, the group handled coal imports on behalf of Coal India, and then gradually began focusing on owning its own mines in India, Indonesia and Australia. The mining activities in Australia have drawn a great deal of controversy and there were fears that the project would be scuttled.[101] But it was finally given the go-ahead. Production has just commenced. Since domestic production of coal is inadequate in meeting demand, the need for imports is immense. This applies to China and almost every other developing country as well.

The present war in Ukraine has caused fuel prices to soar. That has caused many countries to look to using coal once again, causing coal prices to soar as well.[102] That could mean bumper profits for the Adani Group in the coming year, though this will be through the group's overseas holdings, not through the companies listed on Indian exchanges.[103] But that will give the group additional cash flows to service its overseas borrowings.

Need for imported coal

Gautambhai was quick to realize that India would need lots of coal to meet the demand from various sectors. His assumptions were borne out over a period of time. India produces coal, but not enough to meet its various needs. So, it is compelled to import. Moreover, mining in India will not be easy. Protests by environmentalists could scuttle most plans.

Thus, owning and developing coal mines overseas makes immense sense. It de-risks the Adani Group, but more importantly, it de-risks India, giving it an assured source of supply.

At the same time, in order to remain aligned with national priorities, Gautambhai has sought to increase domestic production of coal. But that hasn't been enough, because exploiting coal mines in India can be quite a vexatious process.

And this is where the problem begins.

Gautambhai must battle such issues on three fronts.

Firstly, he has to justify coal imports. The justification is obvious, but it escapes most people, quite often. Indian businesses need coal for power generation, cement and sponge iron, among others. But the most important import is for making steel which uses coking coal. Almost the entire amount is imported. Linked to this is the environment lobby which wants the mining of coal scrapped. But as Gautambhai himself pointed out in his article on 'The Paradoxes at Davos—2022',[104] 'the turmoil over energy [is immense]. Developed nations that were setting targets and giving stern lectures about climate change to the rest of the world now appear to be less censorious as their own energy security is threatened and prices spiral. Very few are willing to admit that there had been an overswing on the side of green solutions and technologies that were still in their nascent stage and that this fragility has been totally exposed by the crisis in Ukraine.'

7.4	
Country-wise coal import sources	
Figures for 2020-21	
Country	Quantity In mn tonnes
Indonesia	92.5
Australia	55
South Africa	31.1
USA	12.2
Mozambique	3.6
Russia	6.7
Singapore	4.5
Others	9.4
Total	215

Source : Ministry of Coal — Provisional Coal Statistics 2020-21
https://coal.gov.in/sites/default/files/2021-06/Provisional-Coal-Statistics-2020-21.pdf

And while he remains a champion for sustainability, he also points out in his talk at the JP Morgan Summit in September 2021.[105] 'The worst-case scenario would be that, in following our need to become green, we adopt a structure that deprives a developing nation's people of hope and of opportunities to better their lives. If so, the search for sustainability will in itself become unsustainable.' You cannot ask a poor villager to go without coal which he uses to cook the family's daily meal.

Secondly, the group has to justify the pricing at which the coal is imported. But that is the easiest thing to do, because there will be a record of prices at which India procures coal from the Adani Group and other parties. True, the group owns coal mines in Indonesia and Australia. But that should be no reason to frown at imports, so long as the prices are comparable with imports from other sources.

Thirdly, justifying coal exploration and extraction of coal from mines within India is not easy. This is proving to be the most difficult. Unfortunately, over the past few decades green activists have been quite vocal about the environmental damage caused because of coal exploration. They oppose every coal mine that the Adani Group plans to develop (more Adani than other group which exploits more coal mines in the country). But then, if one does not exploit Indian mines, India will have to continue importing. India has few other choices. It must import. Or it must allow domestic coal mining—officially.

7.5

Illegal mining continues unabated
(for all minerals excluding atomic and fuel minerals)

States	No. of illegal mining cases registered			
	2010-11	2012-13	2014-15	2015-16**
Andaman & Nico	n.r.	n.r.	n.r.	n.r.
Andhra Pradesh	13,939	16,592	9,379	3,931
Assam	n.r.	n.r.	n.r.	n.r.
Chhattisgarh	2,017	3,238	5,040	2,647
Goa	13	0	0	2
Gujarat	2,184	6,023	5,716	2,280
Haryana	3,446	3,517	5,333	2,288
Himachal Prades	1,213	n.r.	n.r.	n.r.
Jharkhand	199	663	1,162	854
Karnataka	6,476	6,677	8,464	4,725
Kerala	2,028	4,550	4,172	1,459
Madhya Pradesh	4,245	7,169	8,173	6,941
Maharashtra#	34,265	42,918	32,717	13,292
Mizoram	0	16	26	n.r.
Odisha	420	314	104	39
Punjab	754	19	n.r.	n.r.
Rajasthan	1,833	2,861	2,945	1,423
Tamilnadu	277	295	205	25
Telangana*	n.r.	n.r.	3,311	3,129
Uttar Pradesh	4,641	3,266	10,402	4,857
West Bengal	239	479	n.r.	575
Grand Total	**78,189**	**98,597**	**97,149**	**48,467**

Notes : (a) *Data for Telangana available only after 2015 as it is a newly formed state. Andhra Pradesh data, too, is only for the bifurcated region after that year; (b) nr= return not received; (c) **Quarter ending Sept. – 2015. #=However the statement given to the Lok Sabha on 9 March 2017 does not give any value either for the amount of illegal mining material seized or the fines collected for some states, especially Maharashtra. The government has not tabled any further information on illegal mining. No data is available on illegal coal mining.

Sources : (1) Indian Bureau of Mines, Government of India; (2) Reply to Lok Sabha, on 23 August, 2013, Unstarred Question No. 2391 on illegal mining; (3) Lok Sabha Unstarred Question No. 2329, on 9 May, 2016, on illegal mining; (4) Lok Sabha Unstarred Question No.1503, to be answered on 9th March 2017 on illegal mining

Unfortunately, even the courts have not been able to take a balanced view on this subject. In a case involving the Vedanta group[106] the Supreme Court decreed that the Ministry of Environment and Forests (MoEF) should reserve an area of 150-km radius around the Niyamgiri hills which was considered sacred by the local population.

To be fair, the Supreme Court only ordered the government to respect the decision of the local panchayat in September 2013. The twelve gram panchayats (village councils) in turn, prodded by the MoEF, passed a resolution stating that there should be no mining within a 150-km radius from the hilltop of Niyam Raja, the presiding deity of the tribals in that region. The panchayats claimed that 'the entire Niyamgiri hill range is sacred for us and the source of our livelihood'.

But the courts had possibly not realized that a radius of 150-km would mean an area of 70,650 sq. km. This is several times bigger than the area occupied by Mecca (0.4 sq. km) or the Vatican (0.4 sq. km) or the Tirupati city (inclusive of the temple, it accounts for a total of 24 sq. km), and the entire city of Jerusalem (124 sq. km).

Illegal mining

But there is a another more insidious development when it comes to protests against any kind of development activity, and that includes mines, ports or cement plants. There is increasing anecdotal evidence that many of these agitations are financed, either directly or indirectly, by groups engaged in illegal mining, or by groups which seek to thwart the group of a particular industrialist.[107]

Unfortunately, the government does not provide any data on illegal coal mining. And there are reasons to believe that the government even hides the truth when it comes to illegal coal mining.[108] Almost everyone knows that there is illegal mining in Meghalaya.[109] Even the government's investigation agencies found evidence of the ill-gotten funds of the Saradha scam being diverted to finance illegal mining. But official data is silent about illegal coal mining. What is unfortunate is that most of the NGOs, who make so much of a song and dance about industry trampling over tribal rights, or desecrate the environment, have seldom spoken against illegal miners. At the street level, the names of the powerful people who manage illegal mines are well known. But both the government and the NGOs prefer to look the other way.

Yet, if one looks at the data available, total incidents of illegal mining have increased year after year. This is so even after the new government came to power. Data beyond 2017 is just not available, partly because the government has made access to any Lok Sabha answers extremely difficult to retrieve, and also because new rules have been introduced, which do not require maintenance of scrupulous records relating to illegal mining.

The reasons are obvious. There is a huge amount of clandestine money to be made from illegal mining.[110] Naturally, these illegal miners—many of them very close to politicians of all hues and colours—do not want legal mining to develop in these areas. Private sector surveillance would make illegal mining that much more difficult. Hence, they finance organizations which in turn raise all sorts of objections, and even get stay orders from the courts, to prevent exploitation of mines. There are reports that much of Naxalism too is financed by illegal miners.[111]

This has even happened in the case of port development. Dhamra Port was stalled for several years because (it was claimed) that the location was the breeding ground for Ridley turtles.[112] Eventually, the project got cleared, and both the Tatas and L&T built the port. But they had not planned for connectivity the way the Adani Group does. Finally, both investors sold off the port to the Adani Group. Incidentally, Ridley turtles still come to breed along the shores in India.

Synergies—Coal and ports

Coming back to the origins of the coal business, Gautambhai knew that by 2000, the deepwater jetty, and the linkages to the hinterland at Mundra had given him a huge advantage over many other ports. He had begun noticing how the demand for coal to generate power had already started outstripping indigenous supply from Coal India.

The Adani brothers identified this nascent opportunity, and they decided to quit plastic trading altogether and instead focused on coal. Gautambhai had already begun trading in coal since December 1998. He now wanted bigger volumes. He began lobbying with state electricity boards to use his port for importing coal.

Suddenly, coal imports and the port began discovering synergies that continue to play out to this day.

Once that was done, additional business had to be brought to the port quickly. The Adani Group tried talking to his principals to see if they could persuade liners to stop at Mundra. But liners have their own set routes. Changing routes does not take place easily, and getting business to come to Mundra was proving to be a bigger challenge that had been felt earlier.

'Had it not been for Gautambhai's trading instincts, Mundra would never have become a viable port,' declares Atul Chaturvedi, the man who helped Gautambhai in most of his complex trading operations even before Adani–Wilmar was set up.

That is where Gautambhai's experience in handling large volumes of imports and exports came in handy. He was clear that he did not want consignment handling agents (CHA) to develop the port business. He took a decision to direct all ships with his cargo—for export or import—to use the Mundra Port instead of landing them at other ports.

His earlier plans of using shipload-full volumes of consignments proved to be of strategic significance. Gautambhai's access to coal mines, his ability to source coal for the state electricity boards, his ability to consolidate volumes and bring them to Mundra at prices and at delivery schedules that few could match, made Mundra economically viable.

However, one thing became abundantly clear. As mentioned earlier as well, while many other coal traders in India tried acquiring coal mines through cosy deals with the government—which then got exposed as 'Coal Scams'—Gautambhai preferred to import the coal first. When he undertook to exploit Indian mines, it was through open tendering. There has been no cosy transfer of assets from the government to this group. This is something that many critics of the Adani Group often forget.

A quaint situation soon developed. On account of inadequate linkages to the hinterland, coal meant for power generation stations in the eastern part of India also began being imported through Mundra. The time saved through smooth logistics justified the trip to Mundra by ship and then by rail to eastern India.

Seeking mines overseas

There are good reasons to believe that vested interests and rivalry also played a huge role in trying to block the development of coal mines in Australia. This was obvious, because Australia is largely a mining country—its largest export income is from resources exploited from the ground.[113] Moreover, the funding that the protestors appeared to have access to was staggering. They could rope in top-notch cricketers as part of their lobbying and could fund many events that should have cost them a packet.[114] Fortunately, however, Adani had structured his investments in Australia in such a manner that it was possible to withstand the delay caused on account of such agitations.

This was one of the shrewdest strategies that he adopted for mining. The architect of the strategy was, however, Harsh Mishra, who was in charge of identifying a new mine in Australia (now retired). He had worked with the Jindals earlier and knew the mining sector quite well. And when he saw the first mine that had been lined up for him, he promptly rejected it, even though Gautambhai had been advised very forcefully to pick up this mine. His reasons were based on technical problems that the mine would encounter, and also the logistical issues that were bound to crop up. So, Gautambhai asked him to stay put in Australia and identify another mine.

That is when he pounced upon the mine that is currently being exploited. But the asking price, he felt was too high. According to some, the price tag was over $1.5 billion.

So, Mishra spoke with Gautambhai on phone, and they arrived at a figure that would be more reasonable. But the seller wouldn't budge. So, Mishra suggested to Gautambhai that they try another tack. They would pay the seller a small upfront fee— around $500 million—and a higher royalty on sales, which would actually result in a larger amount than what was originally sought. After both sides had gone through the numbers with a fine-tooth comb, the deal was struck.

Mishra was possibly aware intuitively that paying a small sum upfront would mitigate possible future risks. He was aware of how many a mining project got wrecked because some vested interests had put a spoke in the wheel and delayed it for a long period of time. With smaller sums being paid, the interest costs were manageable. Moreover, the selling party, an Australian, too had its skin in the game. It had to work overtime, to get the government to clear the project, because its earnings would come in only as a royalty on sales. Together, the seller and the Adani Group managed to overcome one hurdle after another till the final clearances came in. Had the entire amount been paid upfront, the interest burden on account of the delays would have been so great that it could have made the project almost unviable.

Now, as mentioned earlier, in the aftermath of the war in Ukraine and the sanctions on Russia (a major coal producer), coal prices have zoomed. Gautambhai may actually end up making much more than he had envisaged initially.

Mishra explains, 'Dealing with Gautambhai was one of the causes for the project succeeding. He would listen to the objections his managers raised, and quickly arrive at a decision. The conventional way would be to form a committee to study the implications. Gautambhai decides quickly. And he delegates responsibility without being a micromanager. He likes to know all the details. But he watches the way the manager works and thinks. If things do not go right, he steps in. But, by and large, he trusts his managers, and even helps him in overcoming any problems that he might encounter.'

Mishra, who joined the Adani Group in September 2004, also narrates how Gautambhai first identified him. He gave him a long time to think over the proposal he had made. And when Mishra decided in favour of the Adani Group, he found that all the things negotiated were honoured, with a little more thrown in.

The deal for the Australian mine was clinched in 2010. Today, both the seller and the Adani Group are happy with the way things are turning out. At the time of acquisition, the reserves were estimated at 7.8 billion tonnes. Currently, it is estimated at over 10 billion tonnes. The Indonesian mine, acquired in 2006, has coal reserves of around 300 million tonnes.

Intuition and lateral thinking

'That is what makes Gautam different,' explains Mishra. 'His ability to trust his managers; his intuitive understanding of the deal, whether the price tag makes sense, are legendary. And he takes decisions fast. It is always yes, or no. Sometimes, it is "yes-but-only-if-we-can-bring-down-the-price". His grasp of numbers makes him comprehend the gist of complex mathematical formulae. By the time, we have done our DCF [discounted cash flow] computation, Gautam has already arrived at a number that will be a very good approximation of the actual number.'

Adds Malay Mahadevia, director of APSEZ, 'He has an unbelievable ability to assess business aspects of almost any type without the help of spreadsheets.'

Mishra has a theory. Gautambhai's passion for rummy and solitaire have honed his skills relating to pattern recognition. He listens to people. Lets pieces of information settle down and when a pattern emerges, he intuitively knows what to do. He keeps himself informed on every small detail, because he does not like guessing in the dark.

Gautambhai leveraged his logistics capabilities and knowledge of the coal business and opted for mine development and operations contracts in India for state utilities. The contract was to mine, wash and deliver coal at the power plant operated by state utilities. Gautam plans to leverage his port facilities capable of handling coal in the eastern and western parts of the country to move coal in very large volumes (50,000 to 1,50,000 tonnes) through sea and optimize total cost, an approach which was never thought of by other operators in the past; everyone was moving coal in relatively smaller volumes of 2000–3000 tonne rail racks.

There are several factors that worked in favour of Gautambhai as well. Australia is also a large producer of LNG. But post 2013, global prices of LNG crashed. The gas projects had been designed for market prices of over \$14 per MMBTU (energy equivalent to 1 million British thermal units (1 MMBTU) = 26.8 m^3 of natural gas at a given temperature).[115] Coal mines were not in favour then because everyone expected coal prices to crash. Instead, they have remained stable. And currently, coal prices are zooming.

What about green energy? That will depend on the cost of storage units. Even after battery prices have crashed to less than one-twentieth of the original prices a decade ago, they are still expensive. Moreover, current storage capacity would normally take care of one hour's storage for a normal power grid. Unless that can be increased to ten hours, you cannot rely on unpredictable renewable energy flows. Hydrogen may help. But it must be consumed as soon as it is produced. You cannot store it for peak consumption. Moreover, liquefying and then storing it in cryogenic containers is again expensive. And finally, it is difficult to handle and hazardous to keep.

In the euphoria that green energy created, most countries had stopped investing in coal and oil, explains Ruchir Sharma.[116] Now the world needs coal and oil because green energy has proved to be inadequate. So, with soaring demand, come soaring prices, and King Coal still rules the roost.

In Australia too, the Adani Group is building a 200-km railway line connecting the coal mines to the port for easy evacuation and export. In June 2021, the Adani rail project was said to be ready to connect Adani Carmichael Mine to the North Queensland Export Terminal, opening the potential of future projects in the coming time.[117] The project was delayed by ongoing agitations and by the pandemic. The state governments gave the required approvals to the coal mining projects, boosting production, especially in New South Wales and Queensland.

Bravus, a subsidiary of the Adani Group, will export quality coal from the mine to meet the growing demand for energy. It will ease the process of procuring and transporting high-grade coal with great efficiency.

With India likely to continue importing at least 200 million tonnes of coal annually, Adani's overseas coal mines should have a steady business going, in addition to orders from other Asian and African countries.

8

The Australian Saga: Make-or-Break Gamble

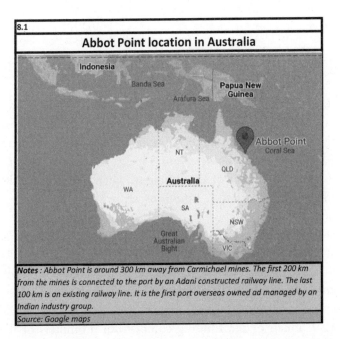

8.1

Abbot Point location in Australia

Notes : Abbot Point is around 300 km away from Carmichael mines. The first 200 km from the mines is connected to the port by an Adani constructed railway line. The last 100 km is an existing railway line. It is the first port overseas owned ad managed by an Indian industry group.

Source: Google maps

No story about Gautam Adani can be complete without dwelling on what happened in Australia. It could have been almost a make-or-break gamble. As mentioned in the earlier chapters, Gautambhai does not like to buckle under a challenge. It stimulates him.

His determination to beat the odds only grows as the challenge becomes greater. This is best evident in the Australian saga.

8.2

The other overseas coal mine in Indonesia

The Adani group has one more overseas coal mining operation. It is located in Indonesia ad was the group's maiden overseas project in coal mining and operations. The move was in line with the group's long-term resolve to support the growing coal demand in energy-starved India.

The journey led to the creation of PT Adani Global, a step-down subsidiary of Adani Enterprises Limited with focus on coal mining, logistics and trading operations in Indonesia. Subsequently the company acquired Exploitation License from the Indonesian government in 2007.

Located in the island of Kalimantan, alternatively known as Borneo, the company has constructed a coal terminal to service its mining operations. The present capacity is 2500 TPH and to be upgraded to 5000 TPH.

The Bunya mines have a Joint Ore Reserves Committee (JORC) - compliant resource of 269 MMT for both mines (combined). Production from the mine during FY 2020-21 was 1.04 MMT

Source: The Adani group

With the benefit of hindsight, Gautambhai can today afford to be sanguine. But while the heat was on, there were times when many thought that he would cut his losses and just leave Australia. The lobbying had become intense. It just made no sense at one level. But in the heat of the moment, when passions run high, nobody cares for reason. Emotions are whipped up. Fears are conjured up.

In a way, what happened in Australia is what happens with most progressive projects in India.[118] A group which seeks to espouse the rights of tribals, or the environment or both, suddenly emerges on the landscape. Such lobbying groups appear to be extremely well-funded. In India, as mentioned in the earlier chapter, much of the funding comes from promoters of illegal mines or illegally grown drugs or hooch. But at times, the funding comes through myriad ways, from vested interest groups, who see the emergence of a competitor or a threat to an existing line of business as a challenge to their very way of managing things.

The funding in Australia could have been variants of the same groups described above—one does not have the bandwidth to investigate and trace the source of funds. The protestors did have access to large funds to mount the type of campaign that lasted several years. They had funds to rope in even top-notch cricketers. But then, given that Australia is a different country, the funding-sources could have been different.

However, by 2012, one thing became clear. That the biggest protests came from people who could not have been affected by the coal mines in any significant way. Officials of the Adani Group were surprised at the responses from the consultation process. Between December 2012 and February 2013, around 25,000 public submissions were received. Only ten submissions were from the regions where the group wished to operate, making it clear that people living in capital cities—and not regional Australia where the mines were located—were waging a battle.[119]

Business first

What makes the Australia investment extremely interesting is that Gautambhai decided to get into coal mining in Australia because it seemed a very attractive business proposition.

The Adani Group already owned a coal mine in Indonesia. It was bought when Gautambhai was still into trading operations, and he used to sell the Indonesian coal to India. But he had observed that India's coal needs were growing (see chapter King Coal). And he knew that Indonesia's output would not be adequate for meeting India's needs. And there was a bigger market in countries beyond India—in Africa and Southeast Asia.

Moreover, it is always a good strategy to diversify risks. Another country source for a coal mine would seem a prudent business practice. Setting up a coal mine in Australia made sense, because this was essentially a country that made export money from selling its mineral output (which included oil and gas). It did make immense sense.

8.3

SCORING A COAL GOAL
Adani funds a way to kickstart job winner for Queensland

Source: "From stop to start -- celebrating 10 years in Australia"

That is where Harsh Mishra, who was then group president (international business), Adani Group, was asked to go to Australia and scout around. Gautambhai was aware of two other Indian players who had opted to set up mining operations in Australia. One was the GVK group, and the other was the Gujarat NRE Coke. Both mining operations eventually folded. Causes could range from not being able to face the heat of local lobbies (that did not want outsiders picking up the coal from their country) or inability to make the business viable. Or it could be that they lacked the experience in mining, which Gautambhai had already acquired.

Of course, the reason given by lobbyists was that the new coal mines would destroy the environment. They did not care to mention the fact that the Adani coal mine was just one of the 124-odd coal mines that were already in existence in Australia.[120] But then every lobby has a stated reason, and the actual reason. Protecting the environment does appear a more plausible platform from which to lobby against any large project. This has happened several times in India too.

Gautambhai succeeded because he had the tenacity. He had the ability to withstand risks that would have drowned many smaller promoters. And, more importantly, he used the right strategies at the right time.

The Australian project itself fell into Gautambhai's lap because of his ability to select the right man for the job and trusting him entirely. As has been pointed out earlier in this book, he deputed Mishra, 'As president of corporate planning, I was given the freedom to negotiate mining assets in Australia. When I finally rang him with a proposal—we pay up to $500 million and a $2 a tonne royalty-based arrangement for twenty years in exchange for about 7.8 billion tonnes of coal—he was on holiday in the UK. I told him that this was probably the largest coal tenement in the world and about three times our budget. I told him that on the other hand, this would represent the Group as a game changer. He heard everything . . . and ended one of the most critical "meetings" in the history of the group in just five minutes with a "Go ahead!" Any other person in his place would have flown out to the mines immediately. In fact, he never visited the mine or met the seller for two months, delaying this to just a couple of days before the deal, which I signed on his behalf.'

8.4		
Port facts		
Abbot Point Port, near the Queensland town of Bowen		
Has been in continuous and safe operation since 1984		
Adani has a 99-Year Lease to 2110 over the Port		
Coal from the Carmichael Mine will be shipped through the Port just as other Queensland mines have done for decades		
Port operations		
Adani acquired the Port operations business from Glencore in 2016 as a separate business to the asset lease		
Has around 180 direct employees and more than 200 contractors		
Coal exports bring billions of dollars in export revenue to Queensland, with these royalties used to fund public roads, schools and hospitals		
Source: "From stop to start -- celebrating 10 years in Australia"		

But within a couple of years, opposition to the projects—coal mining, railway line and the port—began raising its head.

Global trade convolutions

Then came a ray of sunshine. China stopped importing coal from Australia, furious at what it perceived as Australia cosying up with the Americans to needle it (China) on Xinjiang and COVID-19.[121] Coal imports from Australia plummeted. It was a crisis for Australia, which earns its largest foreign exchange from mining operations and the export of minerals and gas.

The human costs began spiralling upwards. Income from coal and gas exports began disappearing. Suddenly, many miners were jobless. By 2021, the growing tensions first began to attract international attention due to the human cost of the standoff, with more than seventy vessels, with a combined crew of 1400 people, left stranded offshore.[122]

Suddenly, at the very apex levels in the Australian government, the Adani project appeared to be a lifeline.

The group had already brought in substantial investments. It could guarantee huge offtake by India, which remained the second-largest market for coal in the world and could soon overtake China's demand. And it opened up the prospect of more trade with India. The Adani Group suddenly became a trade and investment ambassador promoting amity and trade ties between both the countries.

It could be more coincidence, but India's decision to join the Quad—a motley group comprising the US, Australia, Japan and India (with little in common among them)—could have a lot to do with the way India and Australia began seeing complementariness in their relationship.[123] The Adani project was bound to be on the top of the list, because the group's investment, at that point of time, was the largest Organisation for Economic Co-operation and Development (OECD) investment into Australia. After all, the total investment in the Australian project as of now is AU$

7.36 billion (Rs 41,724 crore). This amount included expenditure on the following:

- community donations and sponsorships
- development of community assets such as public roads
- purchase of the ninety-nine-year lease of the Abbot Point terminal
- purchase of the Moray Downs pastoral lease
- construction of the mine and railway
- establishment of the Bowen Rail Company
- construction of the Rugby Run solar farm.

Another coincidence is the warming up of relations between the two countries to the point that they signed an FTA (free trade agreement).[124] All of a sudden, both countries are talking about targeting trade volumes five times higher than current levels—to take their bilateral trade from AU$27.5 billion to AU$100 billion in eight years, the trade ministers of the two countries said on 7 April 2022. This could have significant implications for the economies of both countries as well as geopolitical alignments, particularly in the context of containing China which is currently India's largest trade partner.[125] That may or may not happen. But in the world of geopolitics, such possibilities are always considered.

Hindsight vision

Today, it is easier for Gautambhai to say wonderful things about Australia. He says, 'If there is any one country with which India has enjoyed excellent relations it has to be Australia.'[126] And the champion who has played a great part in shaping such perceptions for Gautambhai is Sir Donald Bradman.

As he puts it, 'How does an individual who received no formal training in cricket go on to become the greatest batsman the world has or will ever know? How does an individual defy all statistics and score 34 test centuries in just 52 tests? How does an individual have the overarching drive to score a triple century in just one day? How does an individual against all odds and irrespective of the batting conditions average 99.94 in every innings played? The Don's legend continues to inspire me in every aspect of business, even today.

'Our journey in Australia is now a decade old. If I were to identify a single point the experience in Australia has taught me—it is the power of a purpose and the need to be able to stand resolute behind what one believes in. . .

'India needs to get electricity to 300 million people that even today struggle to turn on a light and I fundamentally believe that the Adani Group has a role to play to help address this challenge.'

But the period from 2012 to 2018 could hardly be called comforting. Not surprisingly, when the nightmarish lobbying and counter-lobbying was over in 2019, Gautambhai graciously stated, 'Thank you to everyone who has invested so much effort and passion during our first ten years in Australia. Without your persistence and dedication, there would be no story to tell. Thank you to the people of regional Queensland who have warmly welcomed us. Without your support, we would have never achieved our ambitions.' He goes on to say that the Adani Group 'recognizes and thanks the Traditional Owners of the lands on which our projects are located; the Barada Barna, Juru, Jangga, Birriah, and Wangan and Jagalingou people, for their consent and support'.

Honeymoon period

The Australian saga began as a honeymoon, however. Both countries were willing to work together. Australia wanted the investments, and India—especially Gautambhai—wanted access to coal. Samir Vora, then executive director and COO, was tasked with overseeing the project in Australia.

There was excitement in the air. Vora's plan was to develop a thermal coal mine, as well as railway and port facilities which could move the coal from the mine to consuming markets as efficiently as possible. That was the year when one of Queensland's largest infrastructure projects, the Airport Link tunnel, was coming to completion in the capital of Brisbane. That would make travel to the mine and port sites that much more convenient.

In June, Julia Gillard becomes Australia's first female prime minister, replacing Kevin Rudd, after a tumultuous period.

The group appointed GHD, its first contractor for the Australia projects. By August the same year, mine planning commenced. A Heads of Agreement was signed with Linc Energy. Queensland Labor Premier Anna Bligh officially opened the Adani Group's corporate office in Eagle Street, Brisbane. The Carmichael Mine and Rail Project environmental impact statement (EIS) commenced. By November that year the Carmichael Mine and Rail Project received 'Project of Significance' status from the Queensland government, and the Queensland Coordinator-General declares the project a 'coordinated project'.

8.5

Queensland Premier Anna Bligh (right) officially opens Adani's corporate head office in Brisbane, with chairman, Gautam Adani, 19 October 2010

In July 2010, Vora travelled with Gautambhai to view the Carmichael mine site and Abbot Point Port. They were excited by what they saw.

The greenfield Carmichael coal tenements in Central Queensland's Galilee Basin were purchased, and negotiations began to secure the lease over the Port of Abbot Point near Bowen, some 300 kilometres to the northeast of the mining area. Adani's first project partner in Australia was GHD, appointed to undertake due diligence and EIS work. Ambitious time frames were set. GHD was supportive, coaching the Adani Group on the way things were done in Australia.

Gautambhai was impatient. His was the first company in India to build a private port and a critical power plant in Australia—all achieved in a record thirty months.

The Adani team in Australia wanted to have Queensland coal on a ship to India sometime in 2014. Exploration commenced, and results from the Carmichael tenements were very encouraging.

The group commenced its EIS process for the project in October 2010, submitting an Initial Advice Statement to the Queensland Coordinator-General.

Queensland Premier Anna Bligh officially opened Adani's Brisbane corporate head office, which was set up in October.

At around this time, in May 2011, the Adani Group purchased the Abbot Point Port, as a ninety-nine-year lease over the port for AU$1.8 billion. It was sold as part of the Queensland government's privatization programme. It is located north of Bowen in Queensland and has delivered coal from Queensland mines to the world since 1984. The port is a strategic asset for Queensland because it enables mines in the Bowen Basin to develop and expand, supporting the state's growth and prosperity.

EIS snafu

Work began on the Carmichael Coal Mine and Rail Project EIS. This is a statutory requirement before any exploitation of the mine, or the building of the railway line, could begin. Mine camps were set up and drilling commenced to test the impact it would have on the environment.

8.6
Mine facts
Carmichael Mine—165 km north-west of the Queensland town of Clermont
Construction commenced in June 2019
The first stage of the mine will produce 10 million tonnes per annum of high-quality coal that will generate affordable and reliable electricity for communities in India and South-east Asia
Coal from the mine will be railed more than 300 km for export through Abbot Point Port, which is approximately 25 km north of Bowen
Jobs and business opportunities are flowing to regional Queenslanders with more than $1 billion worth of contracts signed and awarded, and heavy machinery built and delivered
The mine will generate billions of dollars for State and Commonwealth Governments in its first 30 years of operation. This money, paid through mining taxes and royalties, will help to build new schools, hospitals and roads for Queensland
Source: "From stop to start -- celebrating 10 years in Australia"

In September, Gautambhai made a second trip to Australia to take a look at the way things were progressing. Recruitment began, and the group appointed a head of mine, head of environment and directors of human resources. The group's Brisbane office reached full capacity, and the search for more space began.

In February 2012, the group purchased Moray Downs. The Carmichael tenements are located on the Moray Downs cattle station which spans more than 1,21,000 hectares. That seemed to complete acquisition of assets required for a unified vision. This would involve operating a vertically integrated model, extracting coal from the Carmichael Coal Mine, transporting it by rail to Abbot Point Port. From here it would be exported to meet demand in offshore markets, where the coal would help address energy poverty experienced by millions of people in countries like India.

But disquiet was building. The Adani venture began to be described as a mega-mine—it did have the largest coal deposits in the world—and fears were stoked about the potential damage to the environment the project would cause. A funding proposal, titled 'Stopping the Australian Coal Boom' was leaked to the media.

It outlined in precise detail how the anti-fossil fuel movement would spend millions of dollars to disrupt the coal industry. It talked about disrupting and delaying infrastructure developments, litigation, creating investor uncertainty, building on existing outrage, and changing the story of coal production as being the backbone of the Australian economy. By 2012, activists would settle on a cause to focus their attention, unleashing a 'disrupt and delay' strategy—on the Adani Group as the centrepiece of the anti-fossil fuel movement.

That had some major fallouts. The Adani Group was informed that the crucial EIS approval would only be possible by August 2012. As a result, all resourcing decisions were slowed to remain in tune with the EIS clearances. During Easter 2012, a draft EIS was submitted.

8.7
Rail facts
Carmichael Rail Network—linking the Galilee Basin to the world
The 200-kilometre narrow gauge rail line will connect to existing rail infrastructure that runs to Abbot Point Port
The Carmichael Mine will be the railway's foundation user
Construction commenced in 2019 delivering new jobs and opportunities for regional Queenslanders
Source: "From stop to start -- celebrating 10 years in Australia"

The feedback from the Federal government, however, was that essential information was missing, and therefore significant work was still required. Later in 2012, the EIS was submitted to the coordinator-general for bilateral assessment under Queensland

and Commonwealth legislation. The EIS was then available for public consultation and was released to government agencies, landholders, community groups, interest groups and stakeholders for public submissions.

The Office of the Coordinator-General compiled a comprehensive submissions register. The Adani Group was subsequently instructed to prepare supplementary material in response to the matters raised in the submissions. The group was surprised at the response from the consultation process. That was when the Adani Group discovered that between December 2012 and February 2013, around 25,000 public submissions were received. Only ten submissions were from the regions where Adani wished to operate, making it clear that people living in capital cities and not regional Australia were waging a battle.

In June, another federal government leadership got formed. Kevin Rudd was reinstated as prime minister for the second time, replacing Julia Gillard. But internal instability saw the Australian Labor Party (ALP) lose the federal election with Tony Abbott installed as prime minister leading a Liberal-National coalition government (LNP). In October, the ALP elected Bill Shorten as leader replacing Kevin Rudd and ushering in a new era of unity.

By February, the 25,000 submissions mentioned above were received as part of the EIS public consultation process. Clearly, momentum was building up against the Adani projects.

Even so, the North Galilee Basin Rail Project EIS work commenced. By March the same year, the Queensland Coordinator-General requested additional information for the EIS. But it did receive the 'first mover' status in the Galilee Basin. By November, the group submitted a supplementary EIS for the Carmichael Mine and Rail Project. But the Queensland Coordinator-General made a request for additional information on the supplementary EIS.

Approvals arrive and then get lost

Fortunately, by December, the EIS for the Abbot Point Port Terminal Zero Project was approved. In May 2014, the Queensland Coordinator-General's EIS evaluation report was issued, and Adani received federal government's approval in July 2014.

However, the approvals came with the strictest environmental conditions in Australian history. For the first time in Australian history, a condition was imposed requiring a groundwater offset, setting the standard for all new mining projects in Australia. The conditions had to be met before construction and operations could start.

8.8
Catching the sunshine
Farm facts
Rugby Run Renewable Solar Farm—near the Central Queensland tow Moranbah
Moranbah averages 320 days of sunshine a year
The site was previously used for low-level cattle grazing
The build took 12 months, Employed more than 175 people at peak construction.
Installed more than 247 000 tier-one grade solar panels, some of which manufactured by the Adani group's renewables business in India
Each panel is 1.95m long and 0.99m wide and weighs 22.2kg
Operations
Generates up to 185,000 MWh each year—enough to power 23,000 h‹
Uses a single-axis tracking system to follow the sun
The site can be run remotely from anywhere in the world
A team of local electricians services Rugby Run
Source: "From stop to start -- celebrating 10 years in Australia"

While all this was going on, POSCO Rail of South Korea signed an MoU for the development of a rail solution. In September

2014, the Queensland Coordinator-General's evaluation report got issued for the North Galilee Basin Rail Project.

The Commonwealth Government approved the North Galilee Basin Rail Project EIS and, by November the same year, the Queensland Deputy Premier Jeff Seeney signed an MoU during the G20 for the state government to invest AU$500 million in the North Galilee Basin Rail Project. In December, a joint venture was formed with Downer to deliver the coal wash plant.

However, the environmental activist organization—the Mackay Conservation Group—did not accept even the conditional EIS clearances. In January 2015, it launched proceedings for a judicial review of the decision.

The review found that there was a procedural error, and in August 2015 the Federal Minister for Environment Greg Hunt asked the Federal Court to set aside the approval. Adani's plans to proceed ground to a halt. A restructuring of the project team was launched, and many of the company representatives from Ahmedabad were sent home.

Activists continued with adverse tactics such as slowing down government processes with Freedom of Information requests, letter campaigns, private members bills raised in parliament by members of the Australian Greens Party and by targeting suppliers.

More setbacks and upheavals

The activists' campaign had gone global. In May 2014, it resulted in Deutsche Bank refusing to provide finance to the Adani projects in Australia. The bank's decision set a precedent. This combined with the uncertainty created by media coverage of the ongoing litigation. As a result, other financiers began to feel pressured.

8.9		
Campaign costs can be huge		
Item	Level 1 lin AU$	Level 2 lin AU$
Litigation	395,000	955,000
The Battle of Galilee	435,000	490,000
Hunter Valley - Enough is Enough!	354,000	260,000
Forward defence in W.A and Victoria	160,000	120,000
Changing the Story of Coal	275,000	390,000
Creating Investor Uncertainty	40,000	180,000
Exposing the Human Aspects of Coal	30,000	70,000
Field Organizing Programme	180,000	940,000
Movement Support	195,000	220,000
Programme Management	130,000	100,000
Totals	**21,94,000**	**37, 25,000**

Notes : These were the investments the Adani Group was seeking when opposition to its coal and port projects began. Prospects are broken down into two levels. Level 1 is the base level of resourcing that is required to have an impact. Level 2 is where the group needs to take the programme to in order to have maximum impact.

Source : pg 3 (pdf pg 19) of book "From stop to start -- celebrating 10 years in Australia

Fortunately, in November 2014, Queensland's capital Brisbane hosted the premier international forum for global economic cooperation—the G20 (Group of Twenty). During the forum, Queensland Deputy Premier Jeff Seeney signed an MoU on behalf of the State Government to invest in the North Galilee Basin Rail Project. The Queensland State election held on 14 February 2015 saw the Australian Labor Party return to Government. The new Labor premier, Annastacia Palaszczuk, confirmed support for the Carmichael Mine and Rail Project, but not for the funding agreement made by Seeney during the G20 forum. On 23 June 2015, the Queensland cabinet confirmed its support for Adani and other projects, with a decision made to encourage an early start-up of coal mining in the Galilee Basin through non-financial State Government support.

Interestingly, instead of the financial support by the state government, a Commonwealth-Government-promoted initiative called the Northern Australia Infrastructure Facility (NAIF) was started. It had a charter to encourage and complement private sector investment that benefits northern Australia. The NAIF would now become a source of finance.

The group promptly began working on applying for a NAIF loan.

But more political upheavals were to rock Australia. In February 2015, Prime Minister Tony Abbott survived a Liberal Party leadership spill, and in Queensland, Labor won the State election, punishing Campbell Newman's LNP Government for public servant job cuts. Annastacia Palaszczuk becomes Queensland premier.

In September, Malcolm Turnbull successfully challenged Tony Abbott in a second spill and became the fourth Australian prime minister in as many years.

8.10

Abbot Point Port: A state development area

Source : "From stop to start -- celebrating 10 years in Australia"

Meanwhile, in January the same year, the Mackay Conservation Group commenced proceedings for a judicial review of the July 2014 Commonwealth Government EIS approval for the Carmichael Coal Mine and Rail Project. In May, federal member for Dawson George Christensen launches a postcard campaign with more than 1000 signatures delivered to Chairman Gautam Adani, declaring support for the Carmichael Coal Mine and Rail Project.

The newly formed ALP State Government, however, confirmed that it would not honour the previous government's agreement to provide AU$500 million in funding.

In August, the judicial review commenced by the Mackay Conservation Group resulted in the loss of the Commonwealth Government EIS approvals, based on a procedural error. But in October, the Commonwealth Government re-approved the Carmichael Coal Mine and Rail Project EIS. Significantly, the Abbot Point Port was now declared a State Development Area.

A rainbow is sighted

In 2016, the Adani Group readjusted its course, outlining an innovative strategy to prioritize the people of regional Queensland and build a long-term future together.

The Adani Regional Content Strategy aimed to enhance the company's ability to make a positive impact in regional communities by delivering jobs, skills development, economic strength and community support.

The strategy set out practical and achievable means for local, regional and traditional owner stakeholders to gain work or business from Adani projects. The strategy also built positive alliances with regional communities. They highlighted the fact that the campaign against the Carmichael Coal Mine was undermining the job prospects and livelihoods of Queenslanders.

Within weeks of its official launch in June 2017, more than 650 businesses signed up to Adani's online supplier platform.

Beneficiaries who received practical benefits from the local supply initiatives included the Queensland towns of Emerald, Clermont, Moranbah, Collinsville, Charters Towers, Rockhampton, Mackay and Townsville.

Political upheavals made the situation more volatile and unpredictable. In July, the federal election saw the Liberal-National Coalition Government returned, but Labor made significant gains.

In January, Queensland Nickel (QNI) went into voluntary administration and 700 Townsville workers lost their jobs.

By February, the Adani Group created its own regional content strategy. This was bolstered by the decision of the Queensland Environment Department to grant clearances to the Carmichael Coal Mine and Rail Project.

By April, the Adani Group saw the authorization of the Indigenous Land Use Agreement with the Wangan and Jagalingou people. And the courts dismissed the plea for a second judicial review brought by the Australian Conservation Foundation.

The strategy gained momentum with the Queensland Department of Natural Resources and Mines approving the mining leases for the Carmichael Coal Mine and Rail Project, and the Adani Group acquired the port operations business from Glencore.

By August, the group received the Commonwealth Government approval for the Great Artesian Basin Offset Strategy. And by October, Premier Annastacia Palaszczuk held a regional cabinet meeting in Townsville and heard the strong community support for Adani first-hand. That in turn led to the Commonwealth Government's approval for the Biodiversity Offset Strategy.

In December, as part of its regional strategy, the Adani Group announced that Townsville would be the location for its regional headquarters in Queensland. And the group applied to the NAIF for $1 billion in funding.

The pace quickens

By November 2017, the Queensland State election saw Labor re-elected, with Annastacia Palaszczuk to serve a second term as Queensland premier. In March the following year, Premier Annastacia Palaszczuk visited India with eight regional mayors, and a presentation was made on Adani's Regional Content Strategy. The premier expressed support for the economic prosperity which the Carmichael Coal Mine would bring to both countries.

The Queensland Department of Natural Resources granted the Associated Water Licence for the Mine, and in June Premier Annastacia Palaszczuk opened Adani's Townsville regional headquarters.

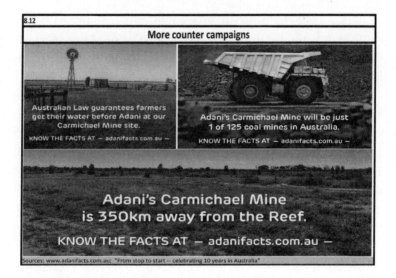

The Adani Regional Content Strategy got launched and the Carmichael Rail land acquisition is finalized. In October, in keeping with its promise to harness green power, the Rugby Run Solar Farm commenced construction, while Rockhampton and Townsville were announced as joint first-in, first-out (FIFO) employee hubs for Adani.

In 2018, in order to become more acceptable, CEO and country head, Jeyakumar Janakaraj embarked on a new strategy to refresh the leadership and 'Australianize' the team. Three key appointments completed Janakaraj's senior team—Kate Campbell as head of communications, followed by Paul Fennelly as head of government and corporate affairs, then Lucas Dow as CEO of Adani Mining.

Dow set about the task of recasting the project to make it more capital efficient. His solution was to shrink the mine in phase one to a 10 million TPA open cut mine with a 200-km narrow gauge railway spur connecting into the existing Aurizon network.

The railway connection plan replaced the earlier plan for a standard gauge railway running from the mine to the port in direct competition with Aurizon.

Meanwhile the 'Stop Adani' movement was ramping up.

The Adani team decided it was time to be proactive in telling the company's side of the story or others would continue to set the narrative.

The company began a campaign to separate fact from fiction, telling its story in print and electronic media and on social media platforms.[127] The Adani Group wanted to be transparent and communicate the truth about its projects in Australia. The truth was that the people at Adani were human, professional and were taking responsibility for their work.

Gradually, understanding of Adani's business operations grew. Members of the public began to reject false information and allegations of illegal behaviour.

In August 2018, a Liberal Party leadership spill saw Malcolm Turnbull defeat Peter Dutton and hold on to his prime ministership. Two days later, Turnbull resigned, and Scott Morrison defeated Dutton in a leadership spill to become the new Liberal leader and prime minister of Australia.

In January, Kate Campbell was appointed as Adani's head of communications. And in April, Paul Fennelly was appointed as Adani's head of government and corporate affairs. Lucas Dow was appointed as CEO of Adani Mining.

By October, the Federal Environment Department engaged CSIRO. Geoscience Australia undertook further reviews of Adani groundwater-related management and research plans despite an extensive peer review already being completed. But by November, the Adani Group became ready to begin construction as soon as the final approvals were received.

The size of stage one of the mine was confirmed as 10 million TPA. Funding for this more capital-efficient project was secured, and by December, Commonwealth approval was received for the mine's Black-throated Finch Management Plan (BTFMP).

Finally, the 'Start Adani' campaign was rolled out with the message, 'If we get the nod today, we can start tomorrow.'

In November 2018, the Adani Group announced that the finance was in place for the Carmichael Coal Mine and Rail Project and that the company was ready to start construction. The activists' campaign to dry up funding support for the Adani project did not succeed.

On 29 November 2018, the Townsville Bulletin reported that the minister for resources and Northern Australia Senator Matthew Canavan had congratulated Adani on its focus and commitment to the project in the face of 'long-standing, ill-informed protest activity'.[128]

In the article, Senator Canavan was quoted as saying, 'Adani's ability to re-scope and finance its Carmichael Mine and Rail Project proves it is a viable, job-creating concern which stands on its own two feet financially and environmentally.'

Back in regional Australia, support for the Carmichael Coal Mine and Rail Project was growing. On 1 December 2018, the *Daily Mercury* quoted federal member for Dawson George Christensen as saying, '[protestors] need to just give it a rest and face reality.

'The job opportunities for North and Central Queensland have won the day and the extreme green blockers to its progress have lost. Protesting is over, the project is on its way and the announcement has been that it's begun; it's now not something they should continue to protest against. It's like protesting against the wind: it's going to blow.'[129]

By December, Townsville's Mendi Group was awarded significant road construction and civil engineering contracts.

More support pours in

By this time, the traditional owners of the Carmichael Coal Mine site publicly expressed dismay at the delays. They had been badly hurt because their future earnings, by way of royalties on each tonne of coal produced, had not been forthcoming. As a result, money that could have supported an entire community had also dried up for almost ten years.

They travelled to Canberra in February 2019 to address parliamentarians, calling on them to not be distracted by activists who had little or no understanding of the project. Native Title applicant Les Tilley was reported in *the Morning Bulletin* on 12 February 2019 saying that the Wangan and Jagalingou people wanted the Adani mine to go ahead, and it was about time their voices were heard.[130]

He was quoted as saying, 'We followed due process under the Native Title Act. Wangan/Jagalingou people have spoken; the ILUA vote count was 294-1.'

Federal member for Capricornia, Michelle Landry, was reported as saying, 'The opportunities and the will of the Wangan and Jagalingou people must be respected. Those actively campaigning against the Carmichael Mine are doing more than creating some noise, they are actively working to undermine the job prospects of Indigenous Central Queenslanders. With Aboriginal unemployment in Rockhampton sitting at 25 per cent and in Woorabinda at 75 per cent, projects with real Aboriginal engagement are so valuable. Adani's ILUA with the Wangan and Jagalingou people will see $250 million in contracts for Indigenous organisations to tender for.'

On 23 May 2019, *the Courier-Mail*[131] reported that it had obtained a letter written by Jangga elder Colin McLennan to Queensland Premier Annastacia Palaszczuk and Deputy Premier, Treasurer and Minister for Aboriginal and Torres Strait Islander Partnerships Jackie Trad on 11 April seeking an urgent meeting. He said, 'We have been working with Adani in partnership to realise these commitments. However, our efforts and expectations are being frustrated by your government.'

They had begun to realize that the Adani Group's Carmichael Coal Mine would deliver AU$250 million in new investment to indigenous businesses.

The project rolls on

The Adani Group had delivered on its promise. Construction of the Carmichael project's roads, railway, accommodation camps and mine infrastructure are close to being completed.

Workers from Townsville and Rockhampton arrive daily by air to the new Labona airstrip. That improved the perception of the locals in favour of the Adani Group.

In return, three years on from the launch of its innovative regional content strategy, Adani continued to focus on creating jobs, skills and economic strength for regional Queensland. More than 1500 people have already been employed and more than AU$1.5 billion worth of contracts awarded to like-minded individuals, small businesses and large organizations in just over twelve months since the project's final approvals were granted.

Those contracts, many delivered during the coronavirus health and economic crisis, recognize and harness regional Queensland's world-class mining equipment, technology and services credentials.

Among the skilled contracting firms to sign up to deliver the Carmichael project are the likes of BMD Group, Martinus, Wagners, Mendi Group, G&S Engineering and Stresscrete.

Against this backdrop of construction, Adani has consolidated its port-operations business. A record 31.96 million tonnes of coal were transported through the Port of Abbot Point in fiscal 2019/20.

The 65 MW Rugby Run solar farm also continued to harness the Queensland sun and power local businesses and homes while demonstrating the efficiency and reliability of the technology.

Positive vibes

Today the Adani Group is focussed on creating positive vibes. Its motto has been, 'Whoever we are and wherever we live, we're all human, and we all want the power to better our lives.'

Australia's world-class coal industry directly employed more than 50,000 people and supported a further 1,20,000 indirect jobs across the country in 2018.

Royalties and tax revenues from Adani projects will now help pay for public infrastructure, creating even more employment and improving people's quality of life.

In Asia, the company talks about supporting developing nations who desperately need affordable energy. Coal from Queensland's Galilee Basin is higher in energy and lower in sulphur than other coal that is mined in Asia.

Together with renewables and other sources of energy, Adani will supply Queensland coal as part of a responsible and sustainable energy strategy while supporting communities and economic growth in regional Australia.[132]

Postscript

Suddenly, the Adani Group has become relevant to the future of both countries. And, sooner or later, this association would spill over into other defence and civil applications. Expect deals in education as well, because Australia has big plans to further tap India's hunger for education, especially vocational education.[133]

9

In Pursuit of the Green-Power Holy Grail

By the time Mundra Port was up and running, Gautambhai had already become the biggest coal trader in India. He had also acquired mines in Indonesia. (The mines in Australia were to come later.)

When the Mundra Port commenced operations, it was but inevitable that coal would form a crucial part of the cargo mix. The other key cargo constituents were crude oil, edible oil and grain.

Coal imports can be messy. You need automated systems[134] to make sure that the coal dust does not fly around and pollute the surroundings, and blacken the faces and hands of the people in the ports. When it is stored, you need water curtains to capture any dust particles that may be flying around. And since coal is highly combustible, you also need to ensure that the coal piles are looked after carefully. Even the slightest friction can generate heat.

It wasn't long before coal terminals sprang up in most of the ports built and operated by the Adani Group.[135] The stage was set for some backward integration.

Since much of the coal was meant for government-owned-and-operated coal plants—usually by the National Thermal Power Corporation (NTPC)—it appeared to be a very exciting business opportunity when the government began inviting private players to set up thermal coal-powered electricity generation plants. One of the first UMPPs (ultra-mega power plants) to be given the go-ahead to invite tenders was the one at Mundra. The terms of the offer were clear. They had to be UMPPs, based on imported coal and should set up super critical turbines. Super critical turbines save on coal consumption leading to lower energy costs, hence resulting in less environmental pollution.

Getting into power generation

The Adani Group had already known what setting up power generation facilities could mean. When Mundra Port was set up, Gautambhai knew that he would need a dedicated power generation facility.

At that time Rajesh Adani used to be actively involved in anything that happened at the port. He recalls, 'When we began to look into how to market the Mundra SEZ, we recognised that we needed to provide customers with land, water, and power. Land and water-needs we were comfortable with. Power represented the missing link.

'So, we said we would commission a 100 MW power plant. At some point, we began to discuss profitability, and someone said getting coal from Jharkhand would be Rs 2000 a tonne but if we imported this from Indonesia then the cost would be around Rs 800 a tonne with superior calorific value.' The relevance of imported coal was obvious.

Imported coal also helped the group stay away from trying to acquire domestic coal mines as a favour from political parties. In retrospect, it allowed the group to stay clear of all coal scams that hit headlines later.

Rajeshbhai adds, 'Then we began to appraise turbine delivery. BHEL would take four years to deliver but if we imported from China, an executive indicated, we would be able to get it 15 per cent cheaper and within a year. Then someone came in with the macro picture that if the country needed to sustain 8 per cent

GDP growth, then it would need to grow its power generation capacity by at least 12 per cent (which was not happening).

'Within minutes, Gautambhai grasped how EBIDTA margins could be moved. Suddenly, the discussion had transformed from creating a 100 MW plant to a 330 MW facility. Within four days, we had transformed our captive power plant support business into an independent power producing division; within six months, we had acquired a coal mine in Indonesia; within months, we had placed orders with Chinese suppliers and deputed 150 Adani executives to work from the shop floors of our vendors and their sub vendors to ensure that the turbines could be delivered on schedule.'

The Chinese on their part set up a mini township for housing their executives who could work side by side with the Adani team. There was a human angle to this as well. There were reports of a few (much celebrated) weddings between Chinese men and Indian women. But that was much before there was acrimony at the official levels on account of border incursions.

Lose some, win some

Thus, when the UMPP at Mundra was announced, the Adani Group bid for it, along with the Tatas. But when the tender was awarded, the bid went in favour of the Tatas. People at the Adani Group were upset and wanted to go in for an appeal or a retendering of the bid. But Gautambhai was adamant. 'It is over and done with,' he is believed to have told his people. 'Now let's focus on other projects,' he reportedly told his managers.

But what Gautambhai began doing was looking up the rule books. He suddenly discovered another route to set up an UMPP. He learnt that he could set up a power plant adopting the case 2 option, which allowed promoters to set up their own power generation facilities if they could acquire the land, set up the plant and enter into a PPA with any state government through a reverse bidding mechanism.

Gautambhai also realized that his own power generating units at Mundra would ensure demand for shipment throughput in range of 30 million tonnes of coal annually. Add to this another 18 million tonnes of coal that Tata Power's Mundra UMPP would require. You have a guaranteed cargo throughput of around 50 million tonnes annually. To ensure that this offtake was handled in the most cost-effective manner, the group set up the world's largest coal receiving facilities capable of handling over 60 million TPA, it has a 17.5-km conveyor belt with capability to discharge 18,000 tonnes of coal per hour.[136]

The Gujarat government was only too happy to look at such plans as it would make the state self-sufficient in power generation.

That is where financing became the next hurdle. Ameet Desai, CEO, Adani Advisory LLP, which advises the entire group on financial matters and investments, remembers how Gautambhai and he sought an appointment with K.V. Kamath of ICICI Bank, to find out whether his bank would be willing to support such a project, and then explained to Kamath how the group would go about setting up 2 x 330 MW plants at Mundra, with an assured supply of coal as its fuel linkage. Gautambhai deliberately kept the size of the project small during these discussions.

'Kamath was convinced of the viability of such a project. Even as the meeting with Kamath was over, and as soon as we got into our car, Gautam quietly told me that I should start preparing for funding another 2 x 330 power plant, thus bringing the total plan to 1,320 MW', Desai adds with a big grin. He then understood that Gautam probably had bigger plans in his mind all along. He only chose to let out some parts of the plan, and reveal other parts at a time when he felt it to be appropriate.

'When he ran into funding constraints once again, the private equity investor 3i Group agreed to pump in the required equity capital. So quick was his response to the injection of funds, that he managed to place orders for the BTG units with a good Chinese supplier, with all warranties in place, at a price that no other power producer in India could get.' Chutzpah, speed, and the ability to take calculated risks were all in display as these plans unfolded.

The Adani Group got its UMPP at Mundra.

Vineet Jain says, 'Gautambhai has fostered a unique culture in our power projects business—he bets on young blood (the average age is only thirty-one), the teachings of Vivekananda represent the inspirational currency of the team (you find them on screen savers everywhere), he has created an environment that *"Achcha kiya to tooney kiya, galat kiya to mainey* (If good work is done, the credit goes to you. If a mistake happens the fault is mine)."

'He spends his best time demolishing silos so that no decision is ever taken on the basis of ethnic origin, language, class, background, school, accent, social status, or previous company worked for. The result? We commissioned India's first super critical power plant (660 MW) in thirty-six months in 2011–12 against our internal projection of thirty-nine months, a global benchmark of forty-eight months and the nearest Indian benchmark of fifty-five months.'

It was only when the first power unit was on the verge of commercial operation, Gautam decided to approach the capital markets for funds. Once again, unlike many other promoters, Gautam likes to get a project running, and then approach the general public for funds through the capital market route.

Ameet narrates, once again with a grin, Gautambhai's reaction to the announcement of the success of the Mundra IPO. The Mundra IPO closed on the evening of 27 November 2006. Ameet and the entire IPO team met Gautambhai and presented him a bouquet of 117 roses to represent the oversubscription by nearly 117 times. Gautambhai congratulated the IPO team, and after the pleasantries were over, asked them to get cracking for Adani Power IPO.

The IPO for power opened on 28 July 2009 when market was passing through a rough patch. But given Gautam's track record of speedy completion of projects boosted investors' confidence in the IPO. It helped in reviving investors' confidence and was oversubscribed by over twenty-one times. The Rs 3000 crore issue, the second biggest public offer after that of Reliance Power in 2008, attracted good investor response and received commitment worth of Rs 63,000 crore from all categories of investors.

Vineet Jain adds, 'Before 2006, we were not in the power generation-transmission business. In just three years, our power projects team created seventeen benchmarks, of which eleven are global. We commissioned four super-critical power plants in 2011–12. We created the world's largest port-based single location power plant at Mundra (4620 MW). And we added the largest power generation capacity by any Indian company in 2011–12. The Adani Group emerged as India's largest private sector power generator within five years of entering an industry with a number of players more than 100 years old. When the joint secretary of the Minister of Power convened a meeting of all public, private and government power generators in India, he started with, "I must request the Adani Group to train 10,000 power engineers across all power companies in India."'

Storm clouds

Unfortunately, there are times when things go wrong. A good example was the manner in which both Gautam and almost the entire power industry got caught unawares when Australia, Indonesia, Mozambique and almost every other coal-producing country decided to benchmark coal prices to international quotes, levy taxes on the market value of coal exported and not on the long-term contracted value.

The Tatas, Adanis and the Jindals had all purchased coal mines in other countries to get a better fix on the guaranteed supply and pricing of coal. To ensure that they could continue getting coal at the price they desired, they even entered into long-term contracts specifying both the quantity and the price at which these mines would export coal to their power plants in India. It was on this basis that they quoted the price at which they would sell power to the government or to state electricity boards. Suddenly, the costing went awry. Almost every power plant in the country that was based on imported coal began bleeding, and the sight of red ink around the figures was not that comforting.

But Gautam was not too perturbed. He knew that his problem had now become a national problem, for which the country itself would have to find a solution. Expectedly, the ministries of power, coal, commerce and even the Prime Minister's Office got actively involved in trying to find a solution to this crisis that confronted not just the power companies, but the entire country. Could a solution be found which would allow the big power-generating companies to get higher prices for imported coal, without passing it on to consumers? Could the PPAs be modified? It was obvious that without being compensated for the higher prices of coal, many power generators might go belly up. Tata Power even said that it was ready to sell its power plant at Mundra at throwaway prices.[137] Clearly, the power companies' problem had now become a national problem.

But how could Gautambhai, who is normally extremely astute when it comes to signing agreements, sign one which did not allow for an increase in coal prices to be reimbursed as a pass-through?

The reason was not difficult to find. Both the Tata and Adani Groups had signed similar PPAs. They had said that they would source the coal from their respective mines overseas— the Tatas from Mozambique and the Adani Group from

Indonesia. The projects were supposed to be quite profitable, when suddenly, export taxes were slapped on the coal that was being sent out. Under normal circumstances, India would have protested, but it had itself created this new financial levy when it came to iron ore exports. Now that other countries were following suit, with similar imposts on coal exports, India remained a mute spectator. 'There was just no provision for any pass-through of escalated costs in the PPA signed,' explains a merchant banker. He adds with a big grin, 'I think they needed better merchant bankers.'

The Adanis thought that the Tata team had done its homework, and so they agreed to the same terms that the Tata Group had consented to. The Tatas in turn had taken the cost of mining and worked out the costs. They did not imagine that export taxes would ever be slapped on export of coal.

But while the Tatas were close to panic and even said that they were ready to sell their Mundra power plant,[138] Gautambhai was sanguine. He knew that the country would need more and more power-generation capacities. He had the double benefit of being aligned to national priorities, and also not being the only power generator singled out for this error made in good faith. That patience worked out in his favour.

In 2013, the CERC (Central Electricity Regulatory Commission) permitted a tariff increase, but the state government challenged this before the Supreme Court. Finally in 2019, the courts agreed that the CERC was right in permitting higher tariffs, and the Adani plant finally got relief.[139]

The event taught Gautam Adani that even if mines overseas were owned by the group, final pricing can never be certain because governments can always slap additional charges. While the Tatas finally decided to give up their mining operations overseas, Gautambhai decided to expand his mining operations both in India and overseas.

9.1		
Adani thermal plants		
Plant	State	MW
Mundra	Gujarat	4,620
Tiroda	Maharashtra	3,300
Kawai	Rajasthan	1,320
Udu[i	Karnataka	1,200
Rajkheda	Chhatisgarh	1,370
Raigarh	Chhatisgarh	600
Totals		**12,410**

Notes : Additional projects being planned in Dahej (Gujarat), Pench (Madhya Pradesh) and Godda (Jharkhand). Expandsion plans are underway at Udupi and Kawai.

Source : *Adani Power brochure on Empowering the nation for a greater future, 2022*

More than any other case, this event confirms that the Adani Group did not receive any special treatment. When, eventually, the Adani Group got a benefit, it was across the board and was applicable to everyone in the same situation. There was no out-of-turn allocation of projects to the group. All of them were won through open bidding and tendering. What made the Adani Group succeed is the speed at which projects could be implemented, thus saving on project costs. Another factor was the beady eye Gautambhai keeps on operational efficiencies. Together, they have made Gautambhai one of the most successful players in the power business.

He also wrested the power distribution licence for Mumbai. The lucrative Mumbai distribution licence came from Anil Ambani who ran into major financial trouble and had to sell off some of his favourite projects. It is now a subsidiary of Adani Transmission Ltd.[140] Adani Electricity Mumbai Ltd (AEML) serves over 3 million consumers spread across 400 sq. kms in Mumbai and its suburbs with 99.99 per cent reliability, one among the highest in the country. Adani Electricity meets close to 2000 MW of power demand in Mumbai's largest and the most efficient power distribution network. It provides world-class customer care services with the help of advanced technologies. Adani Electricity plans to expand its presence in newer geographies in pursuit of India's vision of 'Power for All'.

9.2 Solar, wind and hybrid		
State	Solar (MW)	Hybrid*
Gujarat	4,080	735
Maharashtra		20
Karnataka	300	1,085
Tamil Nadu		648
Andhra Pradesh		175
Telangana	250	700
Odisha		40
Madhya Pradesh	324	12
Chhattisgarh		100
Uttar Pradesh		395
Himachal Pradesh		130
Totals	4,954	4,040

*Notes :Notes: *Hybrid= solar+Wind -- According to Mercom, Adani has a total solar power capacity of 5250 MW in operation*
Breakup between mega solar farms, rooftop solar, wind and hydel not known

Source : Adani Green Energy Limited brochure of 022 -- Transforming tomorrow with sustainable efforts today

By August 2021, Gautambhai also benefitted from the government order allowing them (and other power units in the country) to sell energy on energy exchanges (as merchant power sales) in view of domestic coal supply shortages which led to pockets of power shortages in some parts of the country.[141] The trader in the Adani Group thus had one more opportunity.

During the interim period, Gautambhai participated in almost every tender for coal-based plants and for solar power. All the bids were competitive and open. Some he won, some he lost. But when viewed in totality, the Adani Group has emerged as the largest solar power player in the country—with installed capacities of 5250 MW, says MercomIndia (Mercom),[142] a leading research and consulting firm for India's energy markets.

Solar inadequacy

First, there is no denying that Adani Solar has made amazing progress in India becoming the largest solar power producer in India.

Second, this was possible only because Gautambhai decided to make the pursuit of green power a corporate quest. The country and the world wanted more green power. Except for takeover of stressed power plants, the group decided not to build any fresh thermal power plants. It would focus on enhancing green power capacities.

But here too, the path was not easy. Vineet Jain says, 'One of the most amazing achievements at the Adani Group was the commissioning of Asia's largest photovoltaic solar power plant (40 MW) in 2011.

'There was a deadline to it. If we commissioned prior to 31 December 2011, we would be awarded a tariff of Rs 15 per unit by the government. If we delayed beyond the deadline by even a day, the applicable tariff would be reduced to Rs 9 a unit—a difference of Rs 1250 crore across the period of the contract.

'For some unforeseen reasons, we got part-possession of the land only in June 2011 leaving us only six months to complete it. At that point, Gautambhai said, "*Nahin ho sakta hai toh* (If it's impossible), leave it. I will be happy if we can get this project up and running by March 2012." That is when we moved into emergency mode.

'We assembled a team of the most dynamic professionals from the Group companies. We decided that every single project member would stay on site. Work began concurrently across all fourteen sub-sites within the location. Work continued round the clock. We created a 24-hour control room in Ahmedabad. Emails had to be responded to within minutes and we altered the design of certain equipment without comprising quality and safety.

'The result was that we completed a project that would have normally taken twelve months in only five! When I walked in with the certificate of commissioning issued by the Gujarat government into Gautambhai's office on 28 December, he looked at it for a minute, said, "Unbelievable!" to himself and then hugged me hard. The culture that Gautambhai has created in the power projects team is that if he were ever to call us at midnight with an assignment for a project, the project would be well underway before sunrise.'

In November 2020, Ramesh Nair, CEO, Adani Solar, stated[143] that his company would target a 50 per cent market share. 'We look forward to achieving a higher reach and visibility for our product nationally by increasing power consumption through alternative forms of energy like solar energy.'

For this, it announced the launch of its retail distribution business for India's eastern and NE states with KSL Cleantech Ltd as the official channel partner for the two regions. Adani Solar has now extended its reach to more than 1000 towns for the distribution of solar panels in India.

By 26 May 2021, the company could proudly boast[144] that Adani Solar had been recognized as the top performer in its PV module product qualification program (PQP) for the fourth year in succession.

The North-east beckons

The company was now ready to rapidly penetrate and capitalize on India's eastern and north-eastern renewable energy markets. This market is currently extremely attractive ever since Tripura installed 50,000 rooftop solar panels in 2018[145] making all the neighbouring north-east states clamour for this type of power supply.

It was cheaper to instal rooftop solar than provide grid connectivity, more reliable, and invited no electricity bills after the installation was complete.

Not surprisingly, all the state governments in that region had begun clamouring for rooftop solar. It was environmentally clean, and found immense acceptance with local populations.

Adani Solar envisages an opportunity of 130 MW within the rooftop segment in these regions. The target customers are predominantly in the rooftop, utility-scale, residential, commercial and industrial (C&I) and solar pump segments.

Company sources said that Adani Solar had rapidly expanded its retail presence across the country. Through its retail channel partners, the company has a sizeable presence in Rajasthan, Uttar Pradesh, Delhi, Haryana, Gujarat, Maharashtra, Kerala, Tamil Nadu, Telangana, Andhra Pradesh and Kerala.

While this growth in solar energy is laudable, what is missing is a strategy that could promote both employment and economic development, in addition to providing rooftop solar solutions. This is because rooftop solar offers more bang for the buck, as the German rollout at the turn of the century showed. Hermann Scheer, the energy minister of Germany, discovered that within eight years of the solar rooftop power rollout in that country,[146] there were more people employed in the solar sector than in the engineering sector.

India has more sunlight than Germany, more land and people (hence more houses) too. India's need for employment generation schemes at the grassroots level is enormous.[147] According to a study,[148] a coal-based plant would require 0.5 people per megawatt of installed capacity. In the case of rooftop solar power, you would require 3.5 people. The manpower in the power sector will not reduce but increase, and the nature of jobs will undergo a huge transformation.

Gautambhai has not looked at this area well enough, though his Foundation does a great deal of work at the grassroots level with school managements. It also imparts vocational skills (more in the following pages). According to some studies done by Tata Power, the biggest social transformation takes place when remote villages are given assured supply of quality power. If they can be taught how to earn more, they will become only too happy to pay for this power.

Tata Power should know, because it has embarked on one of the most amazing sustainable projects in Uttar Pradesh, Bihar and Odisha.[149] It is here that Tata Power is setting up community solar power stations, replete with storage units so that power is available 24x7—especially during night-time when the sun isn't shining. It is teaching people how to restructure rural businesses.

NGOs, that Tata Power is associated with, impart vocational skills to people to help them make money through reliable power supply. Girls are taught how an electric sewing machine could allow them to churn out more embroidery, which has a huge market potential. Village flour mill (*chakki*) owners are educated on the amount of money they would save if they opted for reliable solar power instead of depending on diesel gensets when grid power fails. The loss of business and the high cost of diesel can eat away more money than a commitment to purchase solar power.

But then Gautambhai's focus is on large things. It is quite possible that his Foundation will begin looking at ways to make decentralized solar power generation more appealing and profitable for the poorest of households across the country. It is quite possible that the Foundation will work on strategies where school education, vocational education for maintaining and servicing solar power stations, and management of distributed micro-grids will be planned for each rural cluster.[150]

In any case, as MercomIndia points out,[151] investments in the solar sector in India increased by 254 per cent y-o-y in calendar year 2021 compared to calendar year 2020. Effectively, around 10 GW of solar capacities were added bringing the total to 50 GW.[152] Adani Green Energy raised around $750 million, while ReNew Power raised around $610 million through a SPAC deal and another $585 million through green bonds. Azure Power raised $414 million through dollar green bonds.[153]

For the time being it has been good going. The sun is truly shining. But a lot more needs to be done.

Gas distribution

Another aspect of the green energy thrust has been the CGD sector. The Adani Group is the undisputed leader in solar power generation in the country at the time when this book is being written. It is now integrating backwards into producing solar panels, inverters and the paraphernalia that goes into solar systems. But another arm of the group is busy consolidating its hold on gas distribution.[154]

9.3	
CGD - Big business	
Listed companies	
Stokmarket expectations	
Company	Rating
GAIL (India)	OUTPERFORM
Petronet LNG	NEUTRAL
Gujarat Gas	OUTPERFORM
Indraprastha Gas	OUTPERFORM
Mahanagar Gas	NEUTRAL
Gujarat State Petronet	NEUTRAL
Source : Stockmarket analysts	

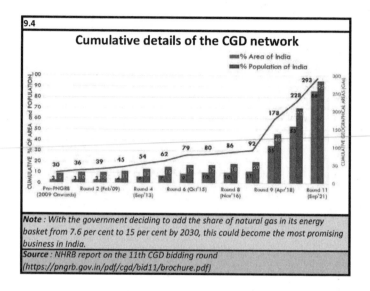

9.4

Cumulative details of the CGD network

Note : With the government deciding to add the share of natural gas in its energy basket from 7.6 per cent to 15 per cent by 2030, this could become the most promising business in India.
Source : NHRB report on the 11th CGD bidding round (https://pngrb.gov.in/pdf/cgd/bid11/brochure.pdf)

The government's CGD network has received about 430 bids in sixty-five geographical areas, which is expected to result in investments worth Rs 80,000 crore, the Petroleum and Natural Gas Regulatory Board (PNGRB) has said.

The Adani Group has bagged most of the city concessions. According to a Nomura report,[155] 'In the private sector, Adani Gas and Torrent Group have been key bidders. Apart from having 17 of its own licenses, Adani Group also has won 19 licenses in its JV with IOC.' Incidentally, Adani Total Gas Ltd has a 50:50 joint venture with Indian Oil Corporation Ltd. More details about the eleventh round of bidding are given a few paragraphs later. And the Adani Group's investments for this sector are also large, as shall be discussed later.

However, it must be reiterated that all the bids were won through open tendering. The Adani Group benefitted because its offers were the most competitive.

However, as Nomura points out in its anchor report,[156] the CGD business is effectively a monopoly business in India. 'GCD is technically regulated by the Petroleum and Natural Gas Regulatory Board (PNGRB), constituted under the PNGRB Act of 2006. The regulator's key mandate is to protect the interests of consumers and entities and to promote competitive markets in petroleum and natural gas [. . .]. The scope of the above regulatory functions is vast. However, even as more than a decade has elapsed since the Board was set-up, the regulator either lacks the powers to perform [its] functions, or for some reason has been thus far unable to exercise the powers it has been granted [. . .], for over 10 years, the regulator has primarily focused on activities [relating to] authorizing and technical standards.'

The PNGRB's powers to decide tariffs were taken away by the courts.[157] In Nomura's view, 'CGD companies' emphasis all along was on winning licenses, and they took the call that they could make up for low open-access tariffs with higher marketing margins, as the regulator has no say in final pricing.' It provides an open field for making profits.

9.5

Operational Highlights 9M FY'22 (Standalone):

Commissioned **70 New Stations**, total CNG Stations now increased to **287**

- Added **52,611** new connections, total PNG home connections surpassed 5.3 lakh mark (**5.31 lakh**)
- Industrial & Commercial connections increased to **5,453** with **487** new Industrial and Commercial connections
- Completed **4,285** Inch Km of Steel Pipeline in New GAs allotted in 9th and 10th rounds
- Combined CNG and PNG volume of **507 MMSCM**, increase of **45% >**
- Combined Exit Volume increased to **2.20 MMSCMD** in Q3 FY22

Financial Highlights 9MFY22 (Standalone) Y-o-Y:

Revenue from Operations increased by **83%** to INR **2141 Cr**

- EBITDA of Rs **673** Cr, up by **28%**
- Reported PBT of Rs **576** Cr, up by **31%**
- Reported PAT at Rs **429** Cr, up by **31%**

Consolidated PAT

Consolidated PAT at Rs **428** Cr, up by **34%**

Other key updates

ATGL wins **14 new** Geographical Areas comprising **56 districts** in **11th** Round of CGD Bidding conducted by PNGRB. This makes ATGL India's largest CGD player.

Source : NHRB report on the 11th CGD bidding round (https://pngrb.gov.in/pdf/cgd/bid11/brochure.pdf)

It will be advisable that the government steps in quickly and empowers its regulators. Without such powers, entrepreneurs could make indecent profits in what is essentially a regulated business.

But it is possible that when the government does tighten up the existing system, and empowers its regulators, the Adani Group might step in to pick up more distressed assets. This is because its operations are among the leanest in the country today. It has a major advantage in owning and managing its own LNG terminals.

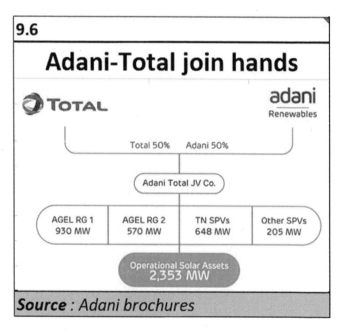

Moreover, it must be noted that the potential for this business is extremely large. India is the third largest energy consumer in the world, says a government report.[158] The share of natural gas in India's energy basket is 7.6 per cent as against 24.7 per cent globally in 2020. The country, adds the government report, aims to increase the share of natural gas in its energy basket from 7.6

per cent to 15 per cent by 2030. That in turn could mean even higher profit margins for the Adani Group.

City gas consumption has been growing at over 7 per cent CAGR (compounded average rate of growth). Imports too are growing at a CAGR of over 5 per cent. Thus, anyone who has an LNG terminal is bound to be making money.[159] Coupled with the distribution licence, the pickings could be larger.

This is reinforced by the Adani Group's announcement on 31 January 2022[160] that 'Adani Total Gas Ltd (ATGL), India's largest private CGD company and a joint venture between the Adani Group and Total Energies, will be investing an additional Rs 20,000 crore in the next eight years.' The company stated that it had won licences to expand its CGD network to fourteen new geographical areas (GAs) in the recently concluded eleventh round of CGD bidding by the PNGRB.

That makes ATGL the largest CGD company catering to fifty-two GAs, nineteen of which are operated along with its strategic JV partner Indian Oil Corporation. These fifty-two GAs account for 15 per cent of the country covering 124 districts across eighteen states and three union territories.[161]

'Now with the authorization of additional fourteen geographical areas, our presence expands from thirty-nine to ninety-five districts,' says Mr Suresh Manglani, CEO, Adani Total Gas Ltd. 'With strong support from the Adani Group and Total Energies, ATGL is committed to the expeditious development of CGD networks across all these new fifty-two districts. ATGL will now be catering to 10 per cent of country's population with cleaner fuel for households as well as for transportation. Therefore, ATGL is fully committed to play a pivotal role in meeting the clean energy needs of India and this strategic expansion is fully aligned with our commitment of Nation Building.'

In other words, ATGL will be reaching out to more than 9 million households, economic transport fuel for vehicles by establishing around 2000 CNG stations and clean fuel to industrial and commercial consumers. To achieve these ambitions, ATGL will be investing Rs 12,000 crore in these fourteen additional GAs, taking ATGL's total commitment in the clean energy sector to Rs 20,000 crore, says the group announcement.

This it means be prepared for a surge in group profits in the coming years. The latest figures confirm such a sentiment.[162]

But all this was before the world was gripped by the Ukraine—Russia war, instigated by the US.[163] As a result oil and gas prices have skyrocketed.[164] Suddenly, for countries like India, gas may not be the cheap green fuel that was one of the key strategies for going green. True, coal prices have also gone up. Will this put a spanner in the CGD business? Will it compel major coal producers—like the Adani Group—to look at coal gasification instead? Nobody knows the answers as yet. But suddenly the future of energy plans, world over, looks a bit perplexing.

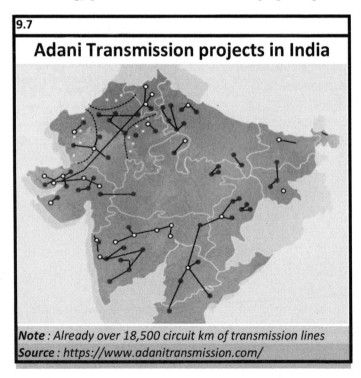

9.7

Adani Transmission projects in India

Note : *Already over 18,500 circuit km of transmission lines*
Source : *https://www.adanitransmission.com/*

Transmission

The achievements of the Adani Group in promoting green energy have not gone unnoticed by the global financing community. On 8 April 2022, the Adani Group announced that IHC public joint-stock company, the Abu Dhabi-based conglomerate, would be investing US$ 2billion as primary capital in three Adani portfolio companies—Adani Green Energy Ltd (AGEL), Adani Transmission Ltd (ATL) and Adani Enterprises Ltd (AEL)—which are all listed on BSE and NSE in India, through the preferential allotment route.[165]

The group's green energy efforts are beginning to pay-off in more ways than one.

The Adani Transmission brochure[166] mentions that it has set for itself an ambitious target to set up 20,000 circuit km (ckm) of transmission lines by 2022. It has already achieved 18,500 ckm of transmission lines by March 2022.[167] The brochure mentions that this will be achieved both organically and inorganically. One can expect takeover of some distressed assets in the power sector in this country. That will make Adani Transmission even larger than it already is today.

The company aspires to be the largest private transmission and distribution company in India. It wants to maintain a 25 per cent share of this market, using the synergies with affordable and reliable power supply and efficiencies that the best of the grids offer.

To conclude: power generation, transmission and distribution are excellent businesses to be in from a long-term perspective. Because they are regulated assets, their rate of return can best be improved time and again through the enhancement of efficiencies. If that can be done, a surge in profits can be expected. That in turn will cause the Adani Group to keep growing as better efficiencies kick in.

And if the group can withstand delays in payments from the government, most regulated businesses promise minimum guaranteed returns, almost like annuities. Once the right papers and guarantees are in place, getting finance is not a problem. Such projects become bankable. Efficiencies do matter. And aligning the group's interests with those of national interests can pay extremely rich dividends. Will CGD remain one of the most profitable lines of business for the Adani Group? That will depend on global pricing, and the growth of the market in the face of climbing prices. Time to wait and see.

10

Aligned with National Interests

Both as a teacher, and more often as a speaker at various fora, I am compelled to remind people that there is one big difference between India and China.

In China, I say, industry and the economy grow because of the government and its proactive stance.

In India, on the other hand, industry and the economy grow in spite of the government.

This has been one of my key themes even in my earlier book, *Game India*.[168]

But, if that is indeed the case, why should anyone get upset when the government begins favouring a few industrialists and helps them grow? The answer to this question should be quite obvious. In China, all industrialists are encouraged. In India, the perception is that a select few enjoy this privilege.

This is what irks economists like Arvind Subramanian. He singles out two industrialists in India—Gautam Adani and Mukesh Ambani—for being recipients of this selective benevolence.[169] He calls them beneficiaries of 'stigmatised capital'.

The charge may be partially relevant. But it is quite possible to look at things differently—by trying to understand why this happens. And, equally important, why this is likely to continue for possibly another decade.

Developing economies and selective favouritism

One reason could be that most successful industrialists (particularly in developing economies) are those who learn how to align business interests with political interests. There is something in the nature of doing business and governance in developing countries that actually fosters such relationships. Even in developed countries like the US, the pharma sector is treated with kid gloves. But the most preferential treatment there is given to the military industry complex. Defence contractors and governments—irrespective of the party that is in majority—work in collaboration (some call it collusion) with members of the ruling party.

By all definitions, India is still a developing economy. Its institutions are still raw. Even those that exist have been weakened by successive governments. Moreover, the backbone that is required—to enforce and ensure the rule of equity and law—is found wanting in many cases.

But then that is what happens with most developing economies. Look at the US a century ago. In fact, as the 2002 movie *Gangs of New York*[170] should remind us, the element of favouritism was rampant till the middle of the twentieth century. It still is, but in more subtle forms.

10.1

John D. Rockefeller Sr

(1839–1937)

Source: Wikipedia –
https://en.wikipedia.org/wiki/John_D._Rockefeller

Robber barons

Consider John D. Rockefeller, for instance. He grabbed one oil concession after another and set up Standard Oil. Then in 1911, the US Supreme Court ruled that Standard Oil must be dismantled for violation of federal antitrust laws. It was broken up into thirty-four separate entities, which included companies that became ExxonMobil and Chevron Corporation, among others. They remain some of the most profitable enterprises in the world. But their origins lie in Standard Oil, and this was possible only because of the enormous support that Rockefeller and the US politicians gave each other.

Can the empires of the beneficiaries of stigmatized capital be broken up? Possibly yes. Provided someone can prove that they are indeed monopolies. When taken as a percentage of market share, they are still small players. When size is considered for being dominant players, it depends on how you define dominant.

So, you need good legislation in place. Then you need good law enforcement agents, who do not buckle under pressure, and finally, you need a good, efficacious adjudication process that can pass orders swiftly and fairly. India has been weak on all the three fronts.

Moreover, it will be difficult to make the monopoly tag stick to Gautambhai for several reasons. Firstly, he does not control over 50 per cent of the ports, power plants, airports or even gas distribution licences. In the case of edible oils, where the organized market is itself very small, the Adani Group owns just a part of that share. Secondly, most of the Adani Group projects were won through an open tender process. There are exceptions to this rule—the Mundra Port for instance. But successive governments were involved in the awarding of the port to Gautambhai, not just a single political party. And when it comes to defence deals, there is no way a tendering system can be put into place.

Moreover, government favoured businessmen have been the norm with most governments in India. And this is true of other nations as well.

Take the case of the Legendary Railroad Tycoons of the US which included names like Cornelius 'Commodore' Vanderbilt, James J. Hill, 'Empire Builder' Edward Harriman, George Gould, Collis P. Huntington, Jay Gould, Jim Fisk, Daniel Drew, Charles Crocker, Jay Cooke, Leland Stanford and Mark Hopkins.[171] Each of these people had excellent political connections and managed to grab land concessions from the US government. That, in turn, allowed them to build the railway network in that country which, at that time, was one of the finest in the world. They made their money by monetizing the land that they grabbed (at ridiculously low prices) before the railway line came up. The land parcels they acquired allowed them to grow into other businesses as well.

Or look at other 'robber barons' like the Rothschilds of Europe (into which one of the sons of the legendary David Sassoon[172] got married). This family actually set the price of gold in the market in those days. They were the people behind some of the largest mining projects, some of which have merged and have amalgamated into Rio Tinto.[173] They called the shots in the banking industry in Europe and even worldwide.

Or take Andrew Carnegie (1835–1919), John Pierpont Morgan (1837–1913), Jay Gould (1836–92), James Fisk (1835–72) and Russell Sage (1816–1906),[174] all of them were called the robber barons, because their money came from 'crime' as we call it today. Cosy relationships with politicians, the police and other law enforcement agencies allowed them to participate in insider trading and land grabs. At that time, they were all part of the game for growth.

Most developing countries have grown this way. This was the case also with the *chaebols* and *zaibatsus* in the eastern part of this world. It is only later, in an attempt to normalize the business climate, that new laws get introduced.

Could that happen in India as well? Difficult to say. But if well-managed countries are studied, such developments do take place. Call it the inevitability of economic evolution.

Not like the chaebols

But there is another charge which Arvind Subramanian makes—the chaebols and the zaibatsus were encouraged to make the country competitive, mostly by becoming export engines for growth. That made them globally competitive as well. This does not appear to have happened in India.

10.2
The 2As: Unprecedented reach?
• Unique in the history of global capitalism?
• Petroleum/petro-chemicals
• Textiles
• Telecommunications
• Retail, online and physical
• Digital platforms
• Financial payments system
• Entertainment
• Education
• Media
• Defence production
• Energy (renewables and conventional)
• Ports and airports
• Power
• Natural gas
Notes : *The two A's are for the two biggest industrialists in India -- Gautam Adani and Mukesh Ambani. The two together cover almost every major sector in the country currently.*
Source : *Arvind Subramanian -- excerpted from a presentation and lecture at Brown University on 8 October 2021, https://www.youtube.com/watch?v=XVXm57tD7tQ.*

Moreover, as Subramanian put it, while almost all the American, European and Oriental entrepreneurs were focused on one or two lines of business, the two stigmatized A's are into almost everything. The chart alongside shows the unprecedented reach the two A's have enjoyed.

Those charges too are a bit unfair. All Indian industrialists in the past have ventured into several lines of business. Take the case of the Tatas and the Birlas. They too were into almost everything a couple of decades after independence. But, with the passage of time, they have learnt to hive off the businesses where they had lost the competitive edge. Even after the streamlining, the number of businesses they are in is quite staggering.

The Adani Group too has been hiving off some uncompetitive or non-core businesses.[175] It won't be long before the Ambanis do this as well.

One reason why many large industry groups in India choose to be in many businesses is probably because this could be the best way to de-risk business. It is like portfolio management. You do not invest all money in just a single company. The general advice is to pick up a basket of companies that balance out industry cycles and policy changes.

India is not known for its consistency of laws. In the past, laws were passed with retrospective amendments. Even as recently as in March 2022, the leading industrial state of Maharashtra tried to fiddle with land classification and land taxes, with retrospective effect from 2006, till the courts stepped in.[176]

Being in several businesses thus protects industrialists from the danger of putting their eggs in one basket. They act as portfolio managers. They do not invest all their money in the shares of just one or two companies. That takes care of failures, or even industry cycles, where if one industry faces a downswing, the other industry could be on the upswing.

Moreover, there is one more reason to suggest why governments that are in a desperate hurry to kickstart the economy prefer to back select industrialists. This is one way of retaining their hold over the licensing of industries on the one hand, yet allowing the country's economy to progress on the other. It may sound complicated. But that is what India can be.

Messy India

Consider, for instance, how difficult India can be. Study the monograph that was recently brought out by Observer Research Foundation and TeamLease, titled 'Jailed for doing Business'.[177] It has some extremely worrying data about how India does its business. The more you look at India, the more you begin to realize that unless the government has political will, doing business will be terribly difficult in India.[178]

10.3			
More opportunities for graft			
India's business regulatory Universe			
	Number of laws	Laws with criminal clauses	Compliances with criminal clauses
Union	678	244	5,239
State	858	599	20,895
Total Number of compliances			
Union	25,537		
State	43,696		
Imprisonment clauses in India's business regulatory universe			
		Laws with criminal clauses	Compliances with criminal clauses
Union		244	5,239
State		599	20,895
Breakdown of imprisonment clauses in India's business laws			
Imprisonment terms		Number of clauses	Percentage of total
Less than 3 months		5,728	21.90%
3 months to less than 1 year		5,855	22.40%
1 year to less than 3 years		11,042	42.30%
3 years to less than 5 years		1,481	5.70%
5 years to less than 10 years		1,821	7.00%
More than 10 years		207	0.80%
Total		26,134	100.00%

Notes : Data denotes the number of laws and compliances applicable to businesses at an aggregate.

Sources : TeamLease Regtech; Jailed for doing Business -- a monograph by ORF and Teamlease - https://www.orfonline.org/jailed-for-doing-business/ -- pg 63 & 64

India's businesses must cope with almost 1536 laws that employers must observe and comply with. 843 of these have jail provisions. But they also have 26,134 compliances, which if flouted could result in imprisonment. The fact that not too many businessmen actually land up in jail suggests that these laws are selectively applied. In most cases settlements take place, which in turn can indicate extortion or bribe taking.

One way of looking at the government's selective preference for certain industrialists could be its way of admitting that it cannot change the system, given the multiplicity of vested interests involved. By picking the most tenacious of entrepreneurs, the government itself ensures three things.

First, it keeps the licensing regime in place, which is great for generating funds for political parties.

Second, it ensures economic growth because the tenacious ones know how to handle government machinery in their own way, especially at the ground level. They know how to handle labour laws, and the inspector raj. And they create jobs as well. That in turn allows the economy to grow.

Third, the favoured entrepreneurs know how to return favours to key people in the political system.

But another way of looking at the reasons given above is that they resemble specious logic that the leftist writer Karl Popper often railed against. Such specious arguments were used even by despots who argued about the fate of the thousands of concubines and servants that were employed in the palaces.

Vexatious litigation

Such specious logic can be driven out only if the law-and-order institutions become stronger. But take a brief look at the vacancies in courts in India.[179] Almost a third of the sanctioned posts of the judiciary—at higher and lower levels—remain vacant. What is sad is that even the sanctioned strength is lower than what ought to be the case in view of the huge backlog of cases in India, making the concept of justice almost farcical.[180] Even recently, media reports talked about a shortage of 50 per cent of judicial vacancies, thus leading to pendency of cases in courts.[181] In April 2022, even the chief justice of India bemoaned the shortage of judges.[182] He said that 'that the judiciary is overburdened, and access to justice would be possible only when sufficient number of courts as well as infrastructure was in place. He said that he was giving priority to fill up the vacancies of judges and improving infrastructure to deal with the backlog of cases.'

10.4	
Court cases in India	
Big numbers may mean nothing	
Adani	62,028
Reliance Industries	33,641
Tata	129,419
Aditya Birla	3,769
ITC	11,132
Government of India	732,330

Note : Based on a simple search on the exact names listed here. The search results could be different for each specific company, or a change in search parametres.

Source :https://indiankanoon.org -- as on 2 March 2022

If one looks at some of the numbers of court cases industry groups and entrepreneurs have to cope with,[183] such an explanation makes sense. We took a sampling from a website[184] by searching 'Adani' and discovered that this name was involved in 62,028 cases. Now this may include other people who had the same Adani family name, and are in no way connected with the Adani Group. But if one refines the search to the name of a company like Reliance Industries, one finds that it is involved in 33,641 cases.

A search on 'Tata' showed up 1.29 lakh cases. And a search on Government of India showed up a staggering 7.3 lakh cases.

It is in keeping with the Law Commission's description of the government as a 'compulsive litigant'—brought out quite succinctly by Vidhi Legal Policy.[185]

This simplistic test shows how many cases get filed. The courts do not have an effective system to disincentivize frivolous or vexatious cases. Everybody knows that many of these cases will eventually be thrown out. But they keep piling up and eventually clog up the system. This is made worse by the limited number of courts and judicial officers as well. All this is exhausting for entrepreneurial time and effort.

India's judicial system does require a major overhaul. But lawmakers remain reluctant to do that, as the present system suits their purpose.[186]

Doing business in India and growing large as well, requires people who know how to handle vexatious court cases as well, some instigated by business rivals and irregular businesses.

This is despite the improvement in the ranking of ease of doing business in India.[187] India's biggest pitfall is the way its judicial systems work.[188] The government does not appoint more judges and create more courts. It does not limit the seeking of adjournments. And, more important, it allows the filing of vexatious cases, so that any person with an axe to grind can file cases against industrialists. At times, these cases are attempts at extortion. Not surprisingly, some of the biggest industrialists have thousands of cases pending against them.[189]

That is where Subramanian's criticism of stigmatized capital may not be entirely fair. To do business in India, you need people who have immense tenacity.

Hopefully, like in the case of the robber barons, wealth generation in India will soon be large enough for powerful industrialists to lobby for institutions to become stronger. Maybe this is India's way of growing.

Eventually, what matters is whether the industrialists are making a good return on capital employed. Is the capital being used profitably?

This is where some analysis of the two industrialists accused of being beneficiaries of 'stigmatised capital' may help.[190]

Regulated businesses can be good

It is true that many of the businesses that Gautambhai is into are regulated businesses, where he may enjoy a natural monopoly. This is true of power generation, transmission and distribution. It is true of roadways. Gas distribution too would also fall into the same basket.

But the big advantage about being in these businesses is that— as mentioned earlier—if your legal documentation is watertight, and the price purchase agreements are carefully structured, if you have the skills required for speedy implementation of projects (time is money) and the deal is signed, it becomes a bankable proposition.

The entrepreneur can now predict the rate of revenue flows into his coffers. The cash flows become long-term annuities. The rates of return can increase if better efficiencies kick in. He can use these cash flow projections to get money from the banks and also plan further diversifications. And if he is Teflon-coated, most of the irritants of payment delays and court cases will just bounce off him.

This is important because governments are known to try renege on payments. It may take some time. Many an entrepreneur has fallen by the wayside on account of such roadblocks. But it is possible to make governments pay up eventually—as has been the case in several disputes relating to power generation and power evacuation. Government have also tried to renegotiate tariffs for solar power. Eventually, no government can go against a well-structured PPA. It is worth recalling that even the much-maligned Enron project could not be cancelled because of the way the legal documents were structured. Eventually, it was Enron's fall in the US that allowed the Government of India to enter into a negotiated settlement, for which too a very high price had to be paid.

An entrepreneur who has the ability to fight it out in courts, and also wait till there is a resolution, has a better chance of succeeding than one who has the right documentation, but does not have the financial strength to cope with delayed payments. It is this kind of fragility that has done many politician-backed entrepreneurs in. They may have had the right ideas and the right drive, but did not have the ability to withstand payment delays or vexatious court cases.

Good profits

10.5

The Adani Group	Group comprises 164 companies (up from 157 of FY20) *(figures in Rs. Cr.)*						over FY2000
	FY=2000	FY-2005	FY-2010	FY-2015	FY-2020	FY-2021	
Sales	2,804	16,655	23,828	72,581	113,846	119,670	42
Income from financial services	26	199	784	4,051	10,672	15,043	585
Total income	2,830	16,854	24,612	76,632	124,518	134,713	47
Capital employed - CMIE	1,228	3,803	51,873	186,052	295,700	328,571	267
Gross capital employed	1,129	3,817	51,860	195,431	303,937	336,776	297
Paid up equity capital (net of forfeited equity capital)	78	309	5,474	17,054	34,776	36,132	461
Reserves and funds less Revaluation reserves	338	1,093	10,112	30,908	25,714	39,220	115
Borrowings	707	2,275	34,645	132,976	202,511	212,976	300
CWIP	350	580	22,492	15,029	10,558	16,578	46
Net capital employed (less CWIP)	778	3,237	29,368	180,402	293,379	320,198	410
Cumulative depreciation on gross fixed assets	6	141	1,629	14,493	40,937	48,448	8,454
PBDITA	177	600	3,417	19,443	30,207	44,731	252
PBDITA on net capital employed (%)	22.7	18.5	11.6	10.8	10.3	14.0	
Return on CMIE definition of capital employed (%)	14.4	15.8	6.6	10.5	10.2	13.6	
Forex earnings	1,171	10,852	6,331	3,690	3,396	3,271	2

Notes : Definitions given below. The Adani group's growth has been remarkable. But it is clearly not as profitable as it was earlier. Moreover, it is important to note CMIE's figures for the Adani Group's exports for FY21 is only Rs 525 crore. It has not included Adani–Wilmar's exports of Rs 2746.16 crore.
We have added this number and made the export number swell to Rs 3721 crore.
CMIE explains its inability to include Adani–Wilmar's export numbers because companies are required to disclose Forex disclosures under details of foreign exchange earnings and outgo' section of the annual report which is usually reported by the companies in their director's report.
Source: CMIE, Prowess

10.6

The Mukesh Ambani Group	Group comprises 207 companies (220 in FY20) *(figures in Rs. Cr.)*						over FY2000
	FY=2000	FY-2005	FY-2010	FY-2015	FY-2020	FY-2021	
Sales	22,609	86,597	217,625	379,246	627,186	569,500	24
Income from financial services	1,136	1,734	4,551	10,907	19,573	30,767	26
Total income	23,746	88,331	222,176	390,153	646,759	600,267	24
Capital employed - CMIE	55,558	78,387	310,609	519,079	1,144,620	1,226,611	21
Gross capital employed	70,327	114,434	392,457	674,554	1,228,049	1,289,339	17
Paid up equity capital (net of forfeited equity capital)	6,292	2,758	12,463	54,816	70,309	71,704	10
Reserves and funds less Revaluation reserves	17,736	46,022	188,222	263,872	512,964	624,405	34
Borrowings	32,912	32,360	118,139	200,484	444,038	368,600	10
CWIP	13,386	4,709	17,694	147,946	79,604	83,810	5
Net capital employed (less CWIP)	63,316	106,946	242,099	524,476	1,140,784	1,205,529	18
PBDITA	7,011	17,614	40,738	49,946	109,563	113,459	15
Cumulative depreciation on gross fixed assets	13,386	33,294	73,633	155,383	200,738	224,630	16
PBDITA on net capital employed (%)	11.1	16.5	16.8	9.5	9.6	9.4	
Return on CMIE definition of capital employed (%)	12.6	22.5	13.1	9.6	9.6	9.2	
Forex earnings	2,210	25,379	104,550	212,651	195,021	137,893	61

Notes: Definitions given below. Among the selected groups covered, the Ambani Group is clearly a market favourite. But the rates of return belie that hype and euphoria.
Source: CMIE, Prowess

Gautambhai has shown that he has both. That is where he is on a more comfortable wicket than many others.

This is where a study of the financials of both the 'stigmatized capital' beneficiaries become important.

Look at the Adani and Ambani charts above. You will notice the following points:

- The Adani Group has logged an unbelievably blistering pace of growth during the past twenty years.
- The Adani sales grew forty-two times during this period compared to twenty-four times for Ambani.
- Other income for Adani grew 585 times, compared to twenty-six for Ambani.
- Total income grew forty-seven times for Adani compared to twenty-four for Ambani.
- Interestingly, total borrowings for Adani grew a mind-boggling 300 times during this period, compared to a modest ten times for Ambani. Critics have talked about the unsustainability of such high growth in borrowings. But they forget an old saying—that it does not matter whether the money is borrowed or is your own money. Money must generate a decent rate of return. It must generate profits that are higher than the commercial rate of borrowing. This is again where Adani triumphs over Ambani. Another interesting fact about the Adani Group is that its borrowings are not entirely from Indian banks. Despite the large debt, borrowings from Indian banks are significantly lower than that for many other industrialists. Thus the systemic risk to the Indian banking system is considerably less than that posed by many other Indian industrialists.

However, 'There has been a significant improvement in the group debt-servicing capacity in recent years due to a jump in group earnings. Besides, a general decline in interest rate in the economy in the last two years has resulted in muted growth in interest cost despite faster growth in borrowings.'[191]

- Profit before interest tax and depreciation before adjustments (PBIDBA) for Adani grew 252 times. Ambani's PBIDBA grew fifteen times.

10.7
Notes for both the tables above:
CMIE's definition of capital employed : *This is a more sophisticated measure which includes paid-up equity capital, paid-up forfeited equity capital, contribution made to capital by government, accumulated reserves, all convertible warrants and all borrowings. However, revaluation reserves and miscellaneous expenses not written off are deducted from the above.*
Gross capital employed = *equity - reserves without revaluation reserves + total borrowings + accumulated depreciation*
Net capital employed = *gross capital employed less CWIP.*
CWIP = *Capital work in progress -- assets which are yet to generate returns. It includes intangible assets under development but newt of impairment.*
PBDITA = *Profit before depreciation, interest, taxes and adjustments.*
Rates of return: *To appreciate rate of return better, it is important to compare them with the commerciual rate of borrowing in the local markets. During the 1990s, for instance, this rate was over 15 per cent. If any promoter earns less than the market rate of borrowing, then one can say that the money with him is not being wisely spent, at least as far as investors are concerned.*

- Except for one year in FY2010, Adani's rates of return have been higher than those of Ambani. In FY2021, return on capital employed for Adani was 14 per cent vs 9.4 for Ambani. And returns on the CMIE definition of capital employed were 13.8 per cent vs 9.2 per cent respectively.
- The one place in which Ambani trounces Adani, hands down, is on the foreign exchange earnings front. Ambani's exports grew sixty-one times, while Adani's only two times (that too after adding Adani–Wilmar's export figures).

One reason for this could be the Adani Group's refusal to show forex earning and instead only shows net forex earnings. In the port business, almost all the income is in foreign exchange. But there are foreign exchange expenses as well. Adani has given the net figures which are exceedingly small. This is where steel exports as well as defence exports, could provide the redeeming quality.

Another reason could be that most of the Adani Group's businesses are focused on domestic services, which do not allow for exports—like the CGD or power distribution businesses. But in this context, it must be stated that even though the Adani Group may not be a big exporter for now, his ports and airports enable exports and imports. Without them, exports would have posed a big challenge.

- And do watch the way Adani has used depreciation funds (which are essentially tax-free money lying with corporate managements) to finance his blistering rate of growth in addition to picking up debt. It is a very interesting method of project financing. Adani's accumulated depreciation grew 8454 times during these twenty years.

- In this context, it is also relevant to quote an August 2022 Reuters report.[192] It points out, quite pertinently, 'While the amount borrowed across the listed companies has more than tripled to 2.3 trillion rupees ($30 billion) over the past decade, aggregate net debt has fallen to about 4 times EBITDA. He has diversified funding sources too, reducing his dependence on state banks, and extended the time available to pay off liabilities: 50 per cent of debt is in capital-markets instruments and repayments stretch from 2026 through 2046. Most of the group businesses, barring property and lending, are captured through listed entities where credit rating agencies see few obvious signs of weakness: Adani is buying cash-generating assets and its bidding behaviour for contracts or acquisitions is not considered aggressive. When cashflows increase, and the rates of return are higher than the interest paid out, borrowing is not such a bad idea at all.'

- Clearly, exports are the one front on which Adani will have to work extremely hard.

Gautambhai will be able to improve significantly on the export number as well, if his Adani–POSCO project goes as well as has been planned. Within a couple of years, or maybe three, the Adani–POSCO project will begin generating profits and exports. There are also the defence-related exports that have already begun to take off.[193]

The synergies that this project will unleash cannot be fully appreciated at this stage. But with the Adani Group's Australian linkages, expect iron ore to be imported from that continent (and through coastal shipping from Indian mines as well) to feed this steel plant, which is likely to be quite large. This could be music to Australia's ears, because it has lost quite a large market on account of Chinese restrictions on Australian imports. Same with coal.

The solar plants will generate the hydrogen at some of the lowest costs in the world. Obviously, the plant will blend Indian ore with imported ore as required from time to time. But being coast based, freight costs are likely to be manageable. With the Adani Group controlling the ships and the ports and the land on which the steel plant is built, expect economies to kick in that few have imagined till now.

Finally, because the group owns many ports along the Indian coast, the steel and cement (even PVC, aluminium and copper) can be shipped to different parts of the country, as well as exported. Expanding the size of the plant will not pose much difficulty, because it will not be tied down to iron ore and coal availability from mines in India alone. The Adani Group's forays into PVC, aluminium and copper are yet to reach a stage that they can be talked about meaningfully. But expect huge revenues and cash flows from these projects as well.[194] In fact, just as the final draft of this book was being sent to the publishers, the news came in that the Adani Group had signed a deal with the state government of Odisha to invest Rs 57,575 crore in that state. The group wants to set up two projects—one for a 4 million TPA Integrated Alumina Refinery and a 30 million TPA Iron Ore (Value Addition) Project.[195]

This could be tricky though. At least two large groups have had to scuttle their plans in that state. POSCO from Korea had to abandon its iron ore to steel plans and Vedanta had to abandon his mining plans including the setting up of a world-class university there. But Adani already has a foothold and a track record in that state. He owns and operates the Dhamra Port, which could unleash synergies with the output from these two projects.

Expect these plans to be the drivers of huge businesses. Moreover, they might be linked to the steel and aluminium plants being set up at Mundra itself. Because the land and the ecosystem are in place over there. But Odisha adds a new dimension to the group's mining, manufacturing and port plans.

To conclude:

- being present in many fields is not a bad idea if one considers all the aspects in a country like India.
- aligning corporate interests to government interests can be an excellent business strategy, especially in developing economies like India.
- so long as the rates of return are not allowed to slip, businesses are suitably derisked, and iron-clad agreements are in place, there should be little to worry about. The Mundra power plant crisis, which took place because of a poorly structured agreement, is a lesson that Gautambhai has learnt. He is more careful in ensuring that all risks have a mitigation strategy.

11

Jettisoning Excess Baggage

As mentioned in the previous chapter, many Indian industrialists opt to pick up several lines of business as a means of de-risking their business. They are opportunity driven. There are very few players like the Bajaj Auto or the TVS groups which are focused only on automobiles or financing automobiles. Or like Infosys which sticks to IT.

The largest IT company, TCS, is part of the Tata Group which is into many businesses. Even Azim Premji, who remains India's biggest philanthropist, has interests in oil and fatty acids, consumer products and lighting, in addition to the group's mainstay, IT.

But one thing common to all groups is a sharp eye to filter out businesses that cease to be relevant to core operations. It could be too small in size compared to the others, hence not warranting that much of management time or attention. Or it could be generating meagre or no profits. Or it could be just part of any management's desire to have a leaner and meaner management team. Such 'burdensome' ventures are invariably hived off.

Hiving off businesses

This is the case with Gautambhai as well. While he started with the plastics and PVC trading business, he gradually gave it up, and shifted to coal. At one time, the brothers were into ship breaking, both in India and the US. But it took too much of management time and effort and that too was given up. Unlike some of his brothers who were into textiles, he chose to stay away from this line of business. Then, as the prospects for coal became bigger and brighter, he went in for coal mining. That in turn became one of the core businesses for his ports when Mundra became operational.

One of the first businesses to be hived off was dealing with ships that were scrapped, and trading in the metal salvaged. Harsh Mishra, former group president, international business, recalls how Gautambhai told him to scout around for mining opportunities—especially in coal. The first opportunity sighted was a US Navy ship dismantling yard which was acquired in 2005 for $5 million. But that did not fit in with Gautambhai's plans—though one of his brothers, Vinod, was still into steel trading. This unit was hived off in 2011.

Seductive aluminium

Since the Adani Group was into mining, a friend, Narayan Chandra of Ashapura Group—who is into mining, real estate and commodity trading in Ahmedabad—requested him to join hands to set up an aluminium project.[196] He had bauxite mines, which he held and operated along with GMDC. To make aluminium you need bauxite, caustic soda and lots of energy. Gujarat—especially the Kutch region—has abundant caustic soda, which is why Tata Chemicals also has its biggest operations there. The Adani Group had its own power plant—a smaller one before the Mundra plant came up.

The plan sounded logical. In keeping with earlier practice, as it was with Adani–Wilmar, both parties would own 50 per cent of the stake—a concept that appeals to Gautambhai immensely. The plan was to tie up with Ashapura Minechem, to set up a Rs 10,000-crore aluminium refinery in Gujarat. The refinery was to produce 1 million tonnes of alumina and 0.5 million TPA of aluminium annually. An alumina extraction unit could be set up in the first phase at a cost of Rs 3500 crore. A smelting unit would come up later, taking the overall project cost to Rs 10,000 crore.

But Gautambhai expected Ashapura to take charge of all operations. Somehow, the bandwidth Ashapura had was limited.

The project failed to take off. Gautambhai also tried setting up a cement plant with Ashapura. But that too did not take off.

Like most good businessmen, Gautambhai is quick to scuttle projects when they don't make economic sense.

Ashapura continues to work with Gautambhai by operating a container freight station at Mundra.[197]

The Ashapura project is probably what Harsh Mishra has in mind when he says, 'Gautambhai will listen to reason. At one point, the Adani Group was pretty firm on entering the aluminium smelting business on the following grounds:

- a large under-consumption of aluminium in India,
- a growing use of the metal,
- a progressive shift in smelting capacities from the west to Asia and
- the presence of bauxite capacities in India to support downstream operations.

'However, he remained intellectually open to contrary opinions: we impressed upon him that this was one business where:

o we would not be able to figure in the top two of the industry in India within a reasonable time frame;

o by the time we got to 5,00,00 TPA capacity the established players would move to enhance capacities in excess of 2 million TPA;

o however hard we tried; our cost of power generation would never be as low as some of the older companies with longstanding assets.

'The result was that even though a lot of planning had matured, the Adani Group withdrew from entering the aluminium smelting business.'

But the idea of using Gujarat for making aluminium stayed with Gautambhai. In December 2021, the group finally announced that it would foray into the production of aluminium.[198] Adani Enterprises Ltd, the flagship company of the diversified Adani Group, has formed a fully-owned unit named Mundra Aluminium Ltd to set up alumina refinery and aluminium smelter. The group has entered into discussions with IOC which already has strategic reserves of oil at Mundra, to join him in producing battery grade aluminium. Such vehicles are already on trial with Mahindra. If all works out, the Adani Group may finally get into aluminium, though into a niche product where he can be a market leader. IOC, it may be recalled, has already tied up with Israel-based start-up Phinergy for development, manufacturing, assembly and sale of aluminium-air batteries.[199] The Adani Group is in discussions with this public sector company.

And now with the recently announced plans of setting up a 4 million TPA integrated alumina refinery in Odisha,[200] the group's involvement with this metal gets even more interesting. It is quite possible that the alumina will be shipped to Mundra, where (solar) power is cheaper and then converted to aluminium.

Also on the anvil is setting up a plant for making PVC through coal.[201] Such technologies have already been in use by Calico Chemicals and Plastics in Mumbai and Chemplast in Mettur. The method is to use calcium carbonate and through electrolysis make calcium carbide. This is then converted into acetylene. This is made to react with hydrochloric acid and chlorine to make vinyl chloride monomer, which is then converted into PVC. Key recruitments have already been made, and the idea of using Gujarat's abundance in chlorine and power, along with coal, could become another big business opportunity. Current plans are to produce 2 million tonnes of PVC.

In June 2022, the group also decided to set up a copper production facility.[202] Kutch Copper, a subsidiary of Adani Enterprises, is setting up a greenfield copper refinery project to produce 1 million TPA in two phases. The project cost is estimated at Rs 6071 crore for the first phase, which will have a capacity of 0.5 million TPA at Mundra, Gujarat.

Add to this the takeover of the Holcim ACC group of companies in India. He has suddenly become the second largest cement manufacturer in India (the largest is the Aditya Birla group).[203] Funding of $5.25 billion as debt financing for this takeover was largely through international bankers.

By getting into these sectors, the Adani Group will be competing with both the Aditya Birla group (which has hitherto dominated the aluminium and cement sectors) and the Sterlite/ Vedanta group (which is a big player in copper production). This is in addition to competing with the Reliance Industries group in areas like green energy, data and 5G. Expect domestic competition to become fiercer in the coming decade.

Retail, ship-breaking and oil exploration

A similar decision was taken with Adani Retail, located in Ahmedabad. 'There is a corridor of opportunity. If you do not pay attention, you may opt for undesirable or sub-optimal path,' is how Devang Desai puts it. It is also the ability to hive off what could become a distraction in the larger scheme of things. That is why he opted to hive off a call centre that he had started. Ditto with a chain of retail stores; there were sixty-four shops that sported the Adani Retail legend. He sold them off to Reliance Industries Ltd. 'If you cannot be Number #2 or Number #3 in any business, it is best to give it away,' says Gautam quite often.

As mentioned earlier, when it came to the ship dismantling business in the US which augmented the steel scrap trading business, he opted out because it took too much of management bandwidth and time and did not have the potential of making this business # 2 or #3 in India.

'Focus on cost, not the market, is what Gautam reminds us quite often,' says Mahadevia. 'You can control the former, not the latter. He is obsessed with cost and speed. At the same time, he is more concerned with how to manage speed, which in turn leads to processes. In many ways, he is an expert at managing chaos.'

Ditto with Welspun Adani. Bal Krishan Goenka is a friend of Gautambhai. Once again, when he pointed to the enormous profits that lay in the oil business, Gautambhai is said to have told him that he had no understanding of the oil business. He could finance the business, but the day-to-day management would be that of Goenka. Once again, in typical Gautambhai style, a 50:50 venture was proposed.

The $1.5 billion (around Rs 7035 crore in 2009) Welspun group was one of the largest steel pipe and home textile furnishings makers in India. He planned merging three promoter-owned investment companies so that he could raise funds.[204]

'We can either borrow money or sell equity of the holding company to meet future cash requirements,' said Goenka, and added that this depends on funding needs in the next growth phase.

Three years later, Goenka began discussions with Gautambhai. By 2014 both had decided to float Adani-Welspun, a 50:50 joint venture. The idea was to invest $1.5 billion in US shale and Canadian oil sands assets.[205] Plans were also drawn up to begin oil exploration.

By 2015, media reports suggest that Welspun had already invested Rs 3000 crore into the energy business, including Rs 500 crore of equity.[206]

All seemed well for some time. But both discovered that the results of exploration weren't that impressive. Finally, both decided to wind up Adani-Welspun.

Gautambhai remains unfazed when he has to take a decision to wind up a business plan that once looked attractive. If the results aren't good, and the prospects don't look promising as well, he does not let friendship cloud his judgement. He decides to cut losses immediately.

That could also explain why he abandoned all initial plans put up before him for the development of Mundra Port. 'He saw Mundra Port as a diagram—of inflow and outflow of cash. Anything that would cause strain on either would need to be modified. Phasing out the port was not even considered earlier,' adds Devang Desai. All the earlier plans put up before Gautambhai involved development and then business generation.

Gautambhai wanted a plan that could do both at the same time. He wanted cash flow and expansion simultaneously. It was also the reason why other possible suitors for the terminal at Mundra were just kept out of the reckoning. Because the others— A.P. Moller, Hutchinson, American President Lines—were in ocean liner businesses as well. P&O was exclusively a terminal operator. That would ensure that there would be little conflict of interest.

Gautambhai has added a couple of additional container terminals and a RORO (Roll-On-Roll-Off) terminal for handling automobile loading and unloading. A large number of liners are now calling at these terminals as they have no clash of interest. A well-thought-out strategy at the time of leasing the first container terminal is paying off handsome rewards to Gautambhai today.

Gautambhai's ability to hive off businesses that have little chance of scaling up are based on a simple logic. 'You should be the least cost producer, which is possible only if you have large capacity,' says Mahadevia. Business logic and people assume prime priority in Gautambhai's mind. Then to facilitate both business and people, processes must be found.

12

Feeding the Nation and Relationships

Gautambhai's focus on agriculture was probably triggered by the deal his group got from the Food Corporation of India (FCI) to handle wheat logistics. Initially, the FCI used to import wheat and pulses through Mundra, which in turn compelled the Adani Group to consider ways to store grain.

12.1		
Huge potential in agriculture		
Opportunity		
USD 80 Bn+ Indian Packaged Food Retail Size	**~10-15%** Low branded penetration	**~18%** Accretive Gross Margin
Key Highlights		
INR 1800 Crores+ Food Basket (c. FY21)	**30% y-o-y volume growth** High growth potential	**Growing faster than Industry** Fortune Atta & Fortune Rice

Note: Segment-wise performance detais for Adani–Wilmar not yet available.
Source: Adani–Wilmar websitge -- https://www.adaniwilmar.com/-
/media/Project/Wilmar/Investors/Quarterly%20Results/AWL%20Q3%20Results-%202021-22

The opportunity came in 2007 when the government floated an international tender for a storage solution. The best bid was by the Adani Group along with the Australian wheat board. Prior to this move, almost all the grain used to be stored in godowns, usually under tarpaulin sheets, which in turn exposed the grain to pests and humidity. The new silo type storage units changed India's approach towards storage altogether. A short video on the company's website tells this story quite evocatively.[207]

By 2007, the Adani Group invested over Rs 650 crore in agri-logistics. It had base depots at Moga, Punjab and at Kaithal, Haryana. Field depots were also set up at five locations—Chennai, Coimbatore, Bangalore, Navi Mumbai and Hubli. All of them were structured under Adani agri-logistics.

At each field storage, systems were put in place to check all grain coming in on all the eight parameters laid down by the government. This included testing the grain for moisture, pesticides, damage, colour and size.

The grain business

The automation allowed the farmer to bring in his grain, get it tested, and send it for storage. The farmer would get a computerized receipt, and the amount to be paid would be determined by the quality and weight of the grain he had handed over for storage. No middlemen were allowed. The entire process—which earlier took farmers around two to three days—was now completed in just two hours.

The grain was then transferred from pre-storage bins to process towers at speeds of 500 tonnes an hour. The silos where the grain was stored had a capacity of 12,500 tonnes each and allowed for top loading and bottom evacuation. This ensured that the wheat that was stored first, also got out first. While the grain was stored, it was airified and fumigated as and when required.

It thus saved the farmer time, got him prompt payment, reduced grain damage, and sped up the entire collection, storage and distribution of grain. Most of all, it professionalized the entire system, leaving little scope for corruption where both the farmer and the government were shortchanged

To evacuate the grain, the group invested in seven dedicated rakes of fifty wagons each. Even the rakes were top loading and bottom evacuation. Each rake could load around 3000 tonnes in four hours and evacuate it at the desired destination at the same speed. This is the kind of technology India should be having almost everywhere. In some ways, Gautambhai was way ahead of his time.

But then Gautambhai was possibly betting on all grain movements from the north coming to Mundra for exports. He was also betting on the reverse traffic—getting imported grain to these warehouses in different parts of the country for offtake so that it could reach the end consumers. The rail connectivity between Mundra and Adipur Junction had just been completed. There was promise of the country's first dedicated freight corridor (DFC) coming up by 2014. This was to connect Rewari in Haryana to JNPT in Mumbai and onward to Dighi.[208] Even by 2022, the DFC had not taken off. Nor has even one of the thirty-six industrial cities planned along both sides of the DFC under the Delhi Mumbai Industrial corridor (DMIC). It would have spurred on the Adani Group's foray into logistics and agriculture. Had that happened, much of north and west India would have seen economic growth of a higher magnitude.

Had he known that the DFC would not be set up by 2014 as had been originally planned, it is possible that Gautambhai might have shelved his plans. But with a port at one end, railway lines in the middle, service industrial townships along the way and suitable storage facilities at the other end, there was only one thing to do—keep pushing up business. The systems, and the determination, coupled with the objectives that the government had for farming, worked in favour of the Adani Group. From wheat, the journey went into edible oil and fruits.

But, once again, luck could be favouring the Adani Group. The ongoing war between Russia and Ukraine jinxed the entire export of wheat to much of the world. India, which has had surplus wheat and rice, thanks to its MSP policy favouring just these two grains, suddenly finds a market for this agri-output. All of a sudden, proper storage evacuation and loading processes are required. Also required are systems that assay the grain received and dispatched. India has become an exporter of grain after a very long time. It used to export rice, but not much wheat. The war and the export demand, at prices that are higher than procurement prices, is forcing the agricultural sector and the government to look more favourably towards the systems the Adani Group has already put in place.

But, once again, the seesaw of policy making nixed grain exports (along with steel). The government did this possibly as on overreaction to rising domestic prices, which is a politically sensitive issue. It could have achieved that by imposing an export tax, or putting limits on exports, or both. But banning exports was not the best move to introduce. Or were there other factors at work? Could it be that if the best grain got exported, the FCI would have to pick up the grain in its warehouses? That grain might have been of substandard quality (there are reports that the government's procurement machinery pays first grade prices for second grade grain[209]). Rather than expose the corruption, the political machinery opted for an export ban.

12.2							
Edible oils domestic production and imports							
	(million tonnes)				(%)		
Oil year (Nov-Oct.)	Oilseed Production	Domestic net availability	Imports	Total availability	Extraction from seeds	Share of domestic supply	Share of imports
2010-11	32.5	9.8	7.2	17.0	30.1	57.5	42.5
2011-12	29.8	9.0	9.9	18.9	30.1	47.4	52.6
2012-13	30.9	9.2	10.6	19.8	29.8	46.5	53.5
2013-14	32.9	10.1	11.0	21.1	30.7	47.9	52.1
2014-15	26.7	9.0	12.7	21.7	33.7	41.4	58.6
2015-16	25.3	8.6	14.9	23.5	34.2	36.8	63.3
2016-17	31.3	10.1	15.3	25.4	32.3	39.7	60.3
2017-18	31.5	10.4	14.6	25.0	33.0	41.6	58.4
2018-19	31.5	10.4	15.6	25.9	32.8	39.9	60.1
2019-20	33.2	10.7	13.5	24.2	32.1	44.0	56.0
2020-21[a]	36.1	11.2	13.15/13.46[b]	24.46/24.77[b]	30.9	46.22/45.64[b]	53.77/54.35[b]

Notes: [a] Based on Fourth Advance estimates from Ministry of Agriculture and Farmers' Welfare
[b] Two projections are made, one is based on current trends of vegetable oil imports from November 20-July 21 and the other based on trends from August '20 to October '20
Sources: Oil Division, Ministry of Consumer Affairs, Food & Public Distribution, Ministry of Agriculture & Farmers' Welfare, DGCI&S, Ind-Ra;
https://www.indiaratings.co.in/PressRelease?pressReleaseID=56462&title=Edible%20Oil%20Inflation%20to%20Remain%20in%20Double%20Digits%20Despite%20Import%20Duty%20Cuts

But the Adani's Groups commitment to food and agriculture continues to be extremely strong. Today, the group deals with a suite of brands—Fortune, King's, Bullet, Raag, Avsar, Pilaf, Jubilee, Fryola, Alpha and Aadhar.[210]

The 'Fortune' cooking oil brand offers the largest variety of oils ranging from soya, rice bran, groundnut, mustard, cottonseed and functional oils. Other products include basmati rice, pulses, soya chunks, *besan*, wheat flour, sugar and ready-to-eat superfood khichdi.[211]

Maybe, once the government gets agricultural warehousing in order,[212] such investments may turn out to be quite profitable, and relevant. It will be interesting to see how things pan out for this activity of the Adani Group.

Adani–Wilmar

Almost as if in synchronized moves, the Adani–Wilmar project also took off from October 2000. That was when Gautambhai realized that he needed to get into edible oil for which he needed a strong raw material (edible oil) sourcing presence in Malaysia and Indonesia.

Atul Chaturvedi, then CEO, Adani–Wilmar Ltd, says, 'He set about scouting for partners while on a trip to Singapore for work. He chanced upon Wilmar. The Wilmar chairman Kuok Khoon Hon could not meet him at a short notice. So, Gautambhai left a leaflet for him. When the chairman saw the leaflet, he was curious and invited Gautambhai for dinner.

'The chairman must have seen the spark in Gautambhai, for within a few days, he was in India to see the proposed location for an edible oil processing plant in Mundra. On the return from Mundra, a joint venture was proposed, and the broad terms of the contract were frozen on the back of an airline boarding pass. The MoU was drafted the following day—Gautambhai went from meeting to MoU in four days!'

Chaturvedi also points out that while the venture was on a 50:50 basis, there were hardly any disagreements. 'But the first major disagreement between the Adanis and Kuok, the Wilmar Chairman, happened within a month of the joint venture being floated. At a time when India's largest refining capacity was 100 TPD, Kuok said we needed to commission a 1000 TPD refining capacity. We thought that this was ridiculous. Kuok said, "You don't understand this business!" He had based this figure on his experience of the market explosion in China. A compromise 600 TPD was agreed upon. Within a year, we raised the installed capacity from 600 TPD to 1,600 TPD and [by 2013] had a 10,000 TPD refining and 9,000 TPD oilseed crushing plant! In those days, India was importing 1–1.5 million tonnes of oil a year. Now it imports 9.5 million tonnes of oil a year.'

Imports continue even today. While the government says that it is keen on stopping imports and giving farmers a better deal, ground realities are different.[213] The Adani Group has designed its strategies in such a way that it benefits either way—through imported edible oil, or through domestic sourcing.

Chaturvedi continues, 'Gautambhai was always thinking of how fast he could turn or accelerate vessel discharge while the Adani–Wilmar joint venture project was being commissioned. He kept pushing the envelope: the result was that he inspired the increase of the pipeline diameter from 6 inches to 16 inches and invested in high-capacity pumps to increase pumping speed from 60 TPH (tonnes per hour) to 400 TPH. As a result, his ships were able to discharge much faster, reduce demurrage and be turned around with speed.'

The lure of apples

Simultaneously, Gautambhai began looking at the apple orchards of Himachal Pradesh.[214] He promptly built the largest cold storage facilities in the country (more details given below). Today, he has created a marvel—with end-to-end logistics for apple growers in that state. It is brought out quite comprehensively in a video the company has prepared.[215]

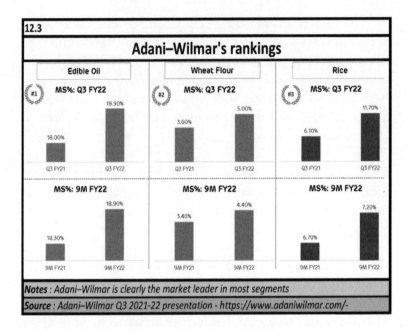

12.3

Adani–Wilmar's rankings

| Edible Oil | Wheat Flour | Rice |

Notes : Adani–Wilmar is clearly the market leader in most segments
Source : Adani–Wilmar Q3 2021-22 presentation - https://www.adaniwilmar.com/-

Today, most agronomists will tell you that the only success story in India—besides the success with milk helmed by Verghese Kurien[216]—of a food chain in agriculture is the work that the Adani Group has done with apples. Limited successes can also be found in sectors like pomegranates and bananas, but not on the same scale as the Adani Group did with apples.

Adani's Agri Fresh looks at farmers in Himachal Pradesh right from the stage of educating farmers about how to grow apples, to advising them on the right use of fertilizers and pesticides. It then trains them on how to pick the apples, what type to pick, and how to put them into boxes (supplied by the company) for onward dispatch to one of the collection centres of the company. More popularly known as Farm Pik, the Adani Group then sends the apples through an entirely automated process where they are first tested for firmness, then washed, cleaned, sorted on the basis of size and colour, and then packed. Today, the largest exports in the Adani Group come from Adani–Wilmar.[217]

To facilitate all this, the group set up, by 2006, the largest storage facilities for fruit in India—at Rampur, Sainj and Rohru in Himachal Pradesh at an investment of Rs 200 crore. All the storage units are temperature and humidity controlled. It thus did away with manual sorting, packing and transportation, which led to huge farm losses on the one hand, and rapacious pricing offered by middlemen on the other.

For the farmers, this meant a twin bonanza. Expenses went down, and incomes went up. To top both benefits, there was another advantage—prompt payments. To make the farmers comfortable with the entire process, the group set up a viewing gallery where the farmers could observe how the apples were being sorted, graded and even priced.

They were given a receipt for the fruit they deposited with the company and invariably got the money into their bank accounts the same day, unless of course, the farmer wasn't connected to a bank or wanted cash. All farmers are informed by SMS of the amounts that are due to them and credited into their accounts.

Continuing education programmes aimed at making farmers better with the best agricultural practices persuaded more farmers to abandon older practices and embrace the new systems. Not surprisingly, the apple crop has increased year after year both in terms of tonnage, and even quality.

What was more endearing to the farming community was the offer of medical facilities, without any charges. This was social and agricultural transformation. It boosted social development, production and distribution.[218] Since the Adani Group had a vested interest in transportation through railways right up to the port, air-conditioned containers (reefers) were also introduced. Today, the company supplies apples all over the world—USA, Canada, Chile, South Africa, EU, China, Australia and New Zealand.

The group does not talk about the incomes from these streams. But according to CMIE data, Adani Agri Fresh accounted for sales of Rs 235 crore and income from financial services of Rs 127 crore in FY 2015. No export figures are given though. In FY20, sales grew to Rs 330.6 crore, financial services stood at Rs 1.5 crore. Once again, no foreign exchange figures are given. In FY21, sales dropped, possibly because of Covid, to Rs 167 crore, and financial services to Rs 2.2 crore. [219]

Volumes required

According to company sources, one reason is that this project is still in its infancy. These practices must be implemented across the country. That is when the money to be raked in will become large. The storage, processing and logistics facilities together could transform agriculture. It will benefit farmers, the companies involved and even the country.

That is when the numbers will grow, and exports will be something to be proud of. In that sense, Gautambhai is ahead of his times even today. He is just creating a blueprint, a proof-of-concept, and a demonstration model which India's policymakers can see, and can then replicate for other crops and regions. After all, agriculture involves over 50 per cent of India's population. That means 50 per cent of votes come from people in this sector. It is hence a core issue for politicians. Gautambhai knows that it is only a matter of time before best practices are introduced in this sector as well. It will then mean greater profits, and immense relevance to the economy.

It is in this context that the three farm laws made a weak and clumsy effort to promote such practices. Unfortunately, the government's political objectives in the three farm laws—now rescinded—caused a blowback. Much of the good that could have been possible was also pushed aside.[220] Yet, there is no denying that the way grain storage and distribution is being managed, and the end-to-end solution for applies are the ways to go for all agricultural produce.

India needs another Verghese-Kurien-like model which empowers the farmers, and also makes the country strong. Unfortunately, the government has not yet come to terms with an empowered farming community. Even NDDB's powers are sought to be whittled down.[221] That is truly unfortunate and regrettable.

12.4									
Adani–Wilmar—edible oil crushing and refining capacities									
Installed Capacity, Actual Production and Capacity Utilization									
Facility	Financial Year 2021			Financial Year 2020			Financial Year 2019		
	Installed Capacity (MT)	Processed Quantity (MT)	Capacity Utilization* (%)	Installed Capacity (MT)	Processed Quantity (MT)	Capacity Utilization* (%)	Installed Capacity (MT)	Processed Quantity (MT)	Capacity Utilizatio n* (%)
Crushing	2,227,500	549,705	25	2,160,000	436,935	20	2,107,500	483,351	23
Refining	5,471,760	3,012,453	55	4,889,360	2,483,970	51	4,128,600	2,516,211	61
Packaged foods	565,500	219,081	39	371,350	148,388	40	196,500	86,820	44
Oleochem	767,700	500,668	65	743,508	523,639	70	738,663	475,270	64

Notes : *Capacity utilization determined on the basis of the actual aggregate production of the relevant product during the relevant period, divided by the average aggregate installed capacity for such product for such period, as adjusted for scheduled and unscheduled downtime.

Source : Adani–Wilmar DRHP filed with SEBI

Thus, Adani's efforts of grain storage and apple harvesting and marketing remain excellent attempts to showcase what is possible.

Wilmar remains a winner

12.5	
ROCP market share	
as of March 31, 2021	
Brand	Mkt share
Fortune	11.50%
Raag	3.30%
King's	2.30%
Aadhar	0.70%
Bullet Lite	0.30%
Alpha	0.10%
Fryola	0.10%
Total	18.30%

Note: ROCP=Refined Oil in Consumer Packs. Much of the market in India is grabbed by the unorganized sector.

Sources: Nielsen Retail Index - MAT March 2021; Adani-Wilmar DRHP-2022

But the scaling up that was not possible with the grain and apple experiments witnessed a full bloom in Adani–Wilmar. It has emerged as the country's largest seller of packaged and branded edible oil, the second largest in wheat flour and the third largest in rice in India. Almost all of them are sold under the Fortune brand, which has by now become a household name.

All these are extremely competitive markets, and the changing capacity utilizations in all these businesses tells you how fluctuating fortunes can be.

The biggest successes are in edible oil. This is where it has become at least three times larger than its closest competitor. Much of this data has been captured from the filings the company made before SEBI.[222] They inform us about how formidable a player Adani–Wilmar has become in India. Excellent sourcing by the group partner Wilmar, good product launches, aggressive marketing have all combined to make this company achieve sales of Rs 29,254 crore in FY20 and Rs 37,077 crore in FY21. Income from financial services were Rs 91 crore and Rs 86 crore respectively; exports account for Rs 2,746.16 crore.[223]

The group has also been active in selling its products through the internet. As page 149 of Adani–Wilmar's DRHP mentions, 'Our online sales through e-commerce platforms increased by 53.30 per cent from ₹2,989.35 million for the financial year 2020 to ₹4,582.82 million for the financial year 2021.'

By now, Adani–Wilmar has expanded its crushing capacity to 22,27,500 tonnes a year, and its refining capacity to 54,71,760 TPA.[224] It has begun moving into value-added products by expanding its oleo chemicals unit in Mundra, developing more value-added soya products and further expanding into mustard, sunflower and groundnut edible oils. Some of this growth could come through plans overseas.

It already has one plant in Bangladesh where it sells edible oil under the brand 'Dhoop Chaon'. Soon it plans to sell pulses in India under the 'Jubilee' brand, basmati rice under the 'Pilaf' brand (which the company has already started) and more such products.

Add to this Adani Logistics grain storage capacities. With the expected wheat crisis emerging in the world, on account of the Ukraine–Russia war, expect this division to become even more active.

But the big business could come from trading in agro-products. 'Currently agro-volumes do not account for much,' says Chaturvedi. 'Most of this trading is confined to cotton and castor seed, and edible oil. The edible oil market is expected to continue growing. This is because India, which used to import 1.5 million tonnes of edible oil in 1996, currently imports significantly larger quantities. And this figure is expected to grow phenomenally as more Indian[s] move into the middle-income bracket and improve their eating habits.'

Gautambhai sees growth in both trading and the port. The group has started trading in soya meal and other agro-commodities like rice, wheat, edible oil and sorghum.

'What makes agro-trading attractive is that for a Rs 10,000 crore turnover, the working capital only Rs 1000 crore,' says Chaturvedi. 'With increasing demands on food products, this business can only grow. And the Adani Group hopes to become one of the foremost players in this field in India.'

For Gautambhai, life yawns out lazily ahead. He knows that time, in its way, will unfold new achievements, and surprises, in the years that lie ahead. As the global economy sinks into more uncertainties, challenges both in terms of global trade and finances are bound to move centre stage. And as food security assumes centre stage among global concerns, the Adani Group's role in agriculture may become all the more relevant and crucial.

Will this affect the global operations and plans of Gautambhai? Will India's ever-increasing needs guarantee more business for one of the most strategically located deepwater ports in the country? Will the changing paradigms in energy spell higher profits for

Adani's power plants? Or will there be newer opportunities. More on this can be found in the following chapters.

These are questions investors will continue to raise. But if the past is anything to go by, each challenge can bring a bigger opportunity.

At sixty, the challenges on hand are still as exciting as they were twenty years ago. Some may even add that life begins at sixty.

To conclude, the Adani Group has made impressive strides in agriculture-related businesses. While it has become the national leader in edible oil and packaged foods through Adani–Wilmar, it has yet to grow large in other segments. Undoubtedly, it is a leader when it comes to apples. But the business is still too small to be monetized, unless it is taken to other agri-produce as well.

This is where government policies will play a major role. For instance, it is possible to believe that had the Adani Group managed to take charge of Ruchi Soya (which eventually went to the Patanjali group), there would have been greater focus on persuading farmers to grow more soya and other edible oil seeds like mustard. That would have reduced India's dependence on imports on the one hand, but also made the farming community prosper on the other. Together, they could have spurred faster economic growth.

However, currently, like most edible oil marketing companies, much of the raw material comes through imports. That is an unwise policy as far as national interests go.[225]

Bigger plans with drones

But Gautambhai has bigger plans in the agriculture space. On 27 May 2022, Adani Enterprises announced that it had signed a definitive agreement to acquire a 50 per cent stake in General Aeronautics Private Limited.[226] This company provides commercial robotic drones and drone-based solutions for crop protection, crop health, precision farming and yield monitoring using artificial intelligence and analytics for the agricultural sector.

The official filing relating to this joint venture merely states, 'The Adani Defence Systems and Technologies Limited shall leverage its military drone and AI/ ML capabilities and work with General Aeronautics for providing end-to-end solutions for the domestic agricultural sector.' Adani Enterprises stated that the indicative time period to complete the acquisition is 31 July 2022. The drone market can be huge for India (and exports as well).[227]

This is an interesting development because the Adani Group already has other collaborations for unmanned aerial vehicles (UAVs)—more specifically with Israel's Elbit[228] and Sweden's Saab.[229] The Adani Group also has plans to step up its export of India-made drones.[230]

This only means that the Adani Group sees a drone market for agriculture that is distinct from that for military purposes. But some technologies may overlap—especially when it comes to reconnaissance and the analysis of images taken on the one hand, and the ability to stay in air for longer periods.

When linked with identification of patches which need to be treated with insecticides/fungicides, or patches that appear to be in need of moisture, there could be synergies with agrochemical companies, some of which could be located at Mundra itself.

When drones work in partnership with weather companies, they provide a better perspective of how much a crop could get damaged, which crops could be grown in specific terrains, and even planting of trees using drones.[231] Expect more plans to be announced about such collaborations, and even plans to take up afforestation in partnership with the government.

This collaboration confirms Adani's plans to continue playing for high stakes in agriculture. This could be one of the most important businesses to determine the political success or failure of any government on the one hand, and to become relevant to the most important political and consumption sector of the Indian economy on the other.

All these technologies will have to work with insurance companies—which must determine differentiated policies for different regions, and meet claims of crop damage. Drones would sharpen the assessment made by such companies. They would also be able to give the government a better picture of what crop yields could be like in the near future.

As might be expected, many of these moves will not be liked by existing middlemen who arrange to make higher claims for crop damage and even arrange to get these claims reimbursed to farmers for a fee. Such moves have hurt farmers and the agricultural insurance companies alike. You can be sure that there will be howls of protest as the Adani Group moves first into finding ways to review crops for identifying yield patterns, crop damage and then into crop-related insurance services as well. A collaboration with weather forecasting companies too cannot be ruled out.

Gautambhai knows that the most crucial activity of national relevance will have a lot more to do with agriculture and allied services. That is where his drone-related collaborations—for manufacture, services and even exports—will play a significant role.

And all these skills could soon find their way into finessing military capabilities as well.

Obviously, this will mean that the executive arm of the government will have to begin working harder to anticipate the kinds of policy changes India requires. Clearly, the job the government has before it is huge. It also needs to popularize the concepts promoted by the Adani Group like grain storage and distribution, fruit collection sorting, processing, packaging and sale, and developing an organized market for agro-produce. Work in these areas has just commenced.

13

The Taste of Goodness

There is a custom in Gujarat which promotes social responsibility, a bit more meaningfully than the corporate social responsibility (CSR) promoted by the government. It has been practised for centuries before any government thought of it, or even made it a law. It is one which requires people who have made money to share some of it with the community. The Gujaratis often do this by adopting a village, or a school or even a family.

This is not to say that other communities do not share the benefits of wealth with their own people. Far from it. Sikhs do this amazingly well through their gurdwaras and their langars—large community kitchens which feed the hungry in their areas. Like the Muslims, the Sikhs are required to give a percentage of their earnings to their religious trusts.

But no community has effectively kept their people away from begging the way the Sikhs (and the Parsis) have. You will seldom find a Sikh (or Parsi) beggar on the streets. The Hindus—by and large—do not have such an organized structure of donations or social welfare. But many individuals do contribute to religious trusts and to temples. In the southern part of this country, the wealthy patronize young artists to keep their cultural heritage alive.

Gujaratis are different in doing this through project adoption. The practice has spread to neighbouring Rajasthan as well. When people make money, they prefer not to give money. Instead, they prefer to adopt a cause. It could be a school. Or just a computer lab in a school. Or a library. They promise money for the cause if certain objectives are met. They even go and inspect the area periodically to ensure that the money is being spent wisely.

It is usually as casual visits, and inquiries like, 'What happened to ....?', 'Where is the calf that we saw six months ago?', 'Did the computers arrive? Can we look at them?' or 'Can we visit the tree we planted two years ago?'

If they find anything amiss, very gently they try to correct the situation. Of course, the implication behind such supervision is the threat that future funding may get curtailed. This deeply ingrained system actually nurtures responsible spending and community upliftment.

And among the Gujaratis, the Kutchis—the community to which the Adanis belong—have invested greatly in educational facilities, hostels for students (especially girls), hospitals and supporting people who can promote vocational education. The idea is to teach people to stand on their feet, and to become wealth generators.

For instance, in Mumbai, there is a group of Kutchis which regularly holds camps for poor people willing to learn how to become plumbers and electricians. The origins of this move could probably lie in the fact that most hardware and medical shops in Mumbai are run by Kutchis. At these camps, they bring trainers who teach the selected people how to become good plumbers or electricians and even give them a kit of tools at one-tenth the market cost (which could be the actual cost of the kit) to help them begin their lives anew as plumbers, carpenters or electricians.

Care, but not charity

Typical of the Kutchis, nothing is given away for free. If a book must be given to a poor student, he is urged to pay at least Re 1 towards the cost of the book. The rest of the money will be provided by the charitable trust. In many ways this is what the Sikhs also do: 'You will get food free of cost. But till it is being prepared, can you polish the shoes of the devotees to have come to the gurdwara?' or 'Can you sweep the floor of the dining hall before food is served for the hungry?'

13.1

Priti Adani at a school supported by her Foundation

Photograph sourced from Adani Foundation

Charity becomes more meaningful when the receiver also contributes towards earning the grant, and thus has his skin in the game. This is a crucial lesson that politicians forget. Subsidies without targets for improvement become a recipe for crippling an entire generation.[232]

These become the core values that communities hand down from generation to generation. The focus is always on how to make people stand on their own feet, to earn with dignity and not become parasites.

It is not surprising therefore to learn that the Adani Group also decided to focus on education and healthcare on a massive scale. Unlike many industrial groups who have focused on colleges or centres of higher education, the Adani Group prefers to begin with school education, especially for the underprivileged, keenly aware that this is the building block on which future lives are made.

The rare exception to this role is the tremendous support the Adani Foundation offers to the GAIMS[233] (or the recent move to set up a private university[234]). Or again, the recent move to go into healthcare as a socially relevant business. The group recently decided to invest[235] Rs 4 billion in the healthcare sector. Expect the group to take over a chain of hospitals or diagnostic centres or plan something that will be big on the national landscape.

13.2

Adani—The social impact a good foundation can make

	2015-16	2016-17	2017-18	2018-19
States	12	12	13	18
Sites	17	20	20	21
Locations	17	22	34	38
Villages/ Wards	1,470	1,470	1,470	2,250
Households	400,000	400,000	500,000	700,000
Beneficiaries				
Direct	438,975	781,722	986,762	1,906,637
Indirect	62,463	1,090,463	1,208,981	1,433,908
Beneficiaries by Thematic Area*				
Education	72,504	79,005	90,373	121,159
Community Health	299,292	391,166	399,301	518,160
Sustainable Livelihood	21,734	108,630	144,959	329,372
Community Infrastructure	21,094	59,466	170,655	379,262
Udaan#	23,335	23,418	49,325	50,353
SuPoshan#		117,072	125,442	487,502
ASDC$	1,016	2,965	6,707	20,829
Notes:				
*Vertical-wise break-up is of direct beneficiaries only.				
#Udaan, SuPoshan and ASDC—more details can be found at https://asiaconverge.com/2019/10/priti-adani-interview-goodness-at-the-grassroots/				
Source: Adani Foundation Annual Report - 2018-19				

The group has also moved into higher education. The group plans to set up a private university have been approved, by the Gujarat government after the state assembly unanimously passed a bill seeking establishment of the university under the Gujarat State Private Universities Act, 2009.[236]

Adani University will start offering programmes from Academic Year 2022 in Ahmedabad.

The group has also set up the Adani Institute of Infrastructure (AII)[237] This institute will focus on training people in building bridges, roadways, railway stations, ports, airports, power plants and even industrial parks. It will be synergistic with the cement, steel, copper and aluminium that the group will be making. With the group taking over road projects from other players—it recently took over the road assets from Macquarrie for Rs 3110 crore[238]— it will be imperative to teach young students more about building roads and bridges, managing cash flows, how to calculate traffic flow to determine toll charges and project cost payback.

Much of this education-related activity is carried out or supervised by the Adani Foundation,[239] which is headed by Pritiben Adani, wife of Gautambhai.[240]

The Foundation itself was established in 1996. And it began championing the cause of the deprived and underprivileged communities.

Today the Foundation's reach covers 3.67 million people in 2410 villages, across eighteen states in India.[241] It focuses on education, community health, sustainable livelihood development and rural infrastructure development along with special projects like *Swachgraha* (a clean house), *Saksham* (capable, competent, potentially viable), *SuPoshan* (nutrition, especially for expectant mothers-to-be) and *Udaan* (flight). Then there is also *Utthan* (upliftment, getting up).[242]

School education

At the heart of all these activities is the *vidyamandir* (the temple of learning) programme.[243] One of the first centres to be started was the Adani Vidya Mandir, Ahmedabad (AVMA). It was the first cost-free school in India to receive NABET Accreditation by the Quality Council of India, a benchmark in the field of education.

Adani Public School, Mundra, is now the first school in Kutch and Saurashtra region to receive the NABET Accreditation. Adani

Vidya Mandirs in Ahmedabad, Bhadreshwar and Sarguja are schools that provide cost-free education to about 2100 students annually. Adani Public School in Mundra, Adani Vidyalayas in Tirora and Kawai, Adani DAV Public School in Dhamra and Navchetan Vidyalaya in Hazira provide subsidized education to students across the country.

Adani Foundation also provides quality education to 1,00,000 children through 600 schools and *balwadis* (playschools for pre-kindergarten children). And this number is growing.

As Pritiben explains, 'School education would possibly be the one activity that I am most concerned about. Of course, this goes hand in hand with skill development, health, and sustainable livelihood development. But the key building block is school education. It is here that the child gets its values and its dreams.'

She adds, 'All our schools are of two types. Some have been set up by us where we adopt the CBSE (Central Board of Secondary Education) curriculum. Then there are schools which belong to state governments, and where we work with the respective state to upgrade the quality of education imparted. Those are usually schools which adopt the SSC (secondary school certificate) curriculum of the home state government. But English remains a compulsory subject even in these state-owned schools. Parents want their children to learn this language because they see it as an aspiration, a window to future growth. However, with both types of schools, our focus remains the same—the child.'

N.V. Vasani, advisor, CSR, Adani Foundation, says, 'Gautambhai once told me that he still remembers his father telling him while he was in fifth class, "Investing in education is investing in a generation." Which explains the group's investment in Adani Vidya Mandir where underprivileged students do not have to pay a single rupee to study.'

She says that in all the government schools that her Foundation adopts (usually in states where the Adani Group has some engagement in a commercial venture like mining or a production/processing plant), there is little attempt to change the teacher. 'The Foundation is aware that even governments have a process in place for the recruitment of teachers. What is missing is motivation, and a sense of accountability. In fact, the government pays quite well, in many cases higher than what the Foundation pays teachers in the schools it runs. But if you adopt a model that focusses on teacher improvement, constant monitoring, and motivation, you can actually transform the quality of their output.'

The Foundation has seen all-round improvement in educational standards even in the government schools adopted by the group. The proof of this is the clamour by parents to get their children admitted into schools managed by the Adani Foundation—even over private schools in those localities. The proof is also there in the outcomes—the children from these schools perform better, and turn out to be the brightest children in their respective communities. And they often feel privileged to teach and guide their peer groups who have not been lucky enough to get into an Adani-supported school.

Vocational approach

All the skill-development and personality-development programmes come under a flagship programme called *Udaan*. Its objective is to encourage young minds to develop an interest in all sorts of enterprises and to encourage them to dream big in life. In other words, it tries to teach children to think big—to fly—which is what Udaan means.

13.3			
Saksham—A profile			
Number of candidates skilled			
Year	Total	Male	Female
2016-17	2,577	1,002	1,575
2017-18	6,623	2,824	3,799
2018-19	20,829	7,910	12,919
Source: 108 stories of transformation – Adani Group			

One way of doing this is by taking students on exposure visits to the group's power plants and ports. This allows students to appreciate the scale of the group's various businesses, and to also begin to orient themselves to the type of role they might want to take up later in their own lives.

More than 2.76 lakh students, teachers and youth from more than 3500 schools and institutes have participated in this project over the past few years.

But Udaan itself has three other components.

One is *SuPoshan*. This is a programme targeted towards breaking the cycle of anaemia in women and malnourishment in children below the age of six years. *SuPoshan Sanginis* (women helper-friends) who are from the community ensure the right medical and social support. This encourages mothers to adopt healthy lifestyles. Today, the SuPoshan programme is spread across fourteen states in more than 3 lakh households.

13.4

GAIMS—A boon for Kutch

Particulars	Status before Registration of GAIMS (As on 26.05.2009)	Status at the time of Hospital Handover (As on 05.07.2013)	Current Status (As on 01.08.2019)
Out Patient Department Chambers	26	32	60
Radiology & Diagnosis Facilities	9	12	22
Operation Theatre	9	9	12
Labour Room	2	4	6
Patient Beds			
In Patient Department / General Ward	186	400	720
Special Wards	50	50	56
Pre-Post Operative Beds	3	10	27
Intensive Care Units	61	70	93
Grand Total	**300**	**530**	**896**

Note: The Adani Group refuses to take any management seats in the medical college attached to this hospital. It has surrendered all such privileges to the state government instead

Source : Adani Foudation

The second is *Saksham.* This is the Adani Skill Development Programme (ASDC) aimed at bridging the skill gap among the youth, to make them employable and thus contribute towards nation building. This programme partners with the government's National Skill Development Corporation (NSDC) and has trained over 30,000 youth (see chart 13.2 in this chapter). Some of its innovative courses include simulator-based crane operation, 3D printing, and welding through augmented reality. 'At the moment, we have over sixty-five Saksham centres operational across eight states in India offering skill training in forty-five trades. Significantly, a large number of the candidates are women,' says Pritiben.

The third part of the Udaan programme is focused on safety and environment. To make this programme relevant, the group has established an occupational health and safety (OH&S) policy and a safety manual. It has identified legal requirements as well—in operation and maintenance activities. Once again, the objective is to ensure the concerns that surround health and safety.

Pritiben adds, 'Our sites go beyond what is required statutorily. We aim to achieve continual improvement year after year. For this, we have won awards and accolades from many organisations and safety forums.'

Healthcare

Linked to all these are the medicare programmes the Adani Group runs. It began with a mobile health van which did the rounds of Mundra and Bhuj regions. Bhuj has been a major focus for the Foundation ever since the earthquake which devastated this region in 2001. Today these medical health care units (MHCUs) can be found in Mundra and Dahej in Gujarat, Tirora in Maharashtra, Kawai in Rajasthan, Surguja and Rajgarh in Chhattisgarh, Dhamra in Odisha, Udupi in Karnataka, Gooda in Jharkhand, and Shimla in Himachal Pradesh. In many places, these mobile units were supplemented and replaced with primary healthcare centres. In Himachal Pradesh, where a major programme of social transformation is under way among apple growers, all healthcare facilities are free of cost.

In 2009, the group got actively involved with GAIMS (Gujarat Adani Institute of Medical Sciences) in Bhuj, which is the first medical college based on PPP principles. The Union government set it up after the Bhuj earthquake devastated countless lives in that region. The hospital was registered in 2009, and was handed over to the group in July 2013.

13.5

The GAIMS Hospital

Picture sourced from the GAIMS website

Spread over 23 acres of land, it offers MBBS and PG courses to aspiring medical professionals. It has over 900 beds which offers free of cost medicare to people in the region. And what many people do not know, because it is seldom advertised, is that the Adani Group has foregone the management quota from day one and handed it over to the Government of Gujarat. This is often a lucrative source of (illegal) money for many managements of such private medical colleges. It also lends clout to the management which can dole out seats to children of powerful people. Moreover, there are no reservations for students from Kutch district despite a heavy demand for such a privilege.

It is possible that as the Healthcare Business division is set up, these activities will be streamlined as charitable activities under the new venture to give it and the professionals who work on such programmes a greater sense of purpose and corporate identity. This sector will soon be making headlines.

Dr Malay Mahadevia asks, 'Despite the challenges, why did the group decide to take up the challenge? The chairman's thoughts were clear from the beginning. Kutch is our *Karma Bhoomi* and we wanted to make life-defining contributions towards giving back to its people.'

In May 2022, the Adani Group announced its intention to get into healthcare as a business activity.[244] Adani Enterprises Limited incorporated a fully owned subsidary—Adani Health Ventures Limited (AHVL). This entity will focus on the business of healthcare-related activities. It would also focus on related activities like setting up, running and administrating medical and diagnostic facilities, health aids, health tech-based facilities and research centres. The group has not yet announced the date from which this business activity will become operational.

There are countless other schemes that the group has come out with—for fisherfolk, for tribals and for the marginalized. But of all of these, the one which will matter most for the future of India will be the work the Adani Group has been doing in school education. This is a sector the government has neglected.[245]

Medicare and school education is what will eventually change India much more meaningfully than many other measures. That will remain the most cherished taste of goodness.

14

The Odyssey Continues

As Gautambhai's family celebrates his sixtieth birthday, the one thought that must be there on everyone's mind is 'sustainability'.

The sustainability of business activities, the sustainability of the group, and equally important, the sustainability of some of these processes—generation after generation.

Looking back, it is quite evident that the man has achieved much—almost unparalleled in India's history. This book is just one small effort to capture the vision, the pace and the journey of this incredible man. No other industry group in living memory (in India at least) has witnessed such a stupendous growth in just twenty years:

- forty-two times in sales
- forty-two times in total income
- 252 times in PBIDTA
- 267 times in capital employed
- The one area where the group has not done very well is in exports which grew only two times over these two decades.[246]

Many of the plans have yet to run their course, and there are indications that the group may more than double in size and operations within the next decade. As mentioned earlier in this book, there is the Adani–POSCO project that could be another game-changer. Then there is the cement business. Healthcare is another big opportunity. And a defence project which could actually turn out to be as big as the rest of the group put together. Then there are plans to build and take charge of more ports—in West Bengal, Sri Lanka, and possibly in the US or the EU. And who knows, Sittwe Port may just fall into the group's hands as the dust begins to settle.

MRO is big business

But the fastest growth could come from Adani's defence projects and from the MRO[247] businesses. An indication of the size of the MRO business can be found from some of the estimates available from Thailand's plans. Quite recently, the group was reported to be considering investing in the Mumbai-based Air Works Group to bolster its civil aviation portfolio.[248]

The Air Works Group is India's largest independent aircraft MRO organization. It services civil aviation companies like IndiGo, Vistara and GoAir among other international airlines like Etihad, FlyDubai, Lufthansa, Turkish Atlantics and Virgin Atlantic. If that happens, it could mean that the government has other plans for AI-SATS, the Air India subsidiary which was also a noticeably big player in the MRO space, but which was not allowed to expand its operations.[249] There is no mention about this subsidiary being sold to the Tata Group along with Air India. This enterprise has the widest range of collaborations with Boeing and Airbus, partly because it was the national carrier, till the airline business was sold to the Tata Group. Second, it also had the widest range of carriers, requiring it to sign such agreements with both the original manufacturers and their MRO partners. It has an immense as yet undiscovered potential.[250]

It may be recalled that the Indian government has, for years, been looking this gift horse in the mouth.[251] The flawed vision of the government has often helped entrepreneurs find business opportunities in such areas. It will be interesting to see how Gautambhai exploits such opportunities. In the MRO space, the

Adani Group could become the nerve centre for all aircraft in Southeast Asia. Access to a private runway very close to the sea could be a benefit not many players have in India.

Defence plans

In the defence space, the opportunities are unbelievable, especially with the government now willing to allow private enterprise to play a role. So, as the future beckons, what are the new goal posts?

Without a doubt, the group is likely to continue its blistering rate of growth. The group has identified three phases of growth.[252] Phase 1 involved trading, ports, and logistics. Phase 2 was concerned with energy and gas utility. Phase 3 according to the group's management will be about transformational opportunities to provide the quantum leap.

This includes working on opportunities created by the seven airports in India which the Adani Group has won through open tenders.

It includes working on the new digital economy and the business opportunities that beckon almost every entrepreneur in the country.

And finally, it also includes water treatment and desalination projects. The last is something that the author is not comfortable with because India does not lack water supply or sources. The country has misused and even abused water. Desalination could only push up costs, and make the urgent need for remedies appear less serious.[253] It may be very good business. But it runs contrary to common sense, or even ethics. Unless, of course, the Adani Group focuses only on the Kutch, Saurashtra and Rajasthan regions where desalination could be justified.

14.1		
Some major defence deals for gthe Adani group		
Identified parners	Deal Size	Details
SAAB of Sweden	$20 billion	https://www.adanidefence.com/newsroom/media-release/Saab-and-Adani-announce-collaboration-plan-for-Aerospace-and-Defence-in-India https://eurasiantimes.com/will-saab-and-adani-defence-win-the-20-billion-Indian-fighter-jet-contract/
Elbit of Israel		https://www.adanidefence.com/businesses/platforms https://elplaw.in/leadership/india-israel-strategic-collaborations-in-the-defence-industry/ https://www.adanidefence.com/newsroom/media-release
Snam of Iti		https://www.indiaglobalbusiness.com/news-in-brief/adani-group-announces-strategic-collaboration-with-italy-based-snam
Airbus	$6.3 bn	https://www.adanidefence.com/newsroom/media-release/Airbus-signs-aircraft-services-MoU-with-Adani-Defence-and-Aerospace
Indamner	MRO business	https://www.indamer.com/ and https://stage.adanidefence.com/MRO
Hindustan Shipyard	Rs.45,000 crore	https://defencewatch.in/hindustan-shipyard-and-adani-defence-to-join-hands-for-rs-45000-cr-submarine-project/

The list given out above does not include all defence deals. But this is where the biggest opportunity and dangers can be found.

The opportunities are obvious.

As a media report points out,[254] between 2016–20, India spent, 'US$331.8 billion on military imports, or 2.6 per cent of gross domestic product (GDP). Although China spent over three times more than India, that accounted for a lower share of its GDP at 1.7 per cent on the military.'

Clearly, India needs to reduce its import bill. A sensible way would be to co-opt the private sector, which could sell to the country, subject to meeting norms, but also export of such defence items, maybe subject (once again) to clearances from the Indian government and the government of the technology partner. India needs to climb up the value chain by moving away from its role of importer of defence equipment to first producing it domestically, and then also exporting such military hardware and other related services.

There will be technologies where the technology supplier or the country the manufacturer is headquartered in, has veto rights. Remember the deal Israel signed with China regarding the purchase of AWACs almost a decade ago. The orders were placed by the Chinese. Money was exchanged. The planes were assembled, and were about to take off. That is when the US cast its veto. The order had to be scrapped, and Israel had to pay damages to China.

Second, India's defence requirements are likely to keep growing. And after the Ukraine–Russia–NATO–USA skirmish, the demand for weaponry will increase. So will the need for R&D in these areas. Then there is the issue of technology transfer. Except for Russia and Israel (and recently even France), technology transfer in defence deals has been scant. Will the private sector be able to negotiate better? That is an opportunity with huge benefits for India.

However, as of now, India's export of arms is pathetically small in the global market. It accounted for barely 0.22 per cent market share. Can India increase this share?

All these pose huge opportunities for India's defence and this sector offers an extremely attractive business proposition. Not surprisingly, almost all major corporates have pitched in. This includes the Tatas, Reliance, Mahindra, Adani, Kalyani Rafael Advanced Systems, Larsen and Toubro, Ashok Leyland and Alpha Design Technologies Pvt Ltd among countless others.[255]

On its part, the Adani Group has chalked out extremely ambitious plans, with some of the best names in the world (see chart 14.1).

The Adani Group has already made its first moves towards defence exports.[256] It knows that the Indian market for drones is large, and that the export potential is also immense.[257] It is only too painfully aware of the late awakening of the country in exploiting the huge potential drones have—from defence application to agriculture and insurance businesses as well.[258] This is another of Adani's businesses that will be watched very closely.

14.2
Adani group's select list of small arms
that are sought to be produced in India
➤ Light Machine Guns -- NEGEV 5.56 x 45mm | 7.62 x 51mm
➤ Carbine / Assault Rifles -- ACE 5.56 x 45mm | 7.62 x 39mm | 7.62 x 51mm
➤ Assault Rifles / Carbines / SMGs -- TAVOR X-95 5.56 x 45mm | 9 x 19mm
➤ Pistols -- MASADA 9X19mm
➤ Sub Machine Gun -- UZI PRO 9 x 19mm
➤ Assault Rifle -- TAVOR 5.56 x 45mm
➤ Sniper Rifle -- GALIL SNIPER 7.62 x 51mm
➤ Two-stage trigger, Sniper Rifle -- DAN .338 | 0.338 Bolt Action
➤ Drones foragriculture through a 50 per cent equity stake in agricultural drone startup General Aeronautics
Sources : Adani group websites and media reports

It also wants to get into small arms manufacture[259] in collaboration with Israel's IWI.[260] The Adani Group (through Adani Land Defence Systems and Technologies Ltd) has purchased a 51 per cent stake in the Gwalior-based arms manufacturing business PLR Systems. The remaining 49 per cent is owned by Israeli Defence company IWI.[261] The list of small arms sought to be produced in India is breath-taking (please refer to chart 14.2).

It has also established, at Mundra, an unmanned aerial vehicle complex in Adani Aerospace Park to build complex aero structures. It specializes in large complex aerostructures and components for the world's leading defence contractors, Indian DPSUs and the DRDO.[262] It hopes to produce the following over there:

- Hermes 900
- Ailerons
- Missile components
- Nacelles (a streamlined body housing a machine, fuel or equipment on an aircraft)

Adani Defence and Aerospace has also announced that it has tied up with Punj Lloyd and US-based Rave Gears to manufacture high-precision aerospace gears.[263] Alpha Design Technologies will provide Adani Defence and Aerospace with a strong tier-1 capability. This is in addition to the list given in chart 14.1.

Ask defence experts about these plans. They will tell you that along with the MRO and other businesses outlined in the charts, these activities of the Adani Group alone should be larger than all the other companies in the group put together. This could happen over the next decade. One of the biggest benefits the Adani Group enjoys is access to a well-constructed private airstrip close to the sea. Defence, aircraft building and MRO projects will love this facility.

Arms is big business. It is one of the two businesses that make the US the global leader—the other one is oil and gas.

Risks galore

But this will come with huge attendant risks.

The bigger one becomes; the more one is compelled to be aligned inextricably with the party in power. The biggest customer will always be the government. There is always the danger of such businesses slipping into what the world calls the military-industrial complex.

Export controls will ensure that even exports will require government clearance (in addition to clearance from the technology partner). Whenever government permissions are required, there is always the danger of reviving the quota raj which crippled the textile sector. The revival of the textile sector in India began only after the quota system was abolished.[264]

This could result in huge compromises, which could become stickier with each passing election. This risk would apply to all private defence players, not just the Adani Group. Since this is a nascent business opportunity for the Indian corporate sector, it will be interesting to watch how both the private sector and the government play their respective roles.

Ideally, the government should lay down some ground rules for this type of business, and even create a separate audit arm along the lines of the Comptroller Auditor General (CAG). Unless strong institutions are created, the military-industrial complex could actually distort this entire sector.

Linked to this is another factor. Till now, all whistleblowing relating to payoffs in defence deals has taken place overseas. No exposure has come from India. Even in the case of the huge number of aeroplanes that Air India acquired, details of the ministry's involvement came out because of a Canadian court. Ditto with Bofors and with the Westland deal.

14.3

The Journey towards sustainability

2000	2010	2015	2020	2025
Coal & Commodity Trading	Thermal Power and Ports	Integration into logistics and transport	- Diversification into 'renewables' and 'distribution' - Technology focus	- Sustainable Infra Asset Owner - Consumer focus

Source : The Adani group profile – Growth with Goodness, February 2022

Now with business and procurement being controlled entirely by Indian entities in India, there is no scope for foreign agencies to know anything about the nature of payoffs. That could become a quagmire. Linked to this is another provision in Indian accounting laws which allows a company not to disclose too many details if the business is related to defence. That provision could make politicians love private defence enterprises.

The need for a strong institutional framework governing all such aberrations needs to be set up urgently.

Beyond defence

The other area that Gautambhai has chalked out for himself is the digital space. As the group's website[265] points out,

- Complete ownership of large land parcels across the country
- Project management capabilities and resources availability
- End-to-end power value chain (generation, transmission and distribution)
- Fibre connectivity and strong network connectivity

- Renewable power generation to ensure sustainability
- As a part of our initial plan, we intend to build data centres in NCR, Mumbai, Chennai and Hyderabad

The right collaborations too are being put into place.

There is the tie-up with EdgeConneX to form AdaniConneX to provide a full range of data centre solutions across India from Hyperscale Campuses to Hyperlocal Edge facilities leveraging EdgeConneX's global expertise. This enterprise will provide high-quality, sustainable data centre solutions, leveraging Adani's expertise in full-stack energy management, renewable power, real estate and experience in managing large infrastructure projects.[266]

Then there is the multi-year partnership with Google Cloud[267] to modernize Adani's IT operations for future scale and group-wide innovation. The strategic collaboration will tap each organization's expertise across infrastructure, technology and industry solutions to modernize the Adani Group's IT operations.

It is in this context that the Adani Group's decision to apply for a limited amount of 5G spectrum begins to assume immense strategic significance. It wants the bandwidth for its captive networks, not to cater to a highly competitive consumer market. It may be recalled that in August 2022, the group acquired the right to use 400 MHz of spectrum in the 26 GHz millimetre wave band. ADNL secured this spectrum for twenty years in the first-ever 5G spectrum auction conducted by the Government of India's Telecommunications Department.[268]

According to the company, this is expected to help create a unified digital platform that will accelerate the pace and scale of the Adani Group's digitization of its core infrastructure, primary industry and B2C business portfolio. The acceleration of digital enablement will lead to material long-term improvement in the rate of return on assets. Acquiring 400 MHz of spectrum is the group's first step in integrating its digital infrastructure portfolio, which includes Data Centres, Terrestrial Fibre and Submarine Cables, Industrial Cloud, AI Innovation Labs, Cybersecurity and SuperApps.

The data business opportunity could be immense. But once again, in the absence of a regulator (despite promises, the government has yet to announce a regulator for the digital space, especially for ecommerce), this could become another Wild West. Without a regulator and without predictability and accountability, caprice could make the digital journey quite bumpy. Already, there are charges of regulatory capture being bandied around. It could be a minefield.

Do bear in mind that even the NPCI[269] has cleverly drafted a clause which clearly states that it overwrites[270] older accounts (no older versions retained), and that it does not keep logs of earlier transactions. One would have thought that only illegal casinos and hawala operators did not keep logs of transactions. To have a government-backed NPCI doing this is extremely worrisome.[271]

Moreover, India operates in the digital space and is attempting to make Aadhaar its key identification document. The entire Aadhaar scheme is riddled with flaws, and there are reports of a huge duplication in Aadhaar numbers and identities.[272] Even the CAG audit has raised red flags about the Aadhaar operation.[273]

Gautambhai will have to take additional care not to allow such inconsistencies, pressures and temptations to tarnish the group's stated values: courage, commitment and trust.

Another activity that has got the media world interested is the group's intent to get into the media business.[274] Adani Enterprises has already created a media company AMG Media Networks, which wants to be in the business of 'publishing, advertising, broadcasting, distribution of content over different types of media networks'. In March 2022, Adani Media Ventures Ltd agreed to buy a stake in Quintillion Business Media Pvt., according to a statement. Quintillion was an Indian partner of Bloomberg LP, the parent of Bloomberg News. But the Quintillion investment is too meagre to demand Gautambhai's attention. So, does he have bigger plans? One does not know at this moment.

Two speeches and an article

Three talks that Gautambhai delivered tell you a little more about his plans.

The first was on 11 November 2021 at a Bloomberg Forum.[275] The second was an earlier talk on 20 September 2021 at a JP Morgan forum.[276] The third was an article that Gautambhai wrote on his LinkedIn blog.[277]

It was in the JP Morgan speech that Gautam Adani stated the following:

'In fact, my belief has only grown stronger and our learnings from this crisis will make both, India, and the Adani Group more resilient, and more prepared to face the future with confidence.

'I am committed to the viewpoint that—*you cannot build long-term value on short-term thinking.* I do recognize that this may not be in alignment with the objectives of a broad risk-driven segment of the investment community.

14.4		
The Adani Group today		
Workforce 23,000+	Renewable Power 5.4 GW*	Transmission 13027 CKT KM
Cargo Handled across Ports 247 MMT	Solar Manufacturing 1.5 GW	Edible Oil 19.3% Market Share
City Gas Distribution 515 MMSCM	Agri Fresh 22000 MT	NBFC 32,500 Customers
Thermal Power Generation 12.41 GW (excluding ATLS 500 MW)	Realty 1.2 MN. SQ. M	Integrated Resources Management 63 MMT
Mining Services 17.5 MMT	Passengers Handled at Airports 3.5 MN. SQ. M	

Notes : These figures relate to FY21. Since then, he has acquired companies, notably, the Holcim-ACC cement facilities in India. That makes him the second largest cement producer in India. Expect these numbers to change radically year after year, because the pace of change has just moved into high gear. The best indicator of the size of the group would be the Bloomberg Billionaires Index, referred to earlier.
Source : The Adani Group profile – Growth with Goodness, February 2022

'If the crisis in 2001 was the bursting of the dot-com bubble, and in 2007 the bursting of the housing bubble, and if in 2020 the crisis was the pandemic, we now have to collectively confront and manage the crisis of climate change.'

'Climate change is indeed extremely important, and needs to be looked at carefully. But "it is impractical to suggest alternatives that the developing world does not have, cannot use and cannot afford. When electricity accounts for about 30 per cent and transportation 29 per cent of the carbon footprint compared to agriculture, which accounts for just 10 per cent of all emissions, it is a paradox. The prosperous man in the brightly lit home with more than one car in his driveway cannot insist that the poor farmer give up his only cow and keep his house dark to save the earth from greenhouse gas emissions. There has to be a more equitable way.'

In a way, he was echoing one of the most strident criticisms against the COP-26 resolutions[278]—that many of the resolutions were a rich man's desire, not a common man's need.

A similar dissatisfaction with the world is evident in the blog that Gautambhai authored, 'As we go through this process there will be pushbacks—and we will run into controversies in other parts of the world. So be it.

'Many will try to stop us building semiconductor plants. Many will dissuade us from investing a larger portion of our GDP in defence. Our principles will come under criticism.

'What we must keep in mind is that many of those who set targets for emissions reductions for India are also those that shy away from acknowledging the disproportionate responsibility borne by a small number of developed countries for the climate crisis. In other words, it is far easier to talk than to walk the talk . . . Instead, let's seek a more stable world order built around countries that are self-confident, self-reliant, and willing to speak to each other in terms of mutual respect rather than coercion and condescension. This is the paradox we must solve!'

Clearly, Gautambhai is aware of the economic opportunities that are arising out of the global effort to combat climate change.

'I believe these opportunities will equate to trillions of dollars over the next two decades, as technologies evolve rapidly. These include next generation high efficiency solar panels, new materials that make massive offshore wind turbines affordable, mainstreaming of carbon capture technologies, various fit-for-purpose battery technologies, smarter and distributed grids, green hydrogen technologies, electric vehicles, plant-based meats and much more.

'I also believe that the advances in digital technologies and machine learning will further stimulate innovation across every single one of these technologies and create their own markets. The sheer power of the economies and policies that will back these developments can compress the timescale required to achieve global energy transition goals. No doubt, several existing industries will be disrupted, and made redundant, but at the same time new industries will be created.

'There is also a real possibility that the marginal price of green power will drop steeply in the future as technologies mature and economies of scale kick in. This will enable the next big manufacturing boom which, in turn, will create new jobs. This is what we should all collectively be aiming for to create an equitable tomorrow.'

Airports

14.5		
Adani airports		
A new opportunity of touching people's lives		
Touching 200 million travellers and non-travellers		
7 airports in a country which needs 200 additional airports		
Benchmarking safe, secure, efficient air-hubs. The first in India		
	Mumbai	
Ahmedabad		Lucknow
Thiruvananthapuram		Mangaluru
Guwahati		Jaipur
Notes : *Offers business opportunities for duty-free shopping, advertising and sponsorships, ground transportation, general aviation, cargo and fuel farm*		
Source : https://adaniairports.com/		

'Today, we are already the world's largest solar power player when we account for our generating, under construction and contracted projects. We have done this in just two years and our Renewables Portfolio has reached our initial target of 25 GW a full four years ahead of schedule. This puts us well on track to be the world's largest renewable power generating company by 2030. This also opens up several new pathways for us including setting us up to be one of the largest green hydrogen producers in the world. Our actions clearly indicate that we are putting our money where our mouth is:

- Over 75 per cent of our planned capex until 2025 will be in green technologies.
- Today, of our EBITDA from utilities, 43 per cent is already from the green business.
- We will triple our renewable power generation capacity over the next four years—from 21 per cent now to a high of 63 per cent. No company is building at this scale.
- Over the next ten years, we will invest over $20 billion [*later raised to $70 billion*[279]] across renewable energy generation, component manufacturing, transmission & distribution.
- We will be the first port business that is ahead of its target to get to net zero by 2025. This business has committed to 1.5-degree pathway through SBTi [science-based target setting].
- We will be the first Indian data centre company that will power all its data centres with renewable energy by 2030.'

He reminded the audience that 'we are now India's largest private sector power producer, largest private port operator, largest private airport operator, largest private consumer gas and electric utility business, largest private electric transmission company and largest infrastructure developer in renewables'.

Gautambhai then goes on to talk about two of their newest and most exciting businesses. The airports business and the Adani Digital businesses.

'The Adani Group's plans for airport-centred growth include metropolitan developments that span entertainment facilities, e-commerce and logistics capabilities, aviation dependent industries, smart city developments, and other innovative business concepts. The best example is our Mumbai airport. Mumbai is on its way to being one of the top five global metropolitan centres of the twenty-first century.

'Also, with India's passenger traffic expected to grow five-fold, our nation needs 200 additional airports to handle 1 billion domestic and international passengers, most of whom will be using an airport, or a route connected to Mumbai. We will not only scale the existing airport but also operationalize the Navi Mumbai International Airport by 2024. This airport will handle 80 million additional passengers. This coincides well with India becoming the world's 3rd largest aviation market. We see airports as catalysts for development and believe that the economic value created by India's cities will be maximized around airports.

'With regards to the Digital business, our upcoming new businesses will include all of our digital-related ventures that now span Data Centres, Industrial Clouds, and the Adani Digital Labs. Earlier this year we established Adani Digital Labs as a part of Adani Enterprises to be able to provide a unified experience to all our end consumers. Today, our end consumer base is growing at 15 per cent. If we can onboard every consumer that is an Adani Consumer on our digital platform, we will potentially have over a billion consumers by 2030. I have very little doubt that every one of our own B2C businesses will be engagements driven on mobile platforms. Therefore, the consumer insights we will obtain through a unified platform will set us on the path to building our own SuperApp platform.'

In the Bloomberg talk[280] he adds a bit more.

'We build infrastructure that enables "flow". And all that flows in this world will need to be clean and green—be it the flow of energy, the flow of goods, the flow of people or the flow of data. Over the past years, we established ourselves in all these flows through our electricity-related businesses, ports and logistics businesses, airport and transport businesses and data-centre-related businesses.

'At Adani, we are doing all we can to make renewables a viable, affordable alternative to fossil fuels. Since our declaration of intent at Davos 2020, we have proven our seriousness by becoming the world's largest solar power developer in a period of just thirty months. By 2030, we expect to be the world's largest renewable energy company without any caveat—and we have committed $70 billion over the next decade to make this happen. There is no other company that has yet made so large a bet on developing its sustainability infrastructure.

'The global consensus appears to be that green hydrogen will be a boon to infrastructure. It is a miracle fuel AND a miracle feedstock. Given India's exponential growth in renewables, producing green hydrogen cheaply could transform India into a net exporter of green energy.

'To that end, the Adani Group is also making major investments in digital infrastructure. Data centres, cloud computing and artificial intelligence vastly improve our access to information, real-time data, and energy efficiency. Science today needs massive computing capabilities and computing capabilities need cloud-based data centers and data centers consume enormous quantities of energy. We believe that India's exponential growth in renewables capacity and our ability to eventually produce clean electricity will make us the greenest choice to warehouse not just India's but perhaps much of the world's data—and aligned with the 'one sun, one world, one grid' principle recently outlined at COP-26.'

In conclusion

The plans that Gautambhai has chalked out for his group are truly breathtaking. At the time when the book is going out to print, not a week passes by without some announcement of something new being done by the Adani Group. The pace he keeps is astonishing. Even though he is sixty years now, he works on several projects, several concepts and strategies constantly. It makes everyone sit up, and work at the tempo he has set for the group.

But the pitfalls are many. Unlike the past, in which the peaks were smaller, and the pitfalls too less dangerous, these are bigger games. But by now Gautambhai is not the small player any more. He is better at assessing risks. And mitigating them.

At present, the immediate focus will be on projects that can generate money quicky—defence and agriculture.

Hydrogen generation[281] and the need to accelerate exports will also be followed up on with the same sense of urgency. Green power means a lot to Gautambhai and has become the Holy Grail for the entire country, if not the world.

It is possible that a lot of attention will be paid to the Adani POSCO venture that was mentioned in the first chapter. This project promises a huge interplay between exports, infrastructure solar and hydrogen.

His decision to take up 50 per cent of the equity in the new venture with General Aeronautics[282] reconfirms his commitment to agriculture, which could be a huge business opportunity and immensely relevant to India.

The defence plans are brilliant. Huge cash, immense national relevance. But frightening possibilities of being compromised—on ethics, on quality and on reputation. These risks apply to all the industrialists who have thrown their hats in the defence ring. But the stakes for Gautambhai will be greater.

Gautambhai has done amazingly well for himself, for his people and for his country. The future is more daunting, even exciting, than ever before. His luck and his intuition have often supported his reputation. He has truly transformed India. And he is determined to transform it further.

Notes

Chapter 1: The Adani Timeline

1   Compiled with the help of the Adani Group's research teams.

2   'Adani Portfolio Companies complete INR 15,400 Cr primary equity transaction with IHC,' *AsiaConverge*, 17 May 2022, https://asiaconverge. com/2022/05/adani-portfolio-companies-get-2bn- investment-rom-ihc/.

3   'ATL to acquire ESSAR's Mahan-Sipat transmission project,' *AsiaConverge*, 3 June 2022, https://asiaconverge.com/2022/06/atl-to-acquire-essars-mahan-sipat- transmission-project/.

4   'Adani: Financial closure of Kutch Copper Limited project,' *AsiaConverge*, 17 August 2022, https://asiaconverge.com/2022/08/adani-financial-closure-of-kutch-copper- limited-project/.

5   'Adani Total Gas Q1 FY23 Results,' *AsiaConverge*, 4 August 2022, https:// asiaconverge.com/2022/08/adani-total-gas-q1-fy23-results/.

Chapter 2: Gautam Adani: The Man Who Changed India

6   Check the site for more information: https://www.dvvmedia.com/en/. The owners of this publishing group have changed hands since then.

7   SEBI. 'Mundra Port and Special Economic Zones,' https://www.sebi.gov. in/filings/public-issues/nov-2007/mundra-port-and- special-economic-zone-limited_9514.html

8   *Bhai* means 'brother'. In Gujarat, it is used after a man's name, which denotes both informality and respect. Family members and very close friends usually use the term. Girls/women have the tag 'ben', which means sister, after their names in the same way.

9   https://asiaconverge.com/2007/10/gautam-adani-man-change-india/

10   Since then, the organizational structure has altered. The last couple of years have seen Gautambhai getting more involved in expanding his industrial

base and becoming more relevant to national objectives. Consequently, few meetings have been possible with the Adani Group post 2019. That is why, a great deal of reliance has been placed on past interviews for Gautambhai's early life. Post 2014, notes and replies from his office and publicly available information have allowed me to bring in additional details.

11   Check Adani–Wilmar website for more information: https://www.adaniwilmar.com/.
Technopark Advisors Pvt Ltd, 'Report on The Indian Packaged Food Industry,' (1 November 2021): 19, https://www.adaniwilmar.com/home/-/media/Project/Wilmar/Investors/Industry%20Report%20-%20Indian%20Packaged%20Food%20-%20compressed.
'Adani–Wilmar Q3 FY-22 results presentation,' https://www.adaniwilmar.com/-/media/Project/Wilmar/Investors/Quarterly per cent20Presentation/AWL per cent20Q per cent203 per cent20Presentation- per cent202021-22.

12   'Adani Highest Bidder for West Bengal's deep sea port,' *rediff.com.* 25 March 2022, https://www.rediff.com/business/report/adani-highest-bidder-for-west-bengals-tajpur-deep-sea-port/20220325.htm.

13   'Adani Group commits to invest Rs 10,000 cr in West Bengal ober the next decade.' *Business Standard*, 20 April 2022, https://www.business-standard.com/article/companies/adani-group-commits- to-invest-rs-10-000-cr-in-bengal-over-next-decade-122042000737_1.html.

14   'POSCO and Adani sign $5 million pact to set up green steel mill in Gujrat,' *Indian Express,* 14 January 2022, https://www.newindianexpress.com/business/2022/jan/14/posco-and-adani- sign-5-million-pact-to-set-up-green-steel-mill-in-gujarat-2406722.html.

15   Refer to the chapter 'An Australian Saga'.

16   Refer to the chapter 'Aligned with National Interests'.

17   'POSCO and Adani sign an MoU for Integrated Steel Mill,' https://www.adani.com/Newsroom/Media-Release/POSCO-and-Adani-sign- MoU-for-Integrated-Steel-Mill.

18   Environmental Justice Atlas, 'POSCO steel plant in Odisha, India,' https://ejatlas.org/conflict/posco-odisha-india.

19   POSCO Maharashtra, http://www.poscomaharashtra.com/in/product/product1.jsp.

20   Aditi Shah and Rajendra Jhadav, 'POSCO's steel plant in India faces disruption, hampering the auto supply chain,' *Nasdaq*, March 2021, https://www.nasdaq.com/articles/exclusive-poscos-steel-plant-in-india-faces-disruption-hampering-auto-supply-chain-2021-03.

21   'Jindal Steel and Power to set-up the largest greenest steel plant in Odisha,' *Business World.* 2 April 2022, https://www.businessworld.in/article/

Jindal-Steel-And-Power-To-Set-Up- Largest-Greenest-Steel-Plant-In-Odisha/02-04-2022-424381/.

22   POSCO newsroom, https://newsroom.posco.com/en/posco-samsung-ct-pif-promote-green- hydrogen-production-project/

23   Arvind Subramanian, 32:15, https://youtu.be/ XVXm57tD7tQ

24   Arjun Srinivas, 'The landscape of India's oligopoly, in five charts,' *Mint*, 19 May 2022, https://www.livemint.com/companies/news/the-landscape-of-india-s-cement- oligopoly-in-five-charts-11652871713817.html.

25   R.N. Bhaskar, 'Why its necessary to develop business and transport along India's coastline,' *Money Control*, 17 August 2017, http://www.moneycontrol.com/news/business/economy/why-its-necessary-to- develop-business-and-transport-along-indias-coastline-2362359.html.

26   Press release issued by the Adani Group on 13 January 2022.

27   APSEZ presentation, p. 13, https://www.adaniports.com/-/media/ Project/Ports/Investor/Investor-Downloads/Investors-Presentation/APSEZ---SRCPL-Presentation_Final.pdf

28   Refer to the chapter 'March of the DNA'.

29   'The best advice I ever got,' *Business Today*, 25 December 2008, https://www.businesstoday.in/magazine/cover-story/story/the-best-advice-i- ever-got-127768-2008-12-25.

30   'Two accused of abducting Gautam Adani 20 years ago go acquitted,' *Indian Express*, https://indianexpress.com/article/cities/ahmedabad/two-accused-of-abducting-gautam-adani-20-years-ago-acquitted-5473592/.

31   Ibid.

32   https://youtu.be/LAi9haE4FRY.

33   'When India's fifth richest man survived a kidnapping and terrorist attack,' *Times Now*, 14 June 2020, https://www.timesnownews.com/business-economy/companies/article/ throwback-when-indias-fifth-richest-man-survived-a-kidnapping-and- terrorist-attack/606122.

34   https://www.bloomberg.com/billionaires/

35   https://www.poetryfoundation.org/articles/69400/tradition-and-the-individual-talent

Chapter 3: The March of the DNA

36   'It is high time India is shedding its sea-blindness,' *AsiaConverge*, 2015, https://asiaconverge.com/2015/10/it-is-high-time-india-is-shedding-its-sea- blindness/.

37   Dinesh C. Sharma, 'George Fernandes and the Infamous IBM exit,' *The Wire*, 1 February 2019, https://thewire.in/government/full-story-george-fernandes-and-the- infamous-ibm-exit.

38 Azim Premji, https://www.medalofphilanthropy.org/premji-azim/.
39 Azim Premji foundations, http://philanthropies.org/azim-premji/.
40 'Billionaires', https://www.bloomberg.com/billionaires/.
41 Lately, however, the Kathiawadi Patels have made their presence felt in this industry and have even begun promoting the Surat Diamond Bourse. Hitherto, there was only the Bharat Diamond Bourse in Mumbai.
42 'The apparel apparition,' AsiaConverge, November 2021, https://asiaconverge.com/2021/11/the-apparels-appaition/
43 The Indian rupee is worth around Rs 75 to a US$ today in May 2022. In 1975, it was worth Rs 8 to a US$ (https://RstoUS$.com/exchange-rate-history-of- Indian-rupee-Rs/). Indians use lakh = 100,000, or a crore = 10,000,000
44 Worth over Rs 1 crore today.

Chapter 5: From Imports to Exports

45 The roles of key management people get modified, from time to time, to meet   a variety of needs that suddenly emerge on the horizon. This is one area that Gautambhai will have to focus on as the group gets larger. Role functions will need a sharper definition. That is how organizations become more professional over the passage of time. But a broad list of key people and the roles they play can be found in chart 2.7.
46 'Gautam Adani: The man who can change India,' AsiaConverge, (2007), https://asiaconverge.com/2007/10/gautam-adani-man-change-india/
47 Check the link for more information on Adani Foundation: https://www.adanifoundation.org/
48 See chart 13.2
49 According to a survey on the following link—https://indiankanoon.org/search/?formInput=adani—in India, the list of the cases can be large. Most of them are frivolous or extortionist in nature. Rivals prop-up people to file cases. Most get dropped or are dismissed by the courts. See chart 10.4. For a list of financial fraud allegations on Adani Group, check the following link: https://nationalviews.com/financial-fraud-allegations-on-adani-group-controversies-case-charges-National views - Aug 2017.
50 R.N. Bhaskar, 'The judiciary series,' AsiaConverge, (2021), https://asiaconverge.com/2021/03/the-judiciary-series/
51 See chart 2.7
52 https://www.brainyquote.com/quotes/louis_pasteur_159478
53 'World Bank Group and S&P's The Container Port Performance Index 2021,' https://cdn.ihsmarkit.com/www/pdf/0522/Container-Port-Performance- Index-2021_report.pdf.

Chapter 6: Mundra: A Gateway to the World

54   Refer to the chapter 'Feeding the Nation and Relationships'.

55   'POSCO and Samsung promote green hydrogen production project,' POSCO newsroom, https://newsroom.posco.com/en/posco-samsung-ct-pif-promote-green- hydrogen-production-project/.

56   https://dancingthroughtherain.com/chance-favors-the-prepared-mind/

57   'Gautam Adani: the man who can change India,' *AsiaConverge*, https://asiaconverge.com/2007/10/gautam-adani-man-change-india/ The entire sequence of events that took place was narrated to the author by Gautam Adani and his team in 2007. Much of it finds expression in an article written immediately thereafter.

58   Ibid.

59   Ibid.

60   'Agents' strike threatens activities at Kandla port,' *Times of India*, 26 June 2003, https://timesofindia.indiatimes.com/city/ahmedabad/Agents-strike-threatens-
activities-at-Kandla-port/articleshow/45608.cms.

61   It is strange and sad that the Indian government (including state governments) opts for a lease of just thirty years. Countries like Australia lease out mines and ports for as many as ninety years. Refer to the chapter 'The Australian Saga'.

62   R.N. Bhaskar, 'Gautam Adani—The man who could change India,' AsiaConverge, https://asiaconverge.com/2007/10/gautam-adani-man-change-india/.

63   'Mundra Port and Special Economic Zone Limited,' https://www.sebi.gov.in/filings/public-issues/nov-2007/mundra-port-and- special-economic-zone-limited_9514.html. R.N. Bhaskar, 'Gautam Adani—The man who could change India,' *AsiaConverge*, 2007, https://asiaconverge.com/2007/10/gautam-adani-man-change-india/

64   'Adani ports abandon Myanmar project, US classifies it as sanctioned country,' *Business Today*, 23 June 2021, https://www.businesstoday.in/latest/corporate/story/adani-ports-abandon- myanmar-project-us-classifies-sanctioned-country-299465-2021-06-23.

65   Gwladys Fouche, 'Nordic-fund KLP divests from Adani ports over links to Myanmar military links,' *Mint*, 22 June 2021, https://www.livemint.com/companies/news/nordic-fund-klp-divests-from- adani-ports-over-links-to-myanmar-military-11624361333090.html.

66   'Adani is the highest bidder for West Bengal's Tajpur deep-sea port,' *Rediff.com*, https://www.rediff.com/business/report/adani-highest-bidder-for-west-bengals-tajpur-deep-sea-port/20220325.htm.

67   Shiv Sahay Singh, 'We will invest over Rs 10,000 cr in Bengal over the next decade, says Adani,' *The Hindu*, https://www.thehindu.com/news/national/other-states/we-will-invest-over-10000-crore-in-bengal-over-next-decade-says-gautam-adani/ article65338313.ece.

68   'AEL and Israel Innovation Authority join hands,' *AsiaConverge*, https://asiaconverge.com/2022/08/ael-and-israel-innovation-authority-join-hands/.

69   'India's Adani to build Sri Lanka port, in competition to Chinese,' https://maritime-executive.com/article/india-s-adani-to-build-sri-lanka-port-in-competition-to-chinese.

70   Sri Lanka Ports Authority, https://wwwslpa.lk/port-colombo/terminals

71   See chart 6.2.

72   Refer to the chapter 'The Australian Saga'.

73   'Adani Ports and Special Economic Zones sees overseas acquisitions,' https://www.marketscreener.com/quote/stock/ADANI-PORTS-SPECIAL-ECO-9059803/news/Adani-Ports-and-Special-Economic-Zone-Seeks-Overseas-Acquisitions-38089148/.

74   'Gulf-based GFH financial group signs pact with Adani for Mumbai's economic zones.' *Economic Times*, 29 June 2015, https://realty.economictimes.indiatimes.com/news/industry/gulf-based-gfh-financial-group-signs-pact-with-adani-for-mumbai-economic-zone/47858917.

75   Dipanjan Roy Choudhary, 'India all set to takeover operations in Myanmar's Sittwe Port after Chabhar,' *Economic Time*, https://economictimes.indiatimes.com/news/defence/india-all-set-to-take-over-ops-in-myanmars-sittwe-port-after-chabahar/articleshow/67437859.cms

76   'Nordic-fund KLP divests from Adani port over links to Myanmar military,' *Economic Times*, https://economictimes.indiatimes.com/industry/transportation/shipping-/-transport/nordic-fund-klp-divests-from-adani-ports-over-links-to-myanmar-military/articleshow/83744386.cms

77   'Adani ports to exit Myanmar investment by June next year,' *Business Standard*, October 2021, https://www.business-standard.com/article/companies/adani-ports-to-exit-myanmar-investment-by-june-next-year-121102701558_1.html.

78   'Bharat Freight Group wins deal to run India-funded Sittwe Port in Myanmar,' https://indiaseatradenews.com/bharat-freight-group-wins-deal-to-run-india-funded-sittwe-port-in-myanmar/.

79   Benjamin Diaz, 'Myanmar groups call out India again this time for contract to develop Sittwe Port,' *Myanmar Times*, 14 July 2021, https://www.myanmar-now.org/en/news/myanmar-groups-call-out-india-again-this-time-for-contract-to-develop-sittwe-port

80   'Tripura will be an economic powerhouse', *AsiaConverge*, https://asiaconverge.com/2019/02/tripura-will-be-an-economic-powerhouse/

81 'Adani's solar partners, KSL Cleantech looking for retail expansion to east and north-east,' https://www.pv-magazine-india.com/2021/11/23/adani-solar-partners-ksl- cleantech-for-retail-expansion-to-east-and-northeast/.

82 https://ioagpl.com/ Refer to the chapter 'In Pursuit of the Green-Power Holy Grail'.

83 R.N. Bhaskar, 'Gautam Adani—The man who could change India,' *AsiaConverge*, https://asiaconverge.com/2007/10/gautam-adani-man-change-india/.

84 'Mundra Port and Special Economic Zone Limited,' https://www.sebi.gov.in/filings/public-issues/nov-2007/mundra-port-and- special-economic-zone-limited_9514.html

85 R.N. Bhaskar, 'Gautam Adani—The man who could change India,' *AsiaConverge*, https://asiaconverge.com/2007/10/gautam-adani-man-change-india/.

86 Refer to the chapter 'The Australian Saga'.

87 Latest available figures, which are at least a couple of years old.

88 For more details on the Adani–Wilmar project, refer to chapter 'Feeding the Nation and Relationships'.

89 For more details on LNG, refer to the chapter 'In Pursuit of the Green-Power Holy Grail'.

90 'Adani defence and aerospace to acquire stake in Bengaluru-based agri-drone start-up,' *Indian Express*, https://indianexpress.com/article/business/adani-defence-and-aerospace- to-acquire-stake-in-bengaluru-based-agri-drone-start-up-general- aeronautics-7941494/

91 'Will Thailand MRO trounce India's plans' and 'Can India become the Asian MRO,' *AsiaConverge*, (2018), https://asiaconverge.com/2018/04/will-thailand-mro-trounce-india-plans/ https://asiaconverge.com/2018/04/can-india-become-the-asia-mro/

92 Adani Defence, https://www.adanidefence.com/newsroom/media-release/ Saab-and-Adani- announce-collaboration-plan-for-Aerospace-and-Defence-in-India.

93 Adani Defence, https://www.adanidefence.com/businesses/platforms https://www.adanidefence.com/newsroom/media-release

94 Adani Defence, https://www.adanidefence.com/newsroom/media-release/ Airbus-signs- aircraft-services-MoU-with-Adani-Defence-and-Aerospace

95 'Adani group announces strategic collaborations with Italy-based SNAM,' *India Global Business*, 9 November 2020, https://www.indiaglobalbusiness.com/news-in-brief/adani-group-announces- strategic-collaboration-with-italy-based-snam

96 'Hindustan shipyard and Adani Defence to join hands for Rs 45,000-cr submarine project,' https://defencewatch.in/hindustan-shipyard-and-adani-defence-to-join- hands-for-rs-45000-cr-submarine-project/

97   See chart 6.2.

98   R.N. Bhaskar, 'Gautam Adani—The man who could change India,' *AsiaConverge*, https://asiaconverge.com/2007/10/gautam-adani-man-change-india/.

99   'India's waterways: a game changer,' *AsiaConverge*, https://asiaconverge. com/2016/11/india-waterways-a-gamechangerrobust- water-transportation-can-help-india-drastically-cut-freight-costs/

Chapter 7: King Coal

100   Refer to the chapter 'The Australian Saga'.

101   Refer to the chapter 'The Australian Saga'.

102   https://www.worldcoal.com/coal/14032022/rystad-energy-coal-prices-soar-to-200-year-high/2.

103   FJPIndia, https://twitter.com/fpjindia/. status/1527543481547116544?s=20&t=DnTARMBpPlZ9yuNH1E2U-w

104   'Paradoxes Davos', https://www.linkedin.com/pulse/paradoxes-davos-2022-gautam-adani/

105   Gautam Adani's speeach at JP Morgan Summit in September 2021, https://www.youtube.com/watch?v=yAbqaXmfdNY.

106   'The Supreme Court and religion: A blinkered perspective,' *AsiaConverge*, April 2016, https://asiaconverge.com/2016/04/the-supreme-court-and-religion-in-india- a-blinkered-perspective-html/.

107   R.N. Bhaskar, 'Sukma Maoists attack', *AaiaConverge*,17 April 2017, https://asiaconverge.com/2017/04/sukma-killings-naxal-violence-illegal- mining/

And 'Kashmiri revolution and land exploitation,' *AsiaConverge*, November 2017, https://asiaconverge.com/2017/11/kashmiri-revolution-and- land-exploitation/.and 'Concealing illegal mining in the North-East', *AsiaConverge*, January 2019, https://asiaconverge.com/2019/01/concealing-illegal- mining-in-thenorth-east/

108   Saket Gokhale, https://twitter.com/SaketGokhale/ status/1554677872618442753?t=K0IUpEbJKq0GFKOxtYGh5g&s=19

109   R.N. Bhaskar, 'Government must not look the other way at these rat hole mines,' *Money Control*, 3 January 2019, https://www.moneycontrol.com/news/opinion/opinion-govt-must-not-look- the-other-way-at-these-rat-hole-mines-3351001.html.

110   'Concealing illegal mining in the North-East', *AsiaConverge*, January 2019, https://asiaconverge.com/2019/01/concealing-illegal- mining-in-thenorth-east/.

111   R.N. Bhaskar, 'Sukma Maoists attack', *AsiaConverge*, 17 April 2017, https://asiaconverge.com/2017/04/sukma-killings-naxal-violence-illegal- mining/.

112   Dharma Port and Olive Ridley turtles—IUCN, https://www.iucn.org/sites/dev/files/content/documents/iucn_dhamra_port_ online.pdf

Researchgate, https://www.researchgate.net/publication/338297888_
THE_DHAMRA_ PORT_AND_THE_CASE_OF_OLIVE_RIDLEY_
TURTLES_THE_ DHAMRA_PORT_AND_THE_CASE_OF_OLIVE_
RIDLEY_ TURTLES_EXECUTIVE_SUMMARY
P. Manoj, 'Adani's Dharma port and Olive Ridley turtles are
growing together,' *Hindu Businessline*, 7 April, 2018, https://www.
thehindubusinessline.com/economy/logistics/adanis-dhamra- port-and-olive-
ridley-turtles-growing-together/article23465686.ece

113 Government of Australia, 'Australia's trade in figures,' Table 2, https://www.
aph.gov.au/ About_Parliament/Parliamentary_Departments/Parliamentary_
Library/pubs/ BriefingBook45p/AustraliaTrade. The protestors did not care
to mention the fact that the Adani mine in Australia was just one more of the
124 odd coal mines that were already in existence in Australia.

114 Refer to the chapter 'The Australian Saga'.

115 'Can India aid Australian growth,' *AsiaConverge*, October 2015, https://
asiaconverge.com/2015/10/can-in.dia-aid-australian-growth/

116 '2022s top 10 trends.' *NDTV*, https://www.ndtv.com/india-news/dr-
prannoy-roy-ruchir-sharma-on-2022s- top-10-trends-full-transcript-2696979

117 Queensland Rail News, 'Can Adani Carmichael mine and rail project chart
the future of coal mining in Australia?' 10 June 2021, https://www.railpage.
com.au/news/s/can-adani-carmichael-mine-and-rail- project-chart-the-future-
of-coal-mining-in-australia.

Chapter 8: The Australian Saga

118 Refer to the chapter 'King Coal'

119 *From stop to start—celebrating 10 years in Australia*, an Adani fact-book brought
out in 2020. Many of the quotes in this chapter have been taken from this book.

120 Ibid.

121 'China's Coal imports from Australia Plummet 98.6%, but India, S.Korea
fill the Gaps,' *Maritime Logistics*, 15 September 2021, ttps://www.
maritimeprofessional.com/news/china-coal-imports-from-australia-370593

122 'The Cold war: Why has China turned its back on Australian coal,' *Mining
Technology*, https://www.mining-technology.com/analysis/the-coal-war-why-
has-china- turned-its-back-on-australian-coal/

123 'What are the Quad countries?', *Fully Defence*, ttps://fullydefence.com/what-
are-the-quad-countries-usa-japan- australia-india/.

124 Australian Government, 'Australia-India Comprehensive Economic Cooperation
Agreement,' https://www.dfat.gov.au/trade/agreements/negotiations/aifta/australia-
india- comprehensive-economic-cooperation-agreement.

125 Piyush Goyal, 'India-Australia trade pact will boost bilateral trade to $100 billion by 2030,' *Business Standard*, https://www.business-standard.com/article/news-ani/india-australia- trade-pact-will-boost-bilateral-trade-to-100-billion-by-2030-piyush- goyal-122040600951_1.html.

126 *From stop to start—celebrating 10 years in Australia*.

127 Australian Government, www.adanifacts.com.au.

128 'Adani financing welcomed by industry groups,' *Townsville Bulletin*, https://www.townsvillebulletin.com.au/subscribe/ news/1/?sourceCode=TBWEB_WRE170_a_ GGL&dest=https%3A%2F%2Fwww.townsvillebulletin.com.au%2Fnews%2Ftownsville%2Fadani-financing-welcomed-by-industry-groups%2Fnews-story%2F8145723b07d11de1a0e01a36029ce0e1&memtype=anonymous&mode=premium.

129 *The Courier-Mail*, https://www.couriermail.com.au/news/queensland/mackay

130 Ibid.

131 Ibid.

132 Bravus Mining & Resources is an Australian company, operating under Australian law, paying taxes and royalties here. We are dedicated to creating jobs and opportunities for regional Queensland communities. The construction of the Carmichael Mine and Rail Projects have already delivered more than $1.5 billion in contracts and 2,000 jobs to benefit regional Queensland. More than 9000 indirect jobs have also been created.

133 Study Australia, https://www.studyaustralia.gov.au/english/study/vocational-education https://www.tafensw.edu.au/.

Chapter 9: In Pursuit of the Green-Power Holy Grail

134 See chart 7.1.

135   See chart 6.5.

136 Refer to the chapter 'King Coal'.

137 Maulik Pathak and Uttam Bhaskar, 'Tata Power offers to sell 51% stake in Mundra port for Re 1,' *Mint*, https://indiatribune.com/tata-power-offers-to-sell-51-stake-in- mundra-for-re-1/.

138 'Tata Power offers to sell 51% stake in Mundra port for Re 1,' *Hindu Businessline*, https://www.thehindubusinessline.com/companies/tata-power-offers-to-sell- 51-of-mundra-plant-for-1/article9732822.ece.

139 'Adani Power Mundra plant central electricity Regulatory Commission cerc tariff,' *Indian Express*, https://indianexpress.com/article/business/economy/adani-power-mundra- plant-central-electricity-regulatory-commission-cerc-tariff-5673489/.

140 Adani Global, https://www.adani.com/businesses/power-distribution.

141 'Tata and Adani plants may get to sell on power exchanges amid coal crisis,' *Business Standard*, https://www.business-standard.com/article/companies/tata-adani-plants-may- get-to-sell-on-power-exchanges-amid-coal-crisis-121083100029_1.html.

142 Mercom India Research, https://mercomindia.com/research-2/

143 Adani Solar, 'Adani Solar partners with KSL,' https://www.adanisolar.com/-/media/Project/AdaniSolar/Media/Media- Releases/webiste---Media-release---Adani-Solar-partners-with-KSL- Cleantech.pdf.

144 Adani Solar, https://www.adanisolar.com/Newsroom/Media-Releases.

145 'Biplab Kumar Das has big plans for Tripura,' *AsiaConverge*, March 2019, https://asiaconverge.com/2019/03/biplab-kumar-deb-has-big-plans-for-tripura/.

146 'Why India not learn from Germany's Hermann Scheer solar power model,' *AsiaConverge*, April 2016, https://asiaconverge.com/2016/04/india-not-learn-germanys-hermann- scheer-solar-power-model/

147 'Praveer Sinha of Tata Power continues to bet on India's plans with divestment from overseas projects,' *AsiaConverge*, August 2021, https://asiaconverge.com/2021/08/fpj-sies-webinar-praveer-sinha-of-tata- power-continues-to-bet-on-india-plans-to-continue-with-divestments-from-overseas-projects/

148 Ibid.

149 'Tata Power is setting up the world's largest rural electrification sustainability project,' *AsiaConverge*, December 2021, https://asiaconverge.com/2021/12/tata-power-is-setting-up-the-worlds- largest-rural-electrification-sustainability-project/.

150 Refer to the chapter 'The Taste of Goodness'.

151 Mercom India Research, 'Investments for Indian solar sector increased,' https://mercomindia.com/investments-indian-solar-sector-increased-2021/

152 Mercom India Research, 'Solar installations in India reach 50 GW,' https://mercomindia.com/solar-installations-india-reach-50-gw/

153 Mercom India Research, India's solar market update 2021,' https://mercomindia.com/product/q4-2021-india-solar-market-update/

154 'City gas distribution network receives 430 bids in 65 areas,' *Telegraph*, https://www.telegraphindia.com/business/city-gas-distribution-network-receives-430-bids-in-65-areas/cid/1843914.

155 Nomura: India Gas: CGDs best way to play gas theme, dated 4 January 2021 156

156 Nomura: India Gas: CGDs best way to play gas theme, dated 4 January 2021 157

157 In its judgment in July 2015, Supreme Court dismissed PNGRB's appeal and upheld the Delhi High Court's verdict that PNGRB does not have power to

determine tariffs. SC also ruled the entire city gas tariff regulation (on which tariff order was issued) ultra vires. The Nomura report mentioned above.

158 PNGRB, '11th CGD bidding round', https://pngrb.gov.in/pdf/ cgd/bid11/ brochure.pdf

159 See chart 6.8.

160 Adani Gas, 'Adani Total Gas Ltd to invest Rs 20,000 cr in CGD sector in the next eight years,' https://www.adanigas.com/newsroom/media-release/ Adani-Total-Gas-Ltd-to- invest-Rs-20000-Cr-in-CGD-sector-in-the-next-eight-years.

161 For details on the LNG Terminals of the Adani Group, see chart 6.3.

162 Adani Gas, 'Adani Total Gas Q3-FY22 results,' https://www.adanigas.com/ newsroom/media-release/Adani-Total-Gas-Q3- FY22-Results.

163 'Ukraine: the war that USA wants,' *AsiaConverge*, https://asiaconverge. com/2022/02/ukraine-the-war-that-usa-wants/.

164 'Oil could climb over $200 a barrel,' *AsiaConverge*, ttps://asiaconverge. com/2022/05/oil-could-climb-to-over-200-a-barrel/

165 Adani Green Energy, https://www.adanigreenenergy.com/-/media/Project/ GreenEnergy/Corporate- Announcement/Board/08042022---Press-Release. pdf?la=en

166 Adani Group, 'Adding Power to your aspirations—2022'.

167 Adani Transmissions, https://www.adanitransmission.com/

Chapter 10: Aligned with National Interests

168 R.N. Bhaskar, *Game India: Game India-seven strategic advantages that could steer India to wealth*, (Delhi: Penguin, 2019)

169 Lecture delivered by Arvind Subramanian on 8 October 2021, https://www. youtube.com/watch?v=XVXm57tD7tQ.
The transcript for this talk can be viewed at https://www.foreignaffairs.com/ articles/india/2021-12-14/indias-stalled-rise.

170 *Gangs of New York*, 2002, https://www.imdb.com/title/tt0217505/ 171 American Rails, 'Railroad Barons,' https://www.american-rails.com/tycoons.html#List.

172 'David Sassoon: the biggest wealth generator of Bombay,' *AsiaConverge*, October 2019, https://asiaconverge.com/2019/10/david-sassoon-the-biggest-wealth- generator-of-bombay/.

173 '15 crazy facts about the Rothschild family', ttps://www.theclever.com/15-crazy-facts-about-the-rothschild-family/.

174 'Robber barons from America's past,' https://www.thoughtco.com/robber-barons-from-americas-past-4120060.

175 Refer to the chapter 'Jettisoning Excess Baggage'.

176 The state introduced non-agricultural taxes in Mumbai and wanted to introduce such taxes for all cities in the state. For more information check link: https://asiaconverge. com/2022/01/new-unfair-and-controversial-real-estate-tax-laws-in- maharashtra/.

177 ORF, 'Jailed for doing business,' 10 February 2022, ttps://www.orfonline. org/jailed-for-doing-business/.

178 'The double-engine growth for Uttar Pradesh must not spread over India,'*AsiaConverge*, https://asiaconverge.com/2022/02/the-double-engine-growth-for-uttar- pradesh-must-not-spread-over-india/.

179 'Understanding vacancies in the Indian Judiciary,' PRS India, 18 November 2021, https://prsindia.org/theprsblog/understanding-vacancies-in-the-indian-judiciary.

180 R.N. Bhaskar, 'The Judiciary series,' *AsiaConverge*, https://asiaconverge. com/2021/03/the-judiciary-series/.

181 Tejeesh N.S. Bhel, '4.5 crore pending cases, 50% judges missing: Why justice in India takes so long?', *Times of India*, 22 October 2021, https:// timesofindia.indiatimes.com/india/4-5-crore-pending-cases-50-judges-missing-why-justice-in-india-takes-so-long/articleshow/87203443.cms.

182 'Judges shortage delaying justice,' *The Hans India*, https://www.thehansindia. com/news/cities/hyderabad/judges-shortage- delaying-justice-738260.

183 See chart 10.4.

184 Indian Kanoon, https://indiankanoon.org.

185 Vidhi Legal Policy, 'Government Litigation,' 2019, https://vidhilegalpolicy. in/wp-content/uploads/2019/05/ GovernmentLitigationFinal.pdf.

186 R.N. Bhaskar, 'The Judiciary series,' *AsiaConverge*, https://asiaconverge. com/2021/03/the-judiciary-series/.

187 'Ease of Doing Business ranking 2020,' https://www.doingbusiness.org/ content/dam/doingBusiness/pdf/db2020/ Doing-Business-2020_rankings.pdf.

188 R.N. Bhaskar, 'The Judiciary series,' *AsiaConverge*, https://asiaconverge. com/2021/03/the-judiciary-series/.

189 Indian Kanoon, https://indiankanoon.org.

190 In 2021, R.N. Bhaskar made the first attempt to look at corporate performance based on CMIE data. It looked at six industry groups in India. These articles can be found at:
https://asiaconverge.com/2021/11/money-makes-the-world-go-round/
https://asiaconverge.com/2021/12/corporate-groups-2-are-they-profitable/
https://asiaconverge.com/2021/12/corporate-groups3-where-did-the-va-go/

191 Krishna Kant, 'Adani Group firm's gross debt rises to Rs 2.2 trillion, shows data,' *Business Standard*, 18 May 2022, https://www.business-standard.com/

article/companies/adani-group-firms- gross-debt-rises-to-rs-2-2-trillion-shows-data-122051601480_1.html.

192 'Gautam Adani takes new tycoon risks,' *Reuters*, https://www.reuters.com/breakingviews/gautam-adani-takes-new-tycoon-risk- next-level-2022-08-09/.

193 Refer to the chapter 'The Odyssey Continues'.

194 Ibid.

195 'Adani group to invest $5.2 billion in Odisha to set-up alumina refinery,' *Business Standard*, https://www.business-standard.com/article/companies/adani-group-to-invest- 5-2-billion-in-odisha-to-set-up-alumina-refinery-122081100404_1.html.

Chapter 11: Jettisoning Excess Baggage

196 Maulik Pathak and Harit Mehta, 'Adani, Ashapura in JV to set up Rs 10,000-cr aluminium refinery,' *Business Standard*, 29 January 2013, https://www.business-standard.com/article/companies/adani-ashapura-in-jv- to-set-up-rs-10-000-cr-aluminium-refinery-108082701022_1.html.

197 Asahpura, http://www.ashapuracfs.com/

198 'Now Adani to venture into aluminium business,' *Hindu Businessline*, https://www.thehindubusinessline.com/companies/now-adani-to-venture- into-aluminium-business/article37987116.ece

199 'Indian Oil buys stake in Phinergy of Israel for manufacturing aluminium air batteries,' *Economic Times*, 4 February 2020, https://energy.economictimes.indiatimes.com/news/oil-and-gas/indianoil- buys-stake-in-phinergy-of-israel-for-manufacturing-of-aluminium-air- batteries/73935714.

200 'Adani group to invest Rs 57,575 cr to set up alumina refinery in Odisha,' *Business Standard*, 11 August 2022, https://www.business-standard.com/article/companies/adani-group-to-invest- 5-2-billion-in-odisha-to-set-up-alumina-refinery-122081100404_1.html.

201 ICIS, 'India's Adani group plans 2m tonne per year coal to PVC plant,' https://www.icis.com/explore/resources/news/2021/05/24/10643486/india-s-adani-group-plans-2m-tonne-year-coal-to-pvc-plant/#:~:text=In per cent20the per cent20coal per cent2Dto per cent2DPVC,is per cent20further per cent20processed per cent20to per cent20acetylene.

202 'Adani group firm Kutch Copper raises Rs 6,017 cr for one million tonne unit,' *Business Standard*, 26 june 2022, https://www.business-standard.com/article/companies/adani- group-firm-kutch-copper-raises-rs-6-071-cr-for-one-mn-tonne- unit-122062600864_1.html.

203 Dev Chatterjee, 'Adani raises $5.25 bn from global banks to acquire Ambuja Cements,' *Business Standard*, 31 July 2022, https://www.business-standard.

com/article/companies/adani-raises-5-25-bn- from-global-banks-to-acquire-ambuja-cements-acc-122073100635_1.html.

204 Baiju Kalesh, 'Welspun to merge investments firms to unlock value, raise funds,' *Mint*, 20 December 2009, https://www.livemint.com/ Companies/7MUOJGrPwtlwGneZ1YozZJ/ Welspun-to-merge-investment-firms-to-unlock-value-raise-fun.html.

205 'Adani-Welspun to invest $i.5 billion in US Shale Canadian oil assests,' *Times of India*, https://timesofindia.indiatimes.com/business/india-business/ adani- welspun-to-invest-1-5-billion-in-us-shale-canadian-oil-sands-assets/ articleshow/45253316.cms?from=mdr.

206 'Welspun Group eyes $5 bn revenue by 2020,' *Business Standard*, 25 october 2015, https://www.business-standard.com/article/companies/welspun-group-eyes-5- bn-revenue-by-2020-115102500149_1.html.

Chapter 12: Feeding the Nation and Relationships

207 Adani Agri-Logistics, ttps://www.adaniagrilogistics.com/ .

208 R.N. Bhaskar, 'DMIC or Delhi-Mumbai corridor will create new best-in-class cities,' *AsiaConverge*, 20 February 2011, https://asiaconverge.com/2011/02/ dmic-delhi-mumbai-corridor-will-create- new-best-class-cities/.

209 'Poverty in Uttar Pradesh and Bihar is not accidental,' *AsiaConverge*, https:// asiaconverge.com/2021/08/poverty-in-uttar-pradesh-and-bihar-is-not-accidental/.
     R.N. Bhaskar, 'The ghostly organisation that should have transformed India's food warehouses,' *Money Control*, 5 July 2019, https://www.moneycontrol. com/news/business/economy/the- ghostly-organisation-that-should-have-transformed-indias-food- warehouses-2352429.html.

210 Fortune oil, https://www.fortunefoods.com/.

211 'Edible oil and food products,' https://www.adani.com/businesses/edible-oil-and-food-products.

212 R.N. Bhaskar, 'Is WDRA a functioning organization?' *AsiaConverge*, 7 August 2017, ttps://asiaconverge.com/2017/08/is-wdra-a-functioning-organisation/.

213 'Policy wath treatment meted out to edible oil reflects the concerns for farmer welfare,' *Free Press Journal*, https://www.freepressjournal.in/analysis/ policy-watch-treatment-meted-out- to-edible-oil-reflects-the-concern-for-farmer-welfare.

214 Farm-pik, https://www.farmpik.com/.

215 Adani Group, 'Farm-pik,' https://youtu.be/j5e9F5b2Tzk.

216 'Remembering Kurien and how much the country owes him,' *AsiaConverge*, https://asiaconverge.com/2021/11/remembering-kurien-and-how-much-the-country-owes-to-him/.

217 See footnotes for chart 10.5.
218 Refer to the chapter 'The Taste of Goodness'.
219 See footnotes for charts 10.5 and 10.6.
220 'Need sensible laws to stop farmer exploitation,' *AsiaConverge*, https://
     asiaconverge.com/2021/09/need-sensible-laws-to-stop-farmer- exploitation/.
221 'Budget 2022: why provisions for agriculture and the poor are laughable
     with no attempt to reward the efficient,'*AsiaConverge*, https://asiaconverge.
     com/2022/02/budget-2022-why-provisions-for- agriculture-and-the-poor-
     are-laughable-with-no-attempt-to-reward-the- efficient/.
222 'Adani Wilmar Ltd', https://www.sebi.gov.in/filings/public-issues/aug-2021/
     adani-wilmar- limited_51577.html.
223 See chart 7.4.
224 See chart 8.8.
225 'The government lets down India's edible oil industry,' *AsiaConverge*,
     https://asiaconverge.com/2022/01/the-government-lets-down-indias-edible-
     oil-industry/.
226 'Adani Enterprises to acquite 50% stake in General Aeronautics,' *Money
     Control*, 27 May 2022, https://www.moneycontrol.com/news/india/adani-
     enterprises-to-acquire-50- stake-in-general-aeronautics-8591541.html.
227 'A droning government wakes up to drones,' *AsiaConverge*, https://
     asiaconverge.com/2021/09/a-droning-govt-wakes-up-to-drones/.
228 Adani Defence, 'Adani-Elbit JV further steps up their presence in the
     international markets,' https://adanidefence.com/newsroom/media-release/
     Adani-Elbit-JV-further- steps-up-their-presence-in-the-international-
     markets.
229 'SAAB-Adani group JV to make drones, military choppers, eyes $1 bn
     jet deal,' *Business Standard*, https://www.business-standard.com/article/
     companies/saab-adani-group-jv- to-make-drones-military-choppers-eyes-1-
     bn-jet-deal-117110500233_1.html.
230 Manu Pubby, 'Defence-Expo 2020: Adani-Elbit JV exports India-made
     military drone,' *Economic Times*, 7 February 2020, ttps://economictimes.
     indiatimes.com/news/defence/defence-expo-2020- adani-elbit-jv-exports-
     india-made-military-drone/articleshow/73998264. cms?from=mdr.
231 Adani Group, Drones in agriculture, https://www.youtube.com/
     watch?v=kDwIt40tSc0
232 R.N. Bhaskar, 'Milk the road to perdition is often through subsidies,' *Money
     Control*, 14 April 2020, ttps://www.moneycontrol.com/news/india/milk-the-
     road-to-perdition-is- often-through-subsidies-5142591.html.

Chapter 13: The Taste of Goodness

233 GAIMS, http://www.gaims.ac.in/About-GAIMS

234 Dev Chatterjee, 'Adani group receives approval to set up university in Ahemdabad,' *Business Standard*, 3 April 2022, https://www.business-standard. com/article/education/adani-group-receives- approval-to-set-up-university-in-ahmedabad-122040300340_1.html.

235 Deborshi Chaki, 'Adani plans $4 bn foray into healthcare,' *Mint*, 2 May 2022, https://www.livemint.com/companies/news/adani-plans-4-billion-foray-into- healthcare-11651431708498.html.

236 Dev Chatterjee, 'Adani group receives approval to set up university in Ahemdabad,' *Business Standard*, 3 April 2022, https://www.business-standard. com/article/education/adani-group-receives- approval-to-set-up-university-in-ahmedabad-122040300340_1.html v

237 AII, https://www.aii.ac.in/.

238 'Adani buys Macquaries Toll Roads for Rs 3,110 crore,' *Times of India*, 5 August 2022, https://timesofindia.indiatimes.com/city/mumbai/adani-buys-macquaries- toll-roads-for-3110-crore/articleshow/93359538.cms.

239 Adani Foundation, https://www.adanifoundation.org/About-Us

240 'Goodness at grassroot,' *Free Press Journal*, https://www.freepressjournal.in/ interviews/goodness-at-the-grassroots.

241 Adani Foundation, 'Nurturing Dreams. Inspiring the Future,' https://www. adanifoundation. org/-/media/Project/Foundation/Newsroom/Adani-Foundation-Brochure. pdf?la=en&hash=AC92A51852C9F514BCD0A05B4AAF7B99.

242 Utthan, https://reports.adani.com/Utthan-Adani-Foundation/index.html.

243 Adani Vidya Mandir, https://reports.adani.com/adanividyamandir/ index.html.

244 'Billionaire Gautam Adani to foray into healthcare business,' *Mint*, 19 May 2022, https://www.livemint.com/companies/news/billionaire-gautam-adani-s- group-to-foray-into-healthcare-business-11652929066543.html.

245 'No atma nirbharta without healthcare,' *AsiaConverge*, November 2021, ttps://asiaconverge.com/2021/11/no-atma-nirbharta-without-healthcare/.

Chapter 14: The Odyssey Continues

246 See chart 10.5

247 'Will Thailand MRO trounce India plans,' *AsiaConverge*, https:// asiaconverge.com/2018/04/will-thailand-mro-trounce-india-plans/.

248 'Gautam Adani to buy stake in Air Works Group: Report,' *Mint*, 29 May 2022, https://www.livemint.com/companies/news/gautam-adani-to-buy-stake-in- air-works-group-report-11653797869290.html.

249 Air India SATS, http://www.aisats.in/.

250 'Can India become the Asia MRO,' *AsiaConverge*, https://asiaconverge.
com/2018/04/can-india-become-the-asia-mro/.

251 Ibid.

252 Adani Group, 'Growth with Goodness, February 2022'.

253 'The Water series,' *AsiaConverge*, https://asiaconverge.com/2019/07/the-
water-series/

254 Ishaan Gera, 'Statsguru: Six charts explaining India's arm import dependence,'
Business Standard, 21 March 2022, https://www.business-standard.com/
article/economy-policy/statsguru-six- charts-explainindia-s-arms-import-
dependence-122032000828_1.html.

255 'Private defence manufacturing companies, India,' https://startuptalky.com/
private-defence-manufacturing-companies-india/.

256 Manu Pubby, 'Defence-Expo 2020: Adani-Elbit JV exports India-made
military drone,' *Economic Times*, 7 February 2020, ttps://economictimes.
indiatimes.com/news/defence/defence-expo-2020- adani-elbit-jv-exports-
india-made-military-drone/articleshow/73998264.

257 https://asiaconverge.com/2021/09/a-droning-govt-wakes-up-to-drones/. 258
Refer to the chapter 'Feeding the Nation'.

259 Adani Defence, 'Small arms', https://www.adanidefence.com/small-arms

260 IWI, https://iwi.net/

261 'Adani Defence buys 51% stake in PLR systems,' *Business Upturn*, ttps://
www.businessupturn.com/companies/adani-defence-buys-51-stake-in-
plr-systems/,

262 Adani Defence, 'Infrastructure', https://www.adanidefence.com/infrastructure

263 Sunil Hebblakar, 'Adani Defence systems technologies takes alpha design,'
EXSoft, 22 April 2019, http://exsoft.org/adani-defence-systems-technologies-
takes-alpha-design/.

264 'Indo count expects to grow in a favourable textiles market,' *AsiaConverge*,
https://asiaconverge.com/2021/08/indo-count-expects-to-grow-in-a-
favourable-textiles-market/.

265 Adani Group, 'Data center,', https://www.adani.com/businesses/data-center

266 Adani Enterprises, 'Adani-ConneX: a new Data Center Joint Venture
formed Between Adani Enterprises And EdgeConneX,' https://www.
adanienterprises.com/newsroom/media-releases/AdaniConneX- a-new-
Data-Center-Joint-Venture-formed-Between-Adani-Enterprises-and-
EdgeConneX.

267 'Adani group selects Google cloud to modernise IT ops for future scale,'
Business Standard, 29 March 2022, https://www.business-standard.com/
article/companies/adani-group-selects- google-cloud-to-modernise-it-ops-for-
future-scale-122032800566_1.html.

268 'Adani and 5G,' *AsiaConverge*, https://asiaconverge.com/2022/08/adani-and-5g/.

269 NPCI, https://www.npci.org.in/

270 'How Aadhar and NPCI together open the doors to major frauds and impersonations,' *AsiaConverge*, https://asiaconverge.com/2018/02/how-aadhaar-and-npci-together-open-the- door-to-major-frauds-and-impersonations/.

271 'Digital payments: NPCI UPI and customer protection,' *AsiaConverge*, https://asiaconverge.com/2022/06/digital-payments-npci-upi-and-customer-protection/.

272 'Aadhar cards: Many ways populations rig numbers, financial transactions,' *AsiaConverge*, https://asiaconverge.com/2020/02/aadhaar-cards-populations-many-ways-rig- numbers-financial-transactions/

273 Neeraj Chauhan and Binayak Dasgupta, 'CAG flags privacy gaps, duplications in Aadhar,' *Hindustan Times*, 7 April 2022, https://www.hindustantimes.com/india-news/cag-flags-privacy-gaps- duplication-in-aadhaar-101649270192669.html

274 'Billionaire Gautam Adani seeks to boost his media investments for expansion plans,' *Mint*, 5 May 2022, https://www.livemint.com/companies/people/billionaire-gautam-adani-seeks- to-boost-his-media-investments-for-expansion-plans-11651751577417.html

275 Adani Group, 'The future of infrastucture is green,' https://www.adani.com/blogs/the-future-of-infrastructure-is-green

276 'India is a beacon of hope in the effort to build a sustainable future,' www.adani.com/blogs/india-is-a-beacon-of-hope-in-the-effort-to- build-a-sustainable-future

277 Gautam Adani, https://www.linkedin.com/pulse/paradoxes-davos-2022-gautam-adani/

278 Vijay Prashad's Chilling Peoples Summit speech, https://www.youtube.com/watch?v=VXp13u4R7ZA

279 IEEFA, 'Adani plans $70-billion investment in renewables over the next decade,' https://ieefa.org/adani-plans-70-billion-investment-in-renewables-over- next-decade/

280 Adani Group, 'The future of infrastucture is green,' https://www.adani.com/blogs/the-future-of-infrastructure-is-green

281 'Hydrogen: the new holy grail,' *AsiaConverge*, https://asiaconverge.com/2022/02/hydrogen-the-new-holy-grail/

282 'Adani Defence to take 50% stake in agricultural drone start-up,' *NDTV*, https://www.ndtv.com/business/adani-defence-to-take-50-stake-in-agricultural-drone-startup-3016181

Acknowledgements

This book would not have been possible without the immense support that I have got for the past 18 years from both Gautambhai and his wife Pritiben. My interactions with Vinod Adani, and his son Pranav have been warm and illuminating. Ditto with my interactions with Rajesh Adani. Ditto for all the Adani professionals who I have interacted with.

Another person whose help, support and advice have always been invaluable is Devendrabhai Amin, former vice president and head of communications of the Adani Group. He retired from the Adani Group a few years ago.

Two other people who were actively involved in writing my earlier book on Gautam Adani were Pankaj Mudholkar and Mudar Pathreya. I owe a lot to both for their support and assistance.

As stated above, I benefitted from several inputs from so many people from the Adani Group—many of them are quoted in this book. The list is long, and hence is not being reproduced here. But each of the Adani professionals I have interacted with, often for years, has taught me much. They helped me understand the enormity of how much can be made possible, and how much more remains to be done.

Outside the Adani Group, I am thankful to market gurus like Nimesh Kampani, Deepak Parekh, Vallabh Bhanshali, Utpal Sheth, and so many others.

I owe thanks to the Free Press group—Ashok and Abhishek Karnani and the rest of the Karnani family—for allowing me time to focus on this book and offering me advice from time to time. Thanks are also due to some cherished friends whom I have consulted for suggestions and even guidance at different points of time. They include (in alphabetical order) Ashok Advani, Swaminathan S.A.Aiyar, Ashfaq Ali, Sucheta Dalal, Dr. Surendra Dhelia, Gaurav Gupta, Pankaj Joshi, Jawahir Mulraj, Santosh Nair, Chandan Parmar, Mitesh Shah, Shardul Shroff, Sitaraman Shankar, Ashim Syal, Sandeep Sharma, Mahesh Vyas and so many other friends who have encouraged me not to give up on this book. Many of them also helped me with my earlier book, *Game India*.

And, most crucially, to Radhika Marwah, my editor at Penguin, who has helped me in so many ways.

And, finally, I owe thanks to my family as well—Chandrika, Dharini, grandson Aayansh and the Khera family for encouraging me and putting up with me.